# MURDEROUS
# WOMEN

True Accounts of Australia's
Worst Female Killers

## LINDY CAMERON & RUTH WYKES

CLAN
DESTINE
PRESS

First published in Australia 2016
by Clan Destine Press

PO Box 121 Bittern
Victoria 3918 Australia

National Library of Australia Cataloguing-in-Publication entry

Author:  Cameron, Lindy & Wykes, Ruth

Title:  Murderous Women:

　　　　True Accounts of Australia's Worst Female Killers

ISBN　(pbk) 978-0-9954394-0-5

　　　　(eBook) 978-0-9954394-1-2

Cover Design:  Willsin Rowe

Design & Typesetting: Clan Destine Press

Printed and bound in Australia by Lightning Source

www.clandestinepress.com.au

# CONTENTS

# MAKE THEM SUFFER

# Introduction

Ours is a world in which the moral compass is set to respect life, to keep it sacred and to treat every day we walk on this earth as a gift. This is as it should be. In Australia our laws protect our rights to live as free citizens; our religious bodies continually remind us of the sanctity of life; and our own individual codes of conduct show us a road map for what is right and what is wrong.

Australian society, in all its diversity, projects a strong message about life. It is enshrined in law that the taking another person's life is wrong, and that if you do, you will be punished.

Capital punishment, however, was abolished in this country many years ago. We do not suggest it, not even for those convicted of the most brutal of murders, and regardless of the number of victims. Nor do Australian citizens have the right to bear arms – of any kind. So the use of firearms, especially handguns, is restricted to the likes of law-enforcement groups, farmers and sporting shooters. Despite these things, or because of them, we don't have a lot of innocent citizens being gunned down because they go about unarmed; or because the 'ultimate punishment' is not an available deterrent. That's not to say we don't have gun deaths, because we do. But they are, more often than not, rival criminals taking each other out.

Our homicide rate – obviously we have one, like every civilised nation – pales into insignificance when compared with some countries. It is much lower per capita, for instance, than the USA or most places in South America..

Most of our murders are committed by a wide variety of other weapons, and methods that do not involve bullets. Traditionally, when Australians kill, they resort to using knives, or blunt instruments, or bare hands, or fire, or poison. The choice of weapon depends on the circumstances and intention. If the murder was accidental – like drunken anger or a flash of pent-up rage – then the nearest weapon will do. One stupid punch can be enough.

But if the murder was intentional then the method of death depends on whether the crime was premeditated *and* well planned, or just premeditated.

For instance, if the first weapon doesn't do the trick, the killer might have to resort to whatever they can lay their hands on – you know, the nearest brick or saucepan if the target is still talking after they've been stabbed; or a plastic bag if they're still breathing after they've been hit with a bat; or a fire to cover tracks, or … you get the drift.

Historically, and generally, speaking, when it comes to killers – and not just Aussie ones – women have tended towards the neat and quiet, have taken the less brutal path, the less bloody option.

Poison, for instance, has been the murder method of choice for women throughout history. It's unobtrusive, it's quiet, it's debilitating, it's easily covered up. Some killers enjoyed watching the slow and agonising death; some used the inexplicable illness as a reason to 'care'.

These days of course, poison as an actual technique of death-dealing is 'so last century' – or the one before. Toxicology tests put paid to most old-fashioned concoctions and autopsies can reveal way too much.

On the other hand, drugs – whether illicit, prescription or over the counter – are a whole other option. Murder can be made to look like suicide or accidental overdose, or at least self-administered before the victim gets in a car and wraps it around a pole, or accidentally sets their house on fire.

So despite the CSI techs and forensic everything, the means by which women can continue to commit quiet, unobtrusive murder have actually grown.

And yet, women themselves seem to be raging against tradition. Since the late 20th century they've been picking up knives, and garrottes, and syringes, and hacksaws; and they've been wielding them in anger, and with vindictiveness and pleasure. It's anyone's guess whether it's a backlash against centuries of being treated like second-class citizens; the stress of modern living; raging out-of-kilter hormones; the freedom to do or be what men have always done and been; weird allergies or iron deficiencies; psychiatric problems; or just plain badness. The bottom line, though, is this: women are getting scarier.

Trying to understand why women kill is … well, it's pointless. Women kill for many of the same reasons that men do – and sometimes it can be explained, and sometimes it can't. Sometimes it can even be understood, but mostly it can't. Because murder for *nearly* every reason is beyond most people's understanding.

We know how easy it is for someone to lash out in anger or take a drunken lunge and just end someone's life. While that is terrible behaviour, and an arrogant way to have the last word in an argument, death was probably not the intention. The intent – as an expression rage, pain, grief or disapproval – was to hurt the other person, not to kill them.

In some states provocation is a legal defence for women who fight back after enduring years of abuse, but killing the abuser is still an extreme form of problem-solving. When she faces court, however, the woman can expect a significant reduction in her jail sentence if it's found that killing was her only way to escape a brutal man or protect her children. As a thinking society we *almost* understand that as a motive.

Murder for greed or pleasure or power or perversion, however, is beyond comprehension.

Killing someone for money or to hide dirty secrets reveals a moral bankruptcy that defies belief. What on earth creates a person who values money or material possessions so much they're prepared to kill to get them, or to cover up the fact they've already taken them?

Perhaps the hardest motive to consider – for understanding it is never going to happen – is the woman who murders for perverse sexual gratification, or for the thrill of the power over another human being. Because these killers don't just kill. They kidnap and hold their victims; they do unspeakable things to them while they're still alive; they defile their remains. And they are never ever sorry.

These killers – women like Catherine Birnie – can impersonate normal, can pretend to be just like you and me, until they start talking about what they did. Then the masquerade is over; there's a different creature talking, one with a disturbing light in her eyes. Is it pride, or power, or the thrill of remembering? Was this the only thing that made her feel like 'somebody' in an otherwise nothing life?

What surprised us most, during the research for this book, was the level of 'overkill' expressed by some women during their crimes. So many of these murders were particularly sadistic and brutal, and went much further than was strictly 'necessary' to end a human life.

Was this a character thing? Was it rage driven? Was it the need of the so-called 'weaker sex' to make sure the job was done, really done, good and proper?

Catherine Birnie's explanation was far more prosaic than that. She told Ruth that killing someone is 'physically hard to do, and that if you're not fit it takes a lot more work'. She claimed she was surprised by how much the human body can endure before it gives up its fight for life.

Of equal surprise to us was the new-millennium trend of partner or pack killings; murders committed by two or more women – for revenge, or fun, or money, or just because they could.

Why do women kill? There are numerous humanistic explanations – terrible childhoods, abandonment or sexual abuse; all landscapes to lives deprived of love. But the majority of children raised in such bleak backgrounds do *not* grow up to become killers.

The women in this book weren't cornered; they weren't fighting for their own lives; they weren't defending someone else; they weren't the victims of the people whose lives they took.

The women within these pages are murderers, pure and simple. They are killers by choice.

In this book we tell the stories of some 20 Australian and New Zealand women who kill. We aim to separate fact from speculation, to look objectively at what happened in each case, and to try and make some sense of the extremes of human behaviour.

Are we any closer to knowing why women kill?

We doubt it. But perhaps we're a little way towards understanding why most women don't.

Ruth Wykes & Lindy Cameron

# PART 1: UNDER HIS SPELL?

Taking a life because you can, and 'playing' with that life before you callously dispose of it, is the most abhorrent form of human behaviour you can imagine. We know about this kind of crime because we have grown up with the legend of Jack the Ripper, and in more recent times have become familiar with the terrible crimes of serial killers.

But when home-grown women team up with sexual sadists and start committing similar crimes on our doorstep, it's too fantastic to believe.

In the 1980s in Australia there were two women, on opposite sides of the country, who teamed up with men to commit crimes that were unthinkable. Then in 2005 a woman attempted to kill her lover's wife, at his request, and left her for dead in the boot of her car.

Were they mad? Were they evil? Was it love? Had they fallen under the spell of dominant, sadistic men?

These women were not held against their will. Neither were they passive witnesses to what their men did to victims. These women helped plan, carry out, then conceal their crimes.

# Don't Ever Call Me Helpless

It's the stillness in her, the calm, when she watches me that frightens me more than anything. I know enough to be aware that her conscience is bankrupt; she is bemused by ordinary human emotions and reactions.

I am her reluctant teacher. I know she mimics my interactions with people to help her pass as ordinary and insignificant. I have become her mask. Yet barely beneath the surface, in those times she is tested, her true character is revealed. When she is real she is cruel, deeply arrogant, manipulative and difficult.

She won't change because she can't. She won't find redemption, and in any case she doesn't want to.

Catherine Margaret Birnie resides in Perth's Bandyup Women's Prison. It has been her home for 30 years, and if public sentiment is any measure of her future, she will remain there for the rest of her life. In 1987 she was imprisoned for abducting, kidnapping, torturing and murdering four Perth women and attempting to murder a fifth. She and her partner David Birnie were kidnappers. They were torturers. They were sexual sadists. They are serial killers.

The first thing you notice about Catherine Birnie is that you don't notice her at all. She blends in, taking up very little space. It isn't until she becomes aware that you haven't recognised her that she makes herself known to you.

She doesn't look scary; neither does she carry an aura of danger. In her everyday life Cathy Birnie is a diminutive woman, only around 160 centimetres tall with tiny features. Her hands are small and well defined, and when she walks it is with the air of someone who doesn't have a care in the world.

Even her face is still and unremarkable when she is relaxed. Her eyes, which have been variously described as cruel, evil and dark, are rarely that; they are part of the mask she wears so successfully. She passes as 'nobody'.

One woman, a social worker who was conducting a workshop at Bandyup, spent some time chatting with Catherine in the library one day. As she was leaving the prison she was talking to a colleague about the 'lovely woman in the library'. She went on to speculate that this nice woman must be one of those people you read about who is in prison for social security fraud. When she learned who she had been talking to she refused to believe it: 'No way! She's like any normal person you'd meet in the street. She couldn't have done that!'

But Catherine isn't like any normal person. She has a native intelligence that enables her to read a person's character very quickly. She also has an intuitive sense of someone's vulnerabilities, and an absolute willingness to play with that. For someone with Catherine's propensity for games, an institution with 180 other women to choose from is a smorgasbord.

Life in prison is relatively comfortable for her. She has gained the right to live in one of the self-care units, which are separate from the main cell blocks and have their own small gardens. She gets access to the daily newspapers and to a computer. All meals are provided; it's still jail, but a self-care unit is as comfortable a place as anyone can find within the prison.

By her own admission she is now a Christian. And while she is quite happy to state that she has found God, her reluctance to expand on this life-changing experience leaves many people cynical. It is far from uncommon for prisoners, especially those serving lengthy jail terms, to convert to Christianity. It is also not uncommon for that to be nothing more than a convenient 'character reference' for their next parole hearings.

Now 58 years old, Catherine is a fading version of the hateful, belligerent woman who stares defiantly out of photos taken after her arrest in 1986. Her face has softened and her hair is grey.

The hateful facial expressions, captured by the news media and police photographers, represent a moment, frozen in time, when she had just been convicted of murder. They are inarguably the reference point by which everybody forms their judgement of Catherine Birnie. After all, the closest most people will ever get to her is by looking at those frozen images. In real life she is softer, less intimidating. But is she any less lethal?

The year 1986 was one in which Australian politics was dominated by the Labor Party. Bob Hawke, the charismatic bloke you'd want to have a beer with, was Prime Minister of Australia. Brian Burke, a man who himself would become intimately familiar with the inside of a prison cell, was Premier of Western Australia. In New South Wales Neville Wran resigned after a decade of leading the state.

Culturally, the Australian Ballet was bravely performing Shakespeare's *Taming of the Shrew* to surprisingly excellent reviews, but the arts event most Australians remember more was the debut of the movie *Crocodile Dundee*. Starring Paul Hogan, it became a worldwide smash. On the small screen an ambitious local soap opera made its debut. Producers and TV executives wondered how it would be received, but *Neighbours* is still entertaining us more than two decades later.

In the sporting arenas around the nation, the Parramatta Eels beat Canterbury Bankstown to become premiers of the New South Wales Rugby League, and in the VFL's 90th year Hawthorn defeated Carlton.

But 1986 was a horrific year for crime. In February a young nurse, Anita Cobby, went missing. When her body was found in a paddock, every ordinary person in New South Wales was stunned, then outraged. Rage was palpable when five men were arrested and details emerged of what they had done to Anita.

In March a car bomb exploded outside Police Headquarters in Russell Street, Melbourne. The bomb killed a policewoman and injured 22 other people. Four men were arrested and sent to prison for the bombings, although one of them was later acquitted on appeal. The apparent motive for the bombings was revenge against the police. The bombers had previously been arrested by the Victoria Police for other crimes.

In July Kevin Barlow and Brian Chambers were hanged in Malaysia. Barlow and Chambers had been caught trafficking 141.9 grams of heroin and, in what Prime Minister Bob Hawke described as a 'barbaric' act, became the first westerners executed under the tough new Malaysian anti-drug laws. They were hanged on 7 July in Pudu Prison.

In August, a beautiful nine-year-old girl, Samantha Knight, went missing in Bondi, Sydney. Despite a huge police investigation and intense media campaign nothing came to light and Samantha wasn't found. Ten years would go by before a real clue led police to start looking at a convicted paedophile, and it would be 17 years after her death that this man would be found guilty of killing her. Samantha's body was never found.

In October 1986 a working-class couple in the Perth suburb of Willagee grew tired of talking about their fantasies and decided it was time to do something about it. In the intimate language of couples they developed a shorthand – a code – for their perverted intentions: 'I've got the munchies'. David and Catherine Birnie started hunting.

It was all well planned beforehand, and it happened so quickly that most of the damage had been done before Perth's police or general community had any real idea that something was wrong. By the time a young, half-naked woman ran into a supermarket in

Willagee and asked them to call the police, at least four young women were dead. Abducted, repeatedly raped, tortured, drugged and murdered.

As police listened with mounting horror to the story being related to them by the frightened young woman, their sense of dread grew. They knew that in the previous several weeks there had been four separate reports of missing women in Perth, and at least one police officer had privately begun to worry that a serial killer was operating in the small, isolated city. Until now it had been a vague fear, but as the story began to unfold that fear gave way to disbelief, then horror.

Willagee is one of Perth's unpretentious suburbs. Situated around 13 kilometres south of Perth, it is a Labor heartland. Australian to its back teeth, its population is 76 per cent Australian-born, 10 per cent of English origin and the rest a smattering of other immigrants. Half the population is married, more than one-third are Catholic and the average house is a separate dwelling.

Developed in 1951, Willagee is named after a small swamp referred to on early maps as 'Wilgee', an Aboriginal term meaning red ochre. This swamp, from which local Aborigines dug ochre, was situated in what is now Kardinya. Most streets are named after those who arrived on *HMS Success* under Captain Stirling in 1827.

David and Catherine Birnie moved into 3 Moorhouse Street, Willagee, in 1984 and were still there in 1986. The house itself was unprepossessing, a modest white-brick building that seemed to be suffering from neglect. The garden was bedraggled, paint was peeling from the walls and bushes had been allowed to grow tall enough to conceal the front windows. A cursory glance from a passer-by would have left you with the impression that this was just another rental property, and that the tenants were terrible gardeners.

But 3 Moorhouse Street was something else altogether: it would become known as Perth's House of Horrors. It became a prison, a torture chamber and a crime scene, a stage upon which unimaginable acts of depravity and sadism would be acted out by the Birnies.

When the Birnies were captured and the extent of their horrific crimes were revealed to a stunned and disbelieving public, there were cries to have the house bulldozed. Nobody could imagine living in that house, not once they knew what had taken place inside those walls. But 3 Moorhouse Street has survived, and today remains structurally identical to how it looked back then. It has been painted and cleaned up, and the garden is healthy and thriving. It looks like a nice house in a pleasant working-class suburb of Perth.

## MARY

Monday 6 October started out like any other week for 22-year-old Mary Neilson. She was a psychology student at the University of Western Australia who was planning to work as a counsellor with the Department of Community Welfare. To earn some extra cash Mary held down a part-time job in a deli.

Mary's parents were both TAFE lecturers, and in October 1986 they were enjoying a holiday in Britain. Mary's Monday began like any ordinary week: she went to work at the deli, and had lectures at university later that day. With a few hours to spare Mary decided to do something about the tyres for her car. She needed new ones.

Like many university students Mary had limited funds and the option of buying cheaper tyres was appealing, so she went to a car wreckers in the southern suburb of Myaree. Here she was served by small, mild-mannered David Birnie, who showed her some tyres and then told her that if she called around to his place he would be able to do her a much better deal. David lived less than five minutes' drive from where he worked. Mary agreed to go and buy the tyres privately from Birnie.

When she knocked on the door at 3 Moorhouse Street, Willagee, she was met at knifepoint by a very different David Birnie who, along with his partner Catherine, dragged her into the bedroom, tore her clothes off her, gagged her and chained her to their double bed. For tseveral hours Mary Neilson was repeatedly raped by David Birnie while Catherine looked on, encouraged him and asked him explicitly what was turning him on the most.

As night fell the Birnies decided they needed to 'remove the evidence' from the house. Still bound, Mary was dragged into their car, driven to Gleneagle Forest, south of Perth, and in the middle of the night was raped again. Then David Birnie took out a nylon cord and wrapped it around Mary's neck. Using a small tree branch to tighten the cord, Birnie strangled Mary Neilson as she lay on the ground begging for her life.

After she had died, the Birnies dug a shallow grave and, before burying her, stabbed Mary. David told Catherine he had read somewhere that this would allow gases to escape as the body decomposed.

Given what is now known about piquerism (a stabbing sexual fetish), it is difficult to believe that there was ever such a pragmatic thought in David Birnie's head. It is far more likely that the act of penetrating his victims with a knife was yet another kick for this depraved man.

When they arrived back in Perth, David and Catherine knew they couldn't leave Mary Neilson's car parked outside their house. David drove the Galant to a riverside car park, opposite police headquarters, where it was found six days later.

Over the years many people have speculated that this, the first known murder committed by David and Catherine Birnie, was unplanned. Experts believe that David impulsively took advantage of Mary Neilson turning up at his workplace and being an 'easy target'. This isn't true. While Mary was in the terrible position of being in the wrong place at the wrong time, David and Catherine had been talking about what they would do, and planning for at least a year.

According to Catherine the murders she committed with her partner David Birnie were thoroughly researched and planned. 'We looked into everything before we started, every little detail ... right down to how long you could leave a car in a certain place before anyone would notice it,' she said. 'We bought this book, it was called *Perfect Murder* or something like that, and we learned a lot from that about what to do.'

Did the Birnies leave Mary Neilson's car so close to police headquarters deliberately? Was it a message to the police and the community? 'No,' scoffed Catherine, 'we did our homework and we found out that that was a car park where the council wouldn't check for days.'

Did they intend to actually murder Mary Neilson? 'She saw our faces, didn't she? She saw where we lived.'

Questions about whether they knew they would kill Mary even before she knocked on their Moorhouse Street door are anticipated. A killer's eyes lock on to those of the inquisitive; cold, expressionless, soulless.

Mary Neilson never stood a chance. From the moment she accepted David's invitation to drop over to his place and negotiate cheaper prices for her tyres, her fate was sealed.

## SUSANNAH

Just two weeks later, on Monday 20 October 1986, David and Catherine Birnie were actively hunting for their next victim. They spent hours driving around the streets of Perth looking for 'the right one'. Unlike some serial killers they weren't drawn to particular physical characteristics, age groups or 'types'; she just had to be female, alone, and vulnerable.

They found her hitchhiking along Stirling Highway in Claremont, a well-heeled area in Perth's western suburbs. Her name was Susannah Candy, and she was 15 years old. It obviously didn't seem dangerous to accept a lift from a mild-looking couple in their thirties, especially since one of them was a woman.

Susannah Candy was an outstanding student at Hollywood High School. Her father, Dr Douglas Candy, one of Perth's most respected ophthalmic surgeons, worked at St John of God Hospital. Susannah lived at home with her parents, two brothers and sister at the time of her disappearance. Dr Candy was protective of his four children and when Susannah started a part-time job in a local restaurant he would meet her after work and walk her home. Dr Candy was worried enough that he asked her to give up her job. But Susannah enjoyed her work and on that Monday night she was alone on Stirling Highway when the Birnies drew up alongside her.

On the pretext of offering Susannah a lift home, the Birnies coerced her into their car and drove back to their Moorhouse Street home. They kept Susannah Candy tied to their bed and committed repeated offences against her, until David Birnie decided it was time to kill her. He produced a nylon rope and put it around her neck, but Susannah became hysterical and fought for her life. Both Birnies forced several sleeping pills down Susannah's throat in an effort to sedate her.

When Susannah was asleep, affected by the drugs, David again put the rope around Susannah's neck. He looked at Catherine and said: 'Prove you love me.'

Without any hesitation Catherine Birnie strangled Susannah Candy to death.

After Catherine Birnie strangled the young girl the couple bundled her into their car and drove her to Gleneagle Forest, where they buried her not far from where they had buried Mary Neilson two weeks earlier.

While being held captive Susannah had been forced to write two letters to her worried parents. In those letters she explained that she was writing to assure them that she was okay, that she just needed some time out to sort through her problems. The letters were sent almost two weeks apart; one posted in Perth and the other from Fremantle. It didn't convince her family; if anything it made them more worried than ever that something terrible had happened.

Susannah's worried family reported her missing to the police. According to a neighbour of the Candy family:

I heard first-hand the appalling treatment that her parents

received at the hands of police. They accused the missing 15 year old, a straight A student with no problems and good references, of variously being a runaway, a prostitute, troubled, drug addled and attention-seeking.

All this in the face of overwhelming evidence to the contrary from fellow students, teachers, the parents, various teen counsellors and her neighbours. The police, either too incompetent or too shiftless to act, upped the ante against the teenager, accusing her of being an accomplished scammer and liar, experienced in hiding aberrant behaviour behind an angelic facade.

In fact, this poor young child was an innocent teenager, being brutally assaulted, and latterly murdered, by the Birnies.

This second-hand account, while perhaps an overstatement in some ways, offers insight into how the police were approaching the reports of the missing women at the time. There had been no bodies found at this stage, and only one other person missing. The only 'evidence' available to police at the time was that Susannah had 'contacted her family' to say she was all right. It isn't altogether surprising that the police were yet to become suspicious that something far more terrible was going on.

## NOELENE

Noelene Patterson lived with her mother in the beautiful riverside suburb of Bicton, near Fremantle. The 31-year-old woman was a former Ansett airline hostess who had worked for the airline for nine years. She then went to work for entrepreneur Alan Bond for two years on his private airline, and in 1986 was working at the Nedlands Golf Club.

Described by those who knew her as elegant, beautiful and popular, Noelene was driving home from work on Saturday 1 November 1986 when her car ran out of petrol. She was stuck on the Canning Highway in East Fremantle, not far from home.

The Birnies had been out hunting that night when they came across Noelene. As it happened they knew her and, according to some reports, had even been to her house to help with wallpapering. They pulled up alongside Noelene and offered to take her to the nearest service station. Relieved to see someone she knew, Noelene accepted the offer.

As soon as she got in the car a knife was held to her throat and Noelene was taken to the Birnies' Willagee home. Bound, gagged, raped and tortured, it had been the intention of the Birnies to kill Noelene that night and dispose of her body in Gleneagle.

But David Birnie developed an emotional attachment to Noelene and kept putting off her murder. He kept her alive for three days. Catherine, on the other hand, took an instant dislike to the beautiful Patterson. In part it was because she sensed David's attachment to Noelene and felt jealous.

After three days Catherine had had more than enough. She held a knife to her own breast and delivered an ultimatum to her partner: 'Her or me – you choose!'

David Birnie gave Noelene Patterson a massive dose of sleeping pills and then strangled her while she slept. The couple then followed a familiar routine – they drove to Gleneagle where they dug a shallow grave and buried Noelene Patterson, but not before Catherine drew some personal satisfaction from throwing sand in the dead woman's face.

## DENISE

Denise Brown was a fun-loving 21-year-old woman who worked as a part-time computer operator. Like many of her friends she loved dancing and nightclubs, and she lived with her boyfriend and another couple in Nedlands. Denise is described by people as having been warm, friendly, trusting and naive.

On Wednesday 5 November Denise had spent the day with a girlfriend at the Coolbellup Hotel. She was waiting for a bus outside the Stoned Crow Wine House in Fremantle that evening when the Birnies pulled up alongside her and offered her a ride home.

It may have been her happy, trusting nature that led her to accept the ride from the Birnies instead of waiting for a bus. In any case, as soon as she was in the car a knife was held to her throat. She was abducted and taken to the Moorhouse residence where, like the women before her, she was raped, time and time again.

Cruelly, the Birnies forced her to make phone calls to tell friends she was okay. It was their way of throwing investigators off any trail, to slow down the inevitability that Denise Brown would be the fourth Perth woman reported missing in the space of 27 days.

The day after abducting Denise Brown from the street, the Birnies decided to kill her. They drugged her, and dragged the bound woman into their car. In a departure from their routine of heading to Gleneagle Forest, the Birnies headed north, and drove more than 60 kilometres to Gnangara Pine Plantation at Wanneroo.

Once they had arrived in the forest David Birnie decided he would rape Denise Brown again while he waited for darkness to fall. During one of the rapes he stabbed her in the neck with a knife, an injury which, while horrific, proved not to be fatal. Catherine Birnie found a bigger knife and handed it to her partner. He stabbed the badly wounded young woman again, this time believing he had killed her.

He set about digging a shallow grave and after he placed Denise Brown's body in it, he was shocked when she sat up, trying to escape. At this point David Birnie grabbed an axe and struck Denise Brown twice on the skull with great force. Then the Birnies covered her body with sand.

## KATE

Just a few days later, on Monday 10 November 1986, 17-year-old Kate was walking along her street in the fashionable suburb of Nedlands. She was on the Stirling Highway when a friendly couple pulled up and asked her for directions. While she was chatting to them the man jumped out of the car, produced a knife and forced her to get in.

She was taken back to Willagee, where she was tied to the bed and raped twice. Kate was forced to phone her parents to say she was all right, and while on the phone she had the presence of mind to draw stick figures on a writing pad, symbolising the phone number she was calling from. It was smart thinking because not only would those stick figures help Kate recall the phone number, it was also evidence that she had been in the house.

The following morning David Birnie left for work, and Kate was left alone with Catherine. Kate convinced Catherine that she desperately needed to use the toilet and eventually Birnie relented and undid the chains. Coincidentally someone knocked on the door while Kate was free from her chains. The distraction gave her the only opportunity she would have, and she escaped through an unlocked window.

Semi-naked, Kate ran through the streets of Willagee until she came to a nearby supermarket in a small shopping centre. Close to hysteria, she demanded that they call the police.

## PAUL FERGUSON

Detective Paul Ferguson had been worried about the reports of missing women, and by 5 November, when Denise Brown was reported missing, he was convinced a serial killer was operating in Perth. Ferguson had checked into the girls' backgrounds: there was nothing to link these women, no secret lovers or married men, no hidden drug use, no reason to run. They all came from good families and were leading normal lives. Until they disappeared.

He was uncomfortable that two of the missing women had apparently contacted family or friends – either through letters or phone calls – after they went missing. This suggested a pattern. His suspicions led him to contact CIB Chief Bill Neilson, who had been in charge of the investigation for serial killer Eric Edgar Cooke in the 1960s. Neilson agreed with him.

Paul Ferguson and Detective Sergeant Vince Katich were working when they heard on the two-way radio that a semi-naked young woman had run into a Willagee supermarket asking for the police. They quickly responded, hoping it was missing girl Denise Brown. They were stunned to find another young woman, and even more stunned when they listened to what she had to tell them.

Kate was an intelligent, observant young woman and she was able to tell the police the address and telephone number of the house in Willagee she had been driven to at knifepoint. She told them about being raped, chained and photographed. But it was when she told them that she had been forced to phone home that the detectives realised they were very, very close to breaking this case.

Ferguson and Katich went to the dishevelled cottage at 3 Moorhouse Street, Willagee, and knocked on the door. Nobody was home. They hid in a panel van in the driveway, and it wasn't long before Catherine Birnie came back from what would be her last free trip anywhere. When the detectives approached her Catherine was tense and cold, but she did tell them where David Birnie worked.

The detectives brought David Birnie home in handcuffs, and then took both him and Catherine to Fremantle police station where they began an intense interrogation. They separated them in different interview rooms, and both Birnies held to the story that Kate had come to their house of her own free will, and had just been partying with them. They stated emphatically that Kate had come to their place the previous evening to share some marijuana, and that one thing had led to another. Both Birnies claimed that David and Kate had consensual sex, and she had stayed the night. They emphatically denied knowing anything about any other missing women.

A search of the house found the handbag and a packet of cigarettes that Kate had hidden in the ceiling to prove that she had actually been there, but there was little to prove the allegation of rape or connect the Birnies with any of the other missing women.

Back at Fremantle police station, Detective Sergeant Katich was beginning to wonder how they would ever get the Birnies to talk. The lack of physical evidence back at Moorhouse Street meant they would need to elicit a confession from at least one of them. At around 7pm Katich said half-jokingly to David Birnie: 'It's getting dark. Best we take the shovel and dig them up.'

To Katich's complete surprise Birnie responded with: 'Okay. There's four of them.'

As soon as she was informed that David had confessed to the crimes, Catherine Birnie capitulated. She confessed her role in the kidnapping, rape and murder of the four dead women, and to her role in Kate's kidnapping and rape.

The Birnies were bundled into a car with the detectives after agreeing to show them where they had buried the bodies. They headed north past Perth city to Wanneroo and then on to the Gnangara Pine Plantation. During the trip David Birnie was relaxed and very chatty. He was so engrossed in making conversation with the police that they were almost at Yanchep before Birnie realised they had gone too far. Catherine, on the other hand, was silent.

They turned back and headed towards the city. As they reached the turn-off from the highway, Birnie directed the detectives to drive about 400 metres into Gnangara Pine Plantation. When they did that he indicated a spot and said, 'Dig there.'

It didn't take police long to uncover the remains of Denise Brown, who had been buried there just five days previously.

The detectives left other police to guard Denise's grave and headed back down the highway with the Birnies, this time heading south. They travelled past the city, then along the Albany Highway until they reached Gleneagle Picnic Area near Armadale.

David Birnie guided the police into the forest and along a narrow track. Up a slight incline, about 40 metres from the track, was where they had buried Mary Neilson. Another kilometre down the same track the Birnies pointed out Susannah Candy's grave. Throughout this trip the police were struck by the fact that the couple showed no emotion, no embarrassment as they led them from one crime scene to another. If anything, the police thought, the Birnies were enjoying being the centre of attention.

After showing the police where they had buried Susannah Candy, Catherine Birnie decided it was her turn. She told police that she wanted to show them where Noelene Patterson was buried. She went to great lengths to describe to the police how much she had disliked Noelene, and stated that she was glad she was dead. As she led police to the final victim, Catherine Birnie walked up to Noelene's grave – and spat on it.

As they were leaving Gleneagle Forest David Birnie paused, looked back, and then said to Detective Sergeant Vince Katich, 'What a pointless waste of young life.'

One of the police officers involved in the investigation, Neville Collard, described the feeling among police that night: 'When they said they had caught the Birnies, the next day they recalled me to work I was on the evening shift. The admission that occurred, I think somewhere around seven or eight o'clock at night, the jubilance in the office and the detectives and shouting and running around saying, "He's admitted to four murders."

'The jubilation that people feel in relation to cracking a really hard case, for me, because I had been in the room with Kate taking statements and interviewing her and going over the facts and going over everything, she was a lucky girl.'

According to Paul Kidd in his book *Never to Be Released*, there was at least one other young woman who was very lucky to be alive after her near encounter with the Birnies. He describes how after the Birnies' capture, a 19-year-old student told police how she was offered a lift by two people who she later recognised as Catherine and David Birnie from photos in the newspapers.

After finishing university for the day, she was walking along Pinjar Road, Wanneroo, when a car pulled up beside her. There were two people in the front and another slumped in the back seat. Later she realised that the person in the back was probably Denise Brown.

She went on:

I felt uneasy. I didn't recognise the car. There was a man driving and a woman in the front seat of the car. The man kept looking down, not looking at me, and the woman was drinking a can of UDL rum and coke. I thought the fact that she was drinking at that time of day was strange. He didn't look at me the whole time. It was the woman who did all the talking. She asked me if I wanted a lift anywhere. I said, 'No, I only live up the road.'

They continued to sit there and I looked into the back seat where I saw a small person with short brown hair lying across the seat. I thought it must have been their son or daughter asleep in the back. The person was in a sleeping position and from the haircut looked like a boy but for some reason I got the feeling it was a girl. I told them again I didn't want a lift because walking was good exercise. The man looked up for the first time and gazed at me before looking away again. By this time more cars had appeared and I started to walk away but they continued to sit in the car. Finally the car started and they did another U-turn and drove up Pinjar Road towards the pine plantation. It wasn't until I saw a really good photo of Catherine Birnie that I realised who they were. Somebody must have been looking after me that day. I don't know what would have happened to me if I had got into that car.

It quickly became obvious to everyone that had Kate not managed to escape from Moorhouse Street, she would have been killed. It was equally apparent that the killings would have continued. David Birnie had a taste for it; he was driven by something inside himself to keep finding women. He had no intention of stopping.

During the police interviews with Kate, and then the Birnies, it became clear that there was a pattern to the crimes. But what wasn't as obvious was how Kate managed to escape.

Catherine's version of the events that led to her arrest are, predictably, very different from Kate's. She told police:

I think I must have come to a decision that sooner or later there had to be an end to the rampage. I had reached the stage when I didn't know what to do. I suppose I came to a decision that I was prepared to give her a chance.

I knew that it was a foregone conclusion that David would kill her, and probably do it that night. I was just fed up with the killings. I thought if something did not happen soon it would simply go on and on and never end.

Deep and dark in the back of my mind was yet another fear. I had a great fear that I would have to look at another killing like that of Denise Brown, the girl he murdered with the axe.

I wanted to avoid that at all costs. In the back of my mind I had come to the position where I really did not care if the girl escaped or not. When I found out that the girl had escaped, I felt a twinge of terror run down my spine. I thought to myself, David will be furious. What shall I tell him?

Kate has grown into a beautiful woman, a mother of three children. At times Kate seems driven by nervous energy; at other times she is a thoughtful, determined woman. Since surviving an ordeal that almost cost her life, Kate seems to have grabbed everything life offers her: she is driven, sometimes loud, opinionated, intelligent, and free – everything Catherine Birnie will never be. Her contempt for the Birnies is never far from the surface and sometimes, in unguarded moments, you can glimpse the scars.

Her recollection of that terrible day is that she outsmarted Catherine Birnie. Chained to the bed, she convinced Catherine that she really needed to use the toilet. Catherine eventually relented, and while Kate was in the bathroom she escaped by squeezing through the small window.

Catherine is reluctant to talk about how Kate actually got away. The story she told the police, in which she described her 'below the surface fears' and wanting the killings to end, is simply incredible. If her story is to be believed she left a young woman, whom she had abducted the night before, to roam around her house while she answered a knock on the door. Maybe she wanted the killings to end, and saw prison as the only way she would ever escape from David. Or maybe she was outsmarted by a young, terrified woman who was willing to do anything to survive.

On 12 November 1986 David and Catherine Birnie appeared in Fremantle Magistrates Court, where they were charged with four counts of murder. They had attracted a hostile crowd, and everyone who entered the courtroom that day had their bags checked. Waiting in the holding cells before their court appearance, the Birnies were heavily guarded by police.

David Birnie was led into court handcuffed to two police officers. He was wearing faded blue overalls, joggers and socks. Catherine arrived in court, cuffed to police, wearing blue jeans and a brown checked shirt. She was barefoot.

As the charges were read out the couple stood together, betraying no emotion. Statuesque. Neither of them had legal representation, and no plea was entered. Bail was refused and the couple was remanded in custody. When the magistrate asked Catherine if she would prefer eight or 30 days to prepare for her next appearance, she looked over at David and said: 'I'll go when he goes'.

On 10 February 1987 a huge crowd had gathered outside Perth's Supreme Court. They were an angry group of people, a microcosm of a community whose horror at the Birnie crimes was manifesting itself in impotent rage. As the prison truck carrying the Birnies arrived, the crowd made their feelings clear. Cries of 'String them up! Hang the bastards' echoed through the crowd. A police guard was there to protect the Birnies as they waited in their holding cells.

David Birnie pleaded guilty to four counts of murder, one count of abduction and one of rape. Through his lawyer he said he wanted to plead guilty to spare the families the long agony of a trial: 'It was the least I could do,' he later told a detective.

Throughout the brief trial Catherine Birnie stood holding her partner's hand. She was not required to plead as her barrister was waiting on the results of a psychiatric report. Catherine Birnie was remanded to appear in court later that month.

Catherine Birnie was found to be fit to plead and on 3 March

1987 she stood in the courtroom and confessed to her part in the murders.

In his sentencing remarks Mr Justice Wallace said to David Birnie: 'Each of these horrible crimes were premeditated, planned and carried out cruelly and relentlessly over a comparatively short period. The law is not strong enough to express the community's horror at this sadistic killer who tortured, raped and murdered four women. In my opinion David John Birnie is such a danger to society that he should never be released from prison.'

When he was sentencing Catherine Birney Justice Wallace said: 'In my opinion you should never be released to be with David Birnie. You should never be allowed to see him again.'

Bill Power was a journalist for a Perth daily newspaper who covered the Birnie trials. His reporting and personal observations of the trial made for compelling reading. In *Never To Be Released* Paul B Kidd highlighted some of Power's more colourful, if somewhat prejudicial, observations. Bill recalled:

'There was nothing distinctive about David and Catherine Birnie when they first appeared in court to face multiple murder charges in the serial killings which brought to an end the mystery of young women going missing off Perth streets.

'They were a rather nondescript, ordinary-looking couple you might find running a petrol station in a country town. David was a weedy little man and Catherine his drab, slightly buxom wife with a very sour face. Both were accompanied by male police officers.

'David Birnie appeared first at the top of the stairs from the holding cell beneath the court and looked totally out of place in the majestic Perth Supreme Court. He was already in the dock glancing around at the massed police, court staff and huge media contingent as Catherine made her way up the stairs to the courtroom.

'The scrawny little serial killer was mesmerising enough but nothing could have prepared me for the moment that Catherine

Birnie appeared at the top of the jarrah staircase leading up to the dock where the charges were to be read out to them.

'If you have ever witnessed a wild cat go off, then try and imagine that same hellcat in the confined spaces of a narrow staircase. Catherine Birnie fought against the guarding police officers and refused to allow any of them to touch her as she screamed and spat her words at them until she reached the dock and spotted her beloved David. Only then did she calm down.

'The unusualness of her appearance continued when David Birnie stood before the court to hear the murder charges read against him and Catherine Birnie was allowed to sit on a small wooden bench immediately behind him. As the judge levelled the horrible case against him, Birnie stood motionless with his hands clasped behind his back.

'What I witnessed next I will take to the grave with me,' Bill Power said. 'As the heinous charges of abduction, rape, torture and murder were being read out against him, Catherine Birnie bent forward, stretched out her right hand and gently stroked the ball of David Birnie's thumb behind his back.

'There has probably never before been such a declaration of undying love in the Western Australian Supreme Court dock.

'It was all over within a few minutes,' recalled Bill Power. 'And the erstwhile angelic Catherine, who moments before had acted out such a show of dedication, was dragged kicking and screaming and spitting down the wooden staircase to a prison van waiting beside the court.

'Perhaps she never wanted another man besides David to touch her.'

When Catherine and David Birnie were captured and brought before the Supreme Court, the mood in Perth was hostile. Crowds gathered outside the court and people were openly calling for the death penalty. Letters were fired off to the local newspapers, talkback radio was alight with people who had nowhere else to take their disbelief or anger. How could this happen in our safe little city?

People were at a complete loss to comprehend. What kind of monsters could do this? Were the Birnies crazy? Evil? How could a woman do this? Perhaps in the torrent of emotions, the most difficult thing of all was to look at Catherine Birnie and to wonder what kind of monster she was.

David Birnie was a lust killer, a psychopath who showed no regard for his victims. Catherine's involvement was explained away as her being personality dependent on her common-law husband. But that's an excuse, and a flimsy one.

We think we can spot misfits in our society. Those people whose social skills are underdeveloped, or who are afflicted with a mental disorder that sees them struggle to fit in with 'the norm'. We also think we would be able to tell if someone were cruel, sadistic, criminal. Yet the most chilling fact about serial killers is that they are rational and calculating – and for most of the time they can participate in society without drawing attention to themselves. As the British serial killer Dennis Nilsen put it, 'A mind can be evil without being abnormal.'

The FBI defines serial murder as the following:

A minimum of three to four victims, with a 'cooling off' period in between;

The killer is usually a stranger to the victim – the murders appear unconnected or random;

The murders reflect a need to sadistically dominate the victim;

The murder is rarely 'for profit'; the motive is psychological, not material;

The victim may have 'symbolic' value for the killer; the method of killing may reveal this meaning;

Killers often choose victims who are vulnerable (prostitutes, runaways etc).

Statistically, the average serial killer is a white male from a lower-to-middle-class background, usually in his 20s or 30s. Many were physically or emotionally abused by parents. Some were adopted. As children, fledgling serial killers often set fires, torture animals and wet their beds (these red-flag behaviours are known as the 'triad' of symptoms). Brain injuries are common. Some are very intelligent and have shown great promise as successful professionals. They are also fascinated with the police and authority in general.

These are, of course, generalisations formed in the United States after years of profiling convicted serial killers. In many respects David Birnie will fit into those statistical norms, but they don't explain Catherine's involvement. Or do they?

Catherine Margaret Harrison was born on 21 May 1951. She was two years old when her mother Doreen died while giving birth to Catherine's younger brother. He died two days later. After the death of her mother and brother, Catherine went to South Africa with her father Harold, who found it too hard to raise his toddler daughter. He sent her back to Perth to live with her maternal grandparents.

A year later she was sent to live with an aunt and uncle and appears to have spent time being shuffled between reluctant relatives. Hers was an unhappy and lonely childhood. Neighbours have remembered Catherine as a sad child, one who rarely smiled, and who had few friends. Her grandparents wouldn't have other children come to visit; some people who knew the family then claim that most parents wouldn't allow their children to associate with Catherine.

When she was still a child Catherine watched her grandmother die from an epileptic seizure. Then at the age of ten she was the subject of yet another custody dispute that resulted in her father, Harold, being awarded sole custody.

Two years later she met a boy, a new neighbour, who was two years older than her, but with whom she felt an immediate affinity. He too was from a disaffected, dysfunctional family; he was a teenage boy who was very angry at the world. Both of them were looking for something and recognised a little of themselves in each other, and it wasn't long before they had fallen in love. His name was David Birnie.

David John Birnie was born on 16 February 1951 to John and Margaret Birnie and was the eldest of six children. They lived in the semi-rural area of Wattle Grove, 13 kilometres east of Perth.

His father was physically disabled and both parents were alcoholics. Neighbours from the time heard rumours of promiscuity, alcoholism and incest. John and Margaret struggled to raise the children due to their low income; at times the authorities would take the children away and place them in care. The family moved in the early 1960s and became neighbours of Catherine and her family. When John and Margaret divorced neither wanted custody of David and he became a ward of the state.

David's was a dysfunctional childhood, and from a relatively young age he displayed signs of an unhealthy sexual appetite. At 15, David left school to become an apprentice jockey for Eric Parnham at a nearby Ascot racecourse. During his time there, some workmates claimed he often physically harmed the horses and developed the tendencies of an exhibitionist. One night, David broke into an elderly lady's house naked, with a stocking over his head, and committed his first rape.

It isn't clear when David and Catherine embarked on their teenage life of petty crime, but they became well known to police. Even as juveniles they were more than willing to show that their regard for the law and respect for society were almost non-existent.

On 11 June 1969 they were charged with 11 counts of theft and breaking and entering. David was sentenced to nine months in prison. Catherine was pregnant at the time and only received probation. The following month, the two appeared before the Supreme Court, charged with another eight counts of theft. Three more years of imprisonment were added on to David's sentence and Catherine received an additional four years of probation.

In July 1970 David escaped from Karnet prison and reunited with Catherine again. It was not long before the two were once again in trouble with the law. They were arrested on 10 July 1970 and charged with 53 counts of theft, breaking and entering, trespassing and illegal operation of a motor vehicle. In their possession, police found wigs, radios, dynamite, detonators and fuses. Catherine admitted to knowing that her actions were wrong, but claimed that she loved David and would do absolutely anything for him. David was sentenced to two-and-a-half years in prison and Catherine was sentenced to six months of imprisonment. Her baby was taken by welfare services.

Catherine's father Harold had been trying to keep her away from David before her imprisonment, but to no avail. While she was serving her time, a parole officer talked to her about how different and much better her life would be if she stayed away from David. The enforced separation from David seemed to have an effect on Catherine, and when she was released she found a job as a domestic servant for a family, the McLaughlins.

She was drawn to their youngest son Donald, became romantically involved with him and married him on her 21st birthday. But tragedy never seemed too far away from Catherine McLaughlin, nee Harrison. Several months later she watched helpless with horror as their seven-month-old son, little Donny, was struck by a vehicle in the driveway of their home. The infant died from his injuries.

Catherine and Donald McLaughlin had five more children and continued with their marriage for a number of years. Meanwhile, David Birnie had been released from prison. He met another woman and they had a baby daughter together.

Did they stay in contact? Did the yearning to be together ever go away? Little is known about those intervening years when David and Catherine were living with their partners and raising children. Catherine and Donald were living in near poverty in Victoria Park, a suburb separated from Perth's CBD by the Swan River. Catherine's father and uncle were living in the house with the couple and five children.

Four weeks after the birth of the youngest baby, Catherine went to hospital to have a hysterectomy. When Donald came to visit her, David Birnie was sitting in the visitors' chair holding Catherine's hand. According to some people she had been seeing David behind her husband's back for almost two years. Soon after leaving hospital she went to visit David one day, then phoned Donald and told him she wasn't coming back.

She changed her surname to Birnie by deed poll, effectively

closing the door on the most stable chapter in her life. And opening the door on a chapter that would send deep chills through a whole city.

At the age of 21 James Birnie, David's younger brother, had to move out of home. His mother had taken a restraining order out against him, and he had just been released from prison, having served five months for indecently interfering with his six-year-old niece.

James told a reporter: '[The six-year-old] led me on. You don't know what they can be like. When I left prison, I had nowhere to go. I couldn't go back to my mother's place because I had assaulted her and there was a restraining order out against me. I had a couple of fights with Mum and the police chased me off. Mum has alcohol problems. So David and Catherine let me move in. They weren't real happy about it and David kept saying that he was going to kill me, to keep me in line.'

James added that David Birnie had few friends, was heavily into kinky sex and had a large pornographic video collection. 'He has to have sex four or five times a day,' James said. 'I saw him use a hypodermic of that stuff you have when they're going to put stitches in your leg. It makes you numb. He put the needle in his penis. Then he had sex. David has had many women. He always has someone.' James' 21st birthday present from David was being allowed to have sex with Catherine.

David Birnie's apparent insatiable appetite for sex began when he was a teenager. It is likely, given that he committed rape at age 15, he was already developing a taste for control and violence. In retrospect, all the danger signs were there; this was a man who would go on to commit progressively worse crimes against women.

Even in prison David tried to find ways to feed his sexual appetite. In June 1993 authorities discovered he had pornography on his personal computer in his special protection unit in Casuarina. The computer was confiscated. More than a decade later he was charged with sexual assault on a fellow inmate.

Because both she and David Birnie pleaded guilty to the charges of abduction and murder there was only a very brief trial, and very little detail of their crimes went on the public record. The psychiatrist who gave evidence about Catherine's mental state and fitness to stand trial, told the Supreme Court that Catherine was totally dependent on Birnie and almost totally vulnerable to his evil influence. He said: 'It is the worst case of personality dependence I have seen in my career.'

Was it really that easy to explain, or to dismiss? Catherine didn't sit by and watch her partner commit these crimes; she was an active participant in them. No matter how much a woman loves her partner, it is not normal to spend significant time planning heinous crimes against other women. Or to abduct strangers. Or to physically restrain them. Or to watch your partner forcefully violate them while you stand around with a camera in your hands. Or to jump into bed and continue the degrading, painful and disgraceful attacks. Or to murder them. Or bury them.

Catherine was an active participant in all the crimes committed by her and David Birnie. It is too simplistic to explain her involvement as merely being under the evil influence of David Birnie.

When the police asked Catherine, after her arrest, why she had helped kill Susannah, she said: 'Because I wanted to see how strong I was within my inner self. I didn't feel a thing. It was like I expected. I was prepared to follow him to the end of the earth and do anything to see that his desires were satisfied. She was a female. Females hurt and destroy males.'

The first part of her statement is probably true. The second part is Catherine being smart – telling the police and mental health experts what she thought they wanted to hear. Her explanation of motive, as told years later, is a little different: 'It's about power. *You* don't know what power is. Nobody knows what power is until you hold somebody's life in their hands, look into their eyes … and take it all away from them.'

Catherine is very aware that people ask 'why?' She claims that people have spent a lot of time trying to understand her, to find a reason for what she did. 'I've filled out those forms – the profile ones. Even the FBI has tried to profile me…and I told them exactly what they wanted to hear. You know – bad childhood, dead mother, stuff they were after.'

Her eyes dance as she relates this; whether it's because she was 'important enough' for the FBI to want to know about her, or because she felt like a naughty child, it's difficult to know. Catherine has had a lifelong contempt for authority, and her way of dealing with it inside the walls of an institution is to manipulate it for her own amusement.

Not long after she was put in prison, Catherine wrote a letter to one of her children. It is an interesting insight into the things that were occupying her thoughts in 1986. In part it reads:

By now you would have heard that I have been charged with murder and other things. Please try to understand that what I did was never meant to hurt anybody but that what I did was because I love David. Love is a very powerful thing & I found out that it can make you do things that you wouldn't do normally. It was because of my love for David that those things happened & went on happening. Be very careful of who you love & to what extent you love that person. I shall never be released from prison because of what has been done. I know this. Even now I won't stop loving David & trying to help him. I am going to see if my lawyer will handle the both of us. I'll always love David no matter what comes out in the court case. He has said he loves one of girls who was murdered & that he also loves me so I'm caught in a trap of loving a man blindly to all his faults. Please go on with your life and try to forget that I was ever your mother because I don't deserve to have children after what I've done to other people's children.

I'll always love you and the other kids but I think it's better if you try to forget me as your mother. I've got to go now as there are more things to be finalized so if I am allowed to I'll write at a [sic] nother time. I do love you and my thoughts are with you always. Don't feel ashamed because I feel all the shame for both of us.

Love Mum

Very little is known about Catherine Birnie's children, as is right. Life in a city as small as Perth would have been almost unbearable for anyone who was associated with the Birnies, let alone members of their family. When news of the arrests broke in the media, five of Catherine's children were living with their father. Her six-year-old son went home from school at lunchtime in tears, having been teased by older children. A relative told a local journalist: 'The children don't want to be judged. They just want some consideration.'

Catherine Birnie's letter is a very small insight into a complex issue. Was she, as she claimed, so in love with David that she was willing to do literally anything for him? She said it was her love for David, not the man himself, that made her commit those crimes. And she held to this line for many years, especially when there were people who were interested enough to ask her why she had committed such unthinkable acts against innocent young women.

Yet her story has changed a little over the years. Whether it's distorted memory, or whether the truth is slowly beginning to emerge, Catherine no longer credits her former partner with so much power when she relates the story to people.

After their arrest both David and Catherine Birnie claimed the only reason they murdered the women was to prevent them from being able to identify their killers. While this may appear a logical, if somewhat chilling confession, it doesn't account for the Birnies' behaviour.

The Birnies were displaying all the signs of being lust killers, for whom the killings had become as important a part of their perverted sexual rituals as the bindings, torture and rape. The fact that Birnie stabbed his fourth victim while he was in the act of raping her was an indication that his sickening violence was escalating, that what he had done in the past was no longer enough to feed his perverse appetite.

The FBI have undertaken extensive research on the crimes of sexual sadists, including interviewing a significant number of offenders and studying the case files. Their findings are used throughout the world as both a reference and an investigative tool. Some of the things they have learned certainly lend weight to the argument that David Birnie was a sexual sadist whose crimes would have escalated had he not been caught. This extract from the FBI's findings is enlightening:

Careful planning epitomizes the crimes of the sexual sadist, who devotes considerable time and effort to the offense. Many demonstrate cunning and methodical planning. The capture of the victim, the selection and preparation of equipment, and the methodical elicitation of suffering often reflect meticulous attention to detail.

The overwhelming majority of offenders studied used a pretext or ruse to first make contact with the victims. The sexual sadist would offer or request assistance, pretend to be a police officer, respond to a classified advertisement, meet a realtor at an isolated property, or otherwise gain the confidence of the victim.

Almost invariably, the victims were taken to a location selected in advance that offered solitude and safety for the sadist and little opportunity of escape or rescue for the victim. Such locations included the offender's residence, isolated forests, and even elaborately constructed facilities designed for captivity.

Almost 77 percent of the offenders used sexual bondage on their victims, often tying them with elaborate and excessive materials, using neat and symmetrical bindings, and restraining them in a variety of positions. Sixty percent held their victims in captivity for more than 24 hours.

The most common sexual activity was anal rape, followed in frequency by forced fellatio, vaginal rape, and foreign object penetration. Two-thirds of the men subjected their victims to at least three of these four acts.

Sixty percent of the offenders beat their victims.

Two men, who offended as a team, used a variety of methods to kill a series of victims. One victim was strangled during sex.

Another was injected in the neck with a caustic substance, electrocuted, and gassed in an oven. A third victim was shot. Twenty-nine of the 30 men selected white victims only. Eighty-three percent of the victims were strangers to the offender. While the majority of the men selected female victims, one-fourth attacked males exclusively. Sixteen percent of the men assaulted child victims only, and 26 percent attacked both children and adults.

These offenders retained a wealth of incriminating evidence. More than one-half of the offenders in our study kept records of their offenses, including calendars, maps, diaries, drawings, letters, manuscripts, photographs, audio tapes, video tapes, and media accounts of their crimes. For the most part, these secret and prized possessions were hidden in either their homes, offices, or vehicles, kept in rental storage space, or buried in containers.

Forty percent of the men took and kept personal items belonging to their victims. These items, which included drivers' licenses, jewelry, clothing, and photographs, served as mementos of the offense, and some of the offenders referred to them as 'trophies' of their conquests. However, none of the offenders retained parts of their victims' bodies, though some kept the entire corpse temporarily or permanently.

Sexually sadistic offenders commit well-planned and carefully concealed crimes. Their crimes are repetitive, serious, and shocking, and they take special steps to prevent detection. The harm that these men wreak is so devastating and their techniques so sophisticated that those who attempt to apprehend and convict them must be armed with uncommon insight, extensive knowledge, and sophisticated investigative resources.

Women's prisons in Perth have never enjoyed equal status, or even equal conditions, with the men's prisons. Part of the reason for this was that in the past so few women committed jailable offences that no government was willing to spend money on funding a separate prison. Part of it was the historic and patriarchal view that the fairer sex was simply not capable of committing terrible crime.

Until 1970 female prisoners were housed in a separate facility at the maximum security Fremantle Prison. Their living quarters were horrific: small, convict-built cells with an adjacent caged, concrete exercise yard no bigger than the average modern bathroom. By 1970 the government understood that the world was changing and there needed to be a separate prison for women.

Bandyup Women's Prison lies to the north-east of Perth's CBD in the Swan Valley. Being the only women's prison in the state, it houses a mix of prisoners, ranging from those women being held on remand, minimum-security prisoners, through to those deemed never to be released. It has the feel of a small community; a confined, disharmonious, dysfunctional community.

Life in Bandyup Prison is dull, repetitive and dehumanising. Imagine arriving in a small, enclosed community – under escort – after leaving your friends and family behind. The gates are closed behind you; you are put into a room, forced to remove all your clothes only to suffer the ignominy of being searched by a complete stranger.

From that moment on your life is completely in the control of other people. You wear the same drab maroon tracksuit as every other inmate, the same shoes or thongs. You will spend 12 hours of every day locked in a small, cramped cell that has an open window through which anyone can look at any time they please. Referred to by your surname, you will have diminished identity and even less free will.

You will have the opportunity to work, and earn up to $50 a week, and you will be able to see family and friends, make phone calls, write letters – but only if the prison authorities grant you those privileges. Your day will start when your cell door is unlocked, and you will trudge through the same, boring routine you did yesterday: shower with your fellow inmates; eat breakfast in the communal dining room; head off to work in the kitchen, laundry, garden or wherever else you spend your day. Lunch, work, recreation (which may include the gym, TV or spending time with your fellow inmates), dinner, then lockdown for the next 12 hours.

There is a shop where you can buy food, cosmetics and other luxuries, as long as you have earned the money or been given some by supportive friends and family.

There is a library where you can borrow books to help while away some of those interminable hours locked up in your cell. Your librarian is Catherine Birnie.

Catherine has adapted amazingly well to her life in prison. During her first few years she spent a lot of time writing to David, and the pair exchanged almost 2600 letters. But she absorbed her surroundings and the forced physical separation from David seemed to encourage her to seek a new way of defining her own identity.

It became a point of pride with Catherine that she stopped writing to David: 'I kept getting letters from David all the time, but I just didn't answer them.' Did she read them? 'If I felt like it.' In light of the general view that Catherine was utterly dependent on David Birnie, it is illuminating that her reasons for not writing to David anymore were so defiant: 'It felt like he was weak ... And I was stronger than him. I didn't need him anymore, and I didn't want to stay in contact with him.'

When asked how she had coped with being in prison, Catherine was forthcoming: 'It was hard at first – really hard. When I first got here women would throw food at me in the dining room ... But that only lasted for the first few months. Then it started to get better.'

According to a former inmate who was in prison with Catherine Birnie in the late 1980s, Catherine's fellow prisoners had mixed feelings about her. 'I thought she was arrogant – she thought she was better than everyone else. I just avoided her ... A lot of the young ones didn't like her, and we just avoided her.

'I don't remember if it actually happened but the girls were talking about throwing sand on her while she was in the shower. But I don't remember her ever actually getting beaten up by anyone.'

This particular inmate had one telling encounter with Catherine: 'I was working in the kitchen and one day I went to the fridge to get something. I could feel someone behind me, and I turned around and saw this big 'thing' standing there. She asked me who I was and I said some smart-arse thing to her, and she said to me "Don't you know who I am? I'm the infamous Cathie Birnie".'

Why did this woman think that 'Cathie' Birnie was big? 'I recall her being tall,' she said. When told that Catherine is only around 160 centimetres tall, this woman was shocked. Birnie's reputation, and her ability to manipulate people in very subtle ways, make her seem bigger than she really is.

Did Catherine have friends in Bandyup or did everyone avoid her? The former prisoner recalls that at that time Catherine had a few middle-aged women who hung around with her 'making teddy bears or something pathetic like that'.

As the years went by more and more inmates came to see Catherine in a more sympathetic light. Media reports that she is 'Queen Bee of Bandyup' are wildly inaccurate.

All the same, it's impossible to spend time with Catherine and not get the feeling that she enjoys her notoriety. In the same conversation where she talked about her decision to ignore David Birnie, Catherine revealed other contacts she has made. 'I wrote to Myra Hindley you know, and she wrote back. We've stayed in touch.'

Catherine was of the opinion that she, Aileen Wuornos and Myra Hindley belonged to an exclusive club. She was convinced that they were the only ones in the world who would understand each other.

Wournos was a convicted American serial killer who killed seven men in Florida between 1989 and 1990. She was sentenced to death and was executed by lethal injection on 9 October 2002.

Myra Hindley and her partner Ian Brady became known worldwide as the Moors Murderers, with British newspapers dubbing Myra 'the most evil woman in Britain'. Brady and Hindley were convicted in 1966 on charges of two counts of kidnapping, child molestation and murder, and Hindley was also found guilty of one charge of being an accessory after the fact. Before she died in prison in 2002 Hindley had launched two unsuccessful appeals to be released from prison, claiming that she was no longer a danger to society. The British justice system and the public disagreed and, right to the end of her.60 years of life, Myra Hindley remained one of the most reviled women in Britain.

Malcolm MacCulloch, professor of forensic psychiatry at Cardiff University, has described Hindley and Brady as the result of a 'concatenation of circumstances' that brought together a 'young woman with a tough personality, taught to hand out and receive violence from an early age' and a 'sexually sadistic psychopath'.

Is this the commonality Catherine sought? Someone who would understand her without passing judgement? Someone who knew what it was like to fall so far under the spell of an evil man that they became capable of anything? Or was it something else altogether? Was it to gloat? To share? Or was it a figment of Catherine's imaginations?

It is well known when the Birnies' killing spree ended, but nobody is certain about when it all began. They have been questioned about the disappearance of at least three other people; but whether their emphatic denials were a case of toying with police or telling the truth may never be known.

On Thursday 30 October 1980 a 12-year-old schoolgirl went to a basketball game in the quiet country town of Collie. It was early evening and as with all country towns, it was safe to wander the streets. Everyone knew everyone, and everyone walked after dark. But for Lisa Mott it was no longer safe.

After the basketball game she was waiting for her lift home in the main street of Collie. Someone saw her talking to the driver of a yellow panel van at about 8.30pm, and then she vanished. Lisa has never been seen since.

Retired CIB detective Reg Driffill was in charge of the investigation into Lisa's disappearance. After the Birnies' arrest in 1986 he interviewed them about Lisa. He knew by then that in 1980, when Lisa went missing, David Birnie was working as a crane driver in Collie. Birnie claimed to know nothing about Lisa Mott.

In 1986, the year David and Catherine are thought to

have.embarked on their killing spree, at least two other women went missing in Perth. Sharon Fulton disappeared from East Perth railway station and Cheryl Renwick went missing from her South Perth unit on 26 May 1986.

Brian Tennant is law reform campaigner and he was in contact with both David and Catherine. In the early 1990s David Birnie began to bargain with authorities for access to Catherine. In July 1992 Brian Tennant claimed that David Birnie told him that he and Catherine had committed other murders, and it would 'be in the public interest' if he were to give information.

When Catherine Birnie was approached about this new information and asked to cooperate, she told authorities she wanted no consideration given to possible prison visits or phone calls from David Birnie. She told Tennant that 'official mind games' had caused her to issue those instructions.

When told the news of Catherine's position David Birnie described it as shattering, leaving his life without meaning or purpose. 'Rather obviously the development means there is absolutely nothing that officialdom can now offer me as an inducement or reward in any other context for there is now nothing I want from Joe (former attorney general Joe Berinson) or his minions.'

Detectives took the highly unusual step of taking David Birnie out of prison and driving him around Perth for about five hours one day, in the hope that he would reveal further information to them. It was a fruitless exercise.

When Catherine is asked directly about whether she was involved in the disappearance of any other women, she just looks at you. Stares. And smirks.

Police and many other people involved in the Birnie murders hold strong suspicions that they killed other women. It is highly improbable that Catherine will ever reveal information, and in spite of the fact that he teased Perth police with hints of 'more', David Birnie can no longer tell authorities anything.

On Friday 7 October 2005 at around midnight, David Birnie was found dead in his prison cell. He had hanged himself. Over the preceding weeks Birnie had been secretly making plans to end his life. He had managed to acquire a length of cord, probably from the prison garment section, and hide it in his cell. He also kept two small plastic ear-drop containers. When Birnie was found by a prison officer doing four-hourly checks he was slumped in a corner of his cell, head forward and legs sticking out in front of him.

Birnie had spent several hours fashioning a noose and then used the air conditioning vent to hang it from. He then placed the ear-drop containers on either side of his neck to increase the pressure of the noose. Detective Senior Constable Shane Graham, who prepared the police report for the coroner, said Birnie had spent a lot of time preparing the noose, and had given a great deal of thought to his weight distribution.

A number of things had occurred in the months and weeks leading up to Birnie's death; all part of the minutiae of life for most people, but much amplified in the prison environment. Up until a few months prior to his death he continued to write to Catherine Birnie in Bandyup, even though it had been many years since she had written back to him. But then his own letters to her stopped.

Birnie had also expressed a desire to meet Kate, the woman who had escaped from their home, and who had led police to capture him and Catherine. He wanted her to visit him in Casuarina so he could talk to her. It was never going to happen.

That contributed to Birnie's depression, as did the investigation he was under after another prisoner claimed he had been sexually assaulted by Birnie. At the same time his antidepressant medication had run out. During the inquest into his death, the coroner made it very clear that this should never have happened. It emerged that a faxed request for David Birnie's medication was not received until 10 days after it was sent. He had not taken any antidepressant medication for three days prior to his suicide.

Another blow to Birnie was when he was told he could have no further contact with Sydney crime writer Amanda Howard. Birnie had been in regular contact with Howard for several years. In her blog on womenincrimeink.blogspot.com, Howard wondered out loud at her own contribution to David Birnie's death:

From that point on, we both wrote weekly. I asked questions and he'd reply with a neatly typed letter. We discussed the case in detail and covered hundreds of other topics. He was interested in politics, religion, and ancient civilizations I solicited his opinion on current crimes and listened with interest to his disgust of other criminals, particularly pedophiles.

After three years of written correspondence, we began telephone conversations. It was a more emotional and expressive form of communication. We talked about his younger years and where he thought he went wrong. We discussed other cases in the news.

When I had asked him about being in jail with a sentence of 'never to be released', he said: 'The first seven years are the hardest. After that, each day is no different.' He seemed resigned to the fact he was never getting out, though he was eligible to apply for parole.

Somehow, in 2005, my role changed from writer to counselor when an investigation of the rape of a fellow inmate began. According to the media, David was the prime suspect. He had confided in me and I saw a downward spiral in his demeanour. No longer an engaging conversationalist, he now was morose and talking about 'the end'.

There the moral dilemma began: Does one convince a serial killer to die, or to live?

I had spent several years getting to know this killer as a person and now he relied on me to get him through each week.

On the day of his suicide he rang me. I did not realize until later that it was a goodbye call. He thanked me for being there as a friend over the years, saying I was the only one who understood him. He also explained that the prison was cutting off our contact. His last words to me were a quotation from Hitchhiker's Guide to the Galaxy: 'They say things can't get any worse, then they do'. (Amanda Howard: Who Weeps for a Serial Killer?)

After his death David Birnie's body lay unclaimed in the state mortuary for more than a month. He was given a secret pauper's cremation, which was carried out at Pinnaroo cemetery in Perth's northern suburbs on Monday 21 November 2005.

It is one of life's ironies that on the night that David Birnie was sitting in his lonely cell at Casuarina Prison making himself a noose, his surviving victim, Kate, was in a Perth hospital giving birth to her second son. After Birnie's death, Kate made the following comments through a media release:

> My family and I are relieved that David Birnie took his own life last night. We are now able to have closure and are looking forward to life without the constant reminder that a criminal such as David Birnie is alive and well in jail at the taxpayer's expense. However, I believe that both David and Catherine Birnie should have received the death penalty for the crimes that they committed, and it has been a travesty of justice that the taxpayers have paid millions of dollars to keep two murderers in jail for at least 18½ years. The knowledge that David Birnie was alive and well in relative comfort while their daughters were dead has been a constant reminder for the families of the women that the Birnies murdered, and the justice system has betrayed these families.

As is their wont, the local media used David Birnie's death.to stir up the issue of crime and punishment. It was almost predictable that even before Birnie had been taken to the mortuary, journalists were leading with stories about whether or not Catherine would be allowed out of prison to attend his funeral. This stirred up a storm with many Perth residents who were outraged that she should be granted such a privilege. People were again calling for the death penalty and demanding that 'that evil woman' never be released.

The small truth that was lost in the media-driven hysteria was that even though Catherine Birnie seemed upset about her former partner's death, she had no intention of requesting to go to his funeral. She didn't see the point.

It was a different story when her former husband Donald McLaughlin died suddenly in the country town of Busselton in 2000, at the age of 59. When she applied to attend his funeral authorities declined her request, but it was a curious insight into the mind of Catherine Birnie nonetheless.

David Birnie's suicide put paid to any debate about whether he should be made eligible for parole in 2007. Debate about Catherine's future was quieted too when the former Labor attorney general Jim McGinty said in 2005 that no matter what the recommendation of the Prisoners Review Board, he would never sign off on her release.

'There are a small number of offenders whose crimes are at the worst imaginable end of the scale who should never be released and Birnie is one of them,' he said. 'I have no sympathy for her. Even though her partner David Birnie committed suicide a year ago and is no longer alive she has forfeited her rights to live as a free citizen.'

Catherine went through the motions of applying for parole but, as she had expected, it was denied.

Asked how long she expected to be in prison Catherine told one woman: 'We wouldn't even be talking about this if we'd done it (committed the crimes) a couple of years earlier.'

Catherine was referring to the abolition of the death penalty in Western Australia, which happened in 1984, only two years before the Birnie murder spree. 'They'd have wanted to see us at the end of a rope.'

What would she do if she ever got out of prison? 'Probably go to work in an old people's home. Something like that.'

Her next possible chance of parole would be 2010, and with a change in government in Western Australia in 2008 came a small glimmer of hope for success.

Catherine Birnie's nephew says she is not a vicious person and she deserves to be released on parole Patrick Turner, who is related to Catherine through her marriage to his uncle, said in 2009 that the 22 years his Aunty Cathy had spent behind bars was a fair price for the crimes she had committed.

'The Catherine we knew would never have [committed these crimes] unless she was under the control of David,' Mr Turner said. 'We let other criminals who have committed murders out after they have served their time.'

'She's kept her nose clean, from what I understand, in prison. She's done everything they've asked of her. She stopped contact with David, we know that for a fact. Personally, if she comes up for parole next year I hope the Parole Board will look at it seriously. She's not as vicious or as callous or as cold-hearted as she is portrayed to be. I don't condone what she did by any stretch of the imagination but that doesn't mean that the love for her that I still have will ever die.'

On the other side of the debate a shrill media has leapt into the fray. An Australian women's magazine *New Idea* ran the headline: 'Australia's Most Evil Woman Begs for Release' and opened with the highly inaccurate but easily digestible:

One of Australia's most notorious serial killers is fighting to be freed from jail – because she claims she is cured of the madness that drove her to kill.

Catherine Birnie, who took part in the murders of four women in Perth in the mid-80s and was sentenced to life behind bars, is making a bold bid for parole. 'Let me out … I'm no longer a danger,' she has pleaded to jail bosses at her WA prison.

The truth was that, as is her legal right, Catherine is entitled to appeal for parole every three years now she has served the mandatory part of her sentence. Prominent QC, Tom Percy, has been calling for her release. Catherine, who was 63 years old in 2016 was 'as quiet as a church mouse', according to Percy and he believes that keeping her locked up is an act of 'pure revenge.' Her fourth appeal was ruled against in March 2016. She will be able to apply for release from prison again in 2019.

# EPILOGUE

Women don't kill, not unless extreme circumstances lead them to do the unthinkable. Or unless they are provoked by relentless abuse. I used to believe that; I believed that women were more caring, more nurturing, and were equipped with better inner resources to cope with life. For the most part I still hold on to that ideal because the majority of women I know, for all their flaws, would never harm anyone.

When I met Cathie Birnie in 1990 I was fascinated. I wanted to know whether she had been under the evil influence of her partner David, or whether there was something different, something missing that made her a callous killer in her own right. It's fair to say that I have never met anyone like Cathie before, so for a long period of time I had no point of reference.

However, over the next eight years I had several encounters with her, and numerous conversations. I was working for the WA AIDS Council during that time and frequently went to Bandyup Women's Prison to conduct workshops. Many of the chats I shared with Cathy were meaningless encounters, banter with someone you know, but at times the talk turned to things that I was less comfortable with, but found strangely fascinating all the same.

In some ways Cathie Birnie massaged my ego. I was very aware that I was in a unique position, having ongoing and, generally, unsupervised contact with someone who was in prison for serial murder. She picked up on my curiosity very early on, and recognised it for what it was. Sometimes she would feed me a morsel, to keep me interested – at other times I felt as though I had overdosed on something very toxic.

Cathie is very passive and almost childish in her day-to-day interactions. Like others who seem to have something missing, she lacks affect when she is relating a story. And while I was usually quite willing to lend her an ear, there were times when her stories rang hollow with me; times I believed she was lying.

Manipulating me. Telling me what she thought I wanted to hear.

When she has a willing audience Cathie is willing to talk at length about murder. Sometimes I got the sense that the six-week murder spree she embarked on with David was the thing that she allowed to define her, almost to shape her whole identity.

In all the time I knew Cathie Birnie, the period of time when she was most animated was when another serial killer was stalking young women in Perth. From January 1996 to March 1997 three young women disappeared from Claremont in the wealthy western suburbs of Perth. Two of the women, Jane Rimmer and Ciara Glennon, were found murdered. The disappearance of the first woman to go missing, Sarah Spiers, remains unsolved.

I was living in Perth at the time and I remember the city being gripped by a palpable fear. Women everywhere were jumpy and hypervigilant. Blonde women throughout the city were dyeing their hair brunette, and nobody walked anywhere on their own. It was awful to experience. It seemed that the only woman I knew who was impervious to the fear, and who had no sense of the negative impact this was having on women, was Cathie Birnie.

She would seek me out when I visited the prison so that she could talk about the latest developments in the case. In fact she was the first person to suggest to me, not long after the first victim, Sarah Spiers, had disappeared, that a serial killer was hunting and that Sarah was his second victim. At the time I thought it was nonsense because the only thing anyone knew was that a young woman had disappeared, and the news was generating a lot of media publicity. Cathie insisted she knew something, and was quite insistent that someone was copying her and David.

At the time I thought it was nonsense. It wasn't until five months later when the Claremont Serial Killer abducted and murdered Jane Rimmer that I began to feel uncomfortable with what I'd been hearing. Was it mind games? Snippets of a truth? Manipulation? For the first time in all my interactions with Cathie I felt a tingle of fear run up my spine.

One exchange I had with her I will stay with me forever. I was in the library alone with Cathie and she was showing me through the selection of books. Being a writer and a bookworm I was genuinely interested in what kinds of books are allowed in prison, and what is forbidden. Cathie knows the library inside out, and we were having a discussion about writers and genres, when she led me to the crime section. It felt somewhat surreal to be standing in a prison library, perusing crime books with a serial killer, but I'm an adventurous woman.

Cathie was chatting about the Lindy Chamberlain book and for some reason I was annoyed with her. It was that small girly voice she was using, and the innocent tone she was taking. I don't even remember now what she said, but I turned to her and said: 'Cathie, don't play the helpless female with me – it gives me the shits.'

A more savvy person than me would have made sure I was between a murderer and the exit door, but I hadn't given it a second thought. I was up against the bookcases, and before I knew it her hands were on me, applying rather uncomfortable pressure. That wasn't what made me think I was experiencing the last moment of my life – it was the physical change in her face: pure rage.

Then through gritted teeth she said: 'Don't ever call me helpless; you forget what I can do.'

She let me go – but it was the most revealing moment I had ever experienced with her. Not because of what she had said to me, or because she had used physical intimidation to frighten me. But because she had let the mask slip, and I had seen what was underneath: rage, callousness, disregard, violence.

Another time she was telling me about how she had saved the life of a fellow prisoner. Apparently the woman in the cell next to her had tried to hang herself one night; Cathie heard her and alerted prison officers, who reached the woman in time to save her.

When I asked Cathie how she could tell what was happening without seeing her, her eyes almost danced: 'You wouldn't have known. But once you've been that close to someone when they're dying, that gurgling sound they make is something you never forget.'

It was then I realised she was remembering a different girl, and a house in Willagee. She hadn't told me that story to convince me she had done a good deed: she was reliving a very bad deed in her mind, and testing me.

I don't understand Cathie Birnie. I have tried to, but she is far too complex – too different – for me to know. I do know this: something is missing in her emotional makeup. Maybe the death of her mother and her subsequent unstable childhood deprived her of those fundamental building blocks on which our values and consciences are shaped. Maybe having her first child taken away by the authorities, and then watching her second child killed in her driveway, were catalysts.

What I do know is that she is a criminal who actively participated in some of the most sadistic crimes known. I have never seen her show one iota of remorse. In all the discussions I have had with her about her crimes she has never shown any embarrassment, shame, regret … And she has never said sorry.

Within the walls of Bandyup Prison Cathie Birnie is a 'model prisoner'. She goes about her daily business with monotony, keeps to herself a lot, is studious, obedient, and generally stays out of trouble. She gets along well with most of her fellow prisoners, many of whom are convinced that she isn't really a bad person; she just got seduced by a really evil man. It's a comfortable fit for many who have to live with her, some of whom can relate to doing bad things to please someone they love.

Is Cathie Birnie a psychopath? I'm not qualified to make that call. I know she sat in her car and lured innocent women into it, fully aware of what she was intending to do to them. She held knives to their throats. She tied them to her bed. She watched her partner violently rape them, took photos, and at times even joined in with the degrading and sickening acts. She watched as they were being murdered, and in one case committed the murder herself. She helped dig their graves, bury them. And she spat on the grave of one of her victims. She has no remorse. She enjoys the notoriety, loves reading about herself in the newspapers.

We were having a conversation one day, talking about ways to deal with some mundane problem that had cropped up in prison. I suggested that she probably didn't have much power to change the situation. Cathie looked at me, smirked and said: 'You talk about power as if you know what it means. You don't know what power is, Ruth. Power is when you hold somebody's life in your hands – and then you end it.'

I walked out of prison that day convinced that Cathie Birnie is beyond redemption.

# How Much Do You Love Me?

Tania crouched down in the corner of the garage. She waited in the semi-darkness for the normal routine of this house to start so she could get her job over and done with. She was dressed in someone else's clothes, in shoes that were a bit too big for her, and she was wearing a bathing cap and balaclava.

Even though it was summer, and she was wearing gloves, it was only six in the morning so her hands were cold. But she just had to hang in there and wait. A couple of times she nearly cut and run, like when she heard noises in the house. But she had to do this; she had to prove herself.

Besides, she was stuck here, in the garage of someone else's house, at the end of a long driveway, miles from home, with no transport – except for the car she was supposed to leave in. And she didn't have the keys to that yet.

At about 6.30 she heard a noise, and then the woman entered the garage through the internal door. Tania watched her, and waited for the right moment.

It was now or never to show him just how much she loved him.

Tania waited until the woman had opened the door to her car, and then she leapt out of the shadows. She grabbed the woman from behind, putting a bag strap around her neck.

The woman fought back. Of course she did. But Tania was taller and stronger. She pulled harder on the strap.

The woman kept struggling and the next thing she knew they were both down on the concrete floor of the garage. But Tania was on top, still had the upper hand, still had the strap around the woman's neck. She pulled hard, tightening the strap, until the woman stopped fighting.

Tania dragged the woman to the back of the car, opened the boot and heaved her into the otherwise empty space.

Tania then got into the driver's seat of the woman's own car, hit the button on the automatic garage door opener and, when the way was clear, drove out and down the driveway. She was buzzing with adrenalin and skidded the tyres a bit but tried to drive carefully, just as the woman would've done if she'd been driving her car instead of lying dead in the boot. Tania headed out onto the local road, then after a while turned onto the Hume Highway and headed towards the city; towards the heart of Melbourne.

She was shit scared; but she kept on going. She had to now. There was nothing else she could do.

Somewhere along the 35 kilometre trip, Tania thought she heard a sound coming from the boot. It might have been a breath; but she ignored it.

At about 7.30am Tania parked the stolen car not far from the Shrine of Remembrance, got out, locked the door and walked away.

Cops see a lot of bad things – it comes with the territory. They have to deal with death, often and in all its ordinary and extraordinary manifestations. The dead may be the victims of traffic accidents, of drug overdoses, of accidents in the home, workplace or public spaces. The police are called in when any loss of life cannot be immediately explained: when it's untimely or the circumstances are unusual; or the doctor called to attend cannot provide a cause of death.

Police also have to endure the ugly and brutal side of death, the incomprehensible kind wrought by the violence of one person on another. The homicide squad gets the worst of that of course; but cops on the hunt for missing people too often find the bad stuff as well – because things don't always turn out the way they should.

On the surface, the daily duty faced by the various state and national Missing Persons Units looks unimaginably daunting. One Australian is reported missing every.15 minutes; that's about 35,000 people a year.

Some people simply wander off and get lost; some are hiding from one side of the law or the other; and some deliberately walk away from a life they can no longer endure. Some people are never seen again because they choose not to be; and some because they're 'missing, presumed dead' either by misadventure or their own hand.

Identifying the reasons why people go missing is as complicated for the police services, and non-government organisations like the Red Cross, as assessing if, how, or even whether the missing person is at risk. Accident, abduction and homicide are always the greatest fears, especially for friends and family; but as outcomes, they are far less common than we might think.

The good news – especially for the hardworking search agencies around the country – is that most 'missing' people either return home, make contact or are located within a few hours; and 95 per cent of the 600 or so who go missing each week are found within seven days.

Despite the huge numbers, only a very small number of the remaining 5 per cent of missing persons cases get labelled with the word 'suspicious'. Even those 'missing, feared abducted' are more likely to have been taken by an estranged family member than a stranger, and, as most homicides are domestic or happen in public situations, most murder victims don't get to be missing first.

When it comes to premeditated murder, however, killers really only have three cover-up choices: accident, mystery or scapegoat. The second option is probably the best bet, especially if the death forever remains a mystery; and of course the best way to ensure that is to make sure the victim is never seen again.

So, among those missing and never found (around 1700 a year), the odds are that more than a few of them didn't leave of their own free will and probably won't ever come home – at least not alive. Given those stats then, there's probably no real way of knowing just how many homicide victims are hidden among all the missing.

While this may be a sad observation of modern life, that we tend to assume the worst, it may also be that we're more aware than ever before of the despicable lengths that some people will go to just to get what they want.

For instance, there's a certain skin-crawling realisation – raised by our suspicion that we've seen something like this before, and usually live on our TV news – that certain missing people will never, ever be seen alive again because they've already fallen victim to the person who reported them missing. We have seen the lie in the eyes of the person in the news conference, tearfully begging for their loved one to come home, or for any information anyone might have *please* about their whereabouts.

By the time 2005 rolled around Narelle Fraser, then a detective senior constable at the Missing Persons Unit, had already worked two such cases, both now ranked among the state's most high profile. These investigations were no more important to Victoria Police itself than any other, but they had attracted serious media attention because of their unusual nature and the probability that the missing were unlikely to still be alive.

When a person goes missing in 'suspicious circumstances' the search parameters change; other police departments, like homicide, become involved. And the public – through the TV news and newspapers – are asked for assistance, for information, for anything. The public itself becomes involved, and therefore interested; and the media, in turn, provides the updates so 'the story' becomes high profile on every level.

The point at which the search for a missing person becomes an investigation into their disappearance is usually the point at which foul play becomes the highest likelihood.

Given that most murder victims are killed by someone who knows them, it stands to reason that if foul play is suspected in a missing person case it means the police probably already have a suspect; and that suspect is most likely someone close to the one who's missing; and it will be for any one of the reasons that people kill someone they know: hate, greed, jealousy, anger, revenge, love.

Yes, even love.

Back in April 2002, Detective Senior Constable Narelle Fraser and her colleagues were searching for a missing husband and wife. This search soon became an investigation into the disappearance of Margaret Wales-King and her husband Paul King. This eventually and tragically became the so-called Society Murders of Margaret and Paul by their son Matthew Wales.

Two years later DSC Fraser joined the search, along with a large complement of police who volunteered for the job, of the Mornington Peninsula's huge Teurong landfill site for the remains of Anna and Gracie Kemp – the mother and child brutally murdered and disposed of by Gracie's father John Sharpe.

That case had also begun as a missing person case, instigated by Anna Kemp's family in New Zealand who'd not heard from her. It turned into a search for Anna *and* Gracie after John Sharpe claimed his wife had 'left him' and then 'returned' two days later for their daughter. It also ended in a double-murder charge, and the heartbreaking search among tonnes and tonnes of rubbish for Anna and Gracie.

Fraser said the search of the tip was gruelling, difficult and at times revolting, but ended with a bizarre sense of elation for all the police concerned when they found the remains of 41-year-old Anna and her 20-month-old daughter.

'I was beside myself with relief, and with the knowledge we had found Anna and Gracie and they were not going to end their lives buried in a tip like pieces of rubbish.'

Both John Sharpe and Matthew King had appealed to the public for help.

In February 2005, Senior Detective Fraser was involved in another missing wife case; one that had turned very quickly into an investigation into the 50-year-old's disappearance.

It was a Sunday, February 13, and the police had been searching for Maria Korp, wife and mother, for nearly four days. Her husband Joe had reported her missing from their Mickleham home the previous Wednesday evening. She had failed to collect their 11-year-old son from school at 3.45pm and had not been seen by anyone since early that morning. A worried Joe Korp had gone to the Craigieburn police station to report his wife missing just after 7.30pm on Wednesday 9 February.

On that following Sunday morning, a car matching the description of Maria Korp's also-missing Mazda 626 was reported 'found' by a Parks & Gardens worker. It had been sitting in the same spot near Melbourne's Shrine of Remembrance for at least two days, possibly longer.

Senior Detective Fraser and two colleagues approached the abandoned car, on Dallas Brooks Drive, at about 10.30am. They noted that the seats were strewn with the contents of a handbag, but the car was locked and empty.

The stench emanating from the boot of the vehicle, however, was sickeningly familiar to the officers. There's probably no worse smell in the world than the breakdown of a human body in decay.

It was also summer and, although the weather for the previous few days had been in the low twenties, the car had been sitting there in the open since Wednesday. The attending police were concerned that their search for the missing woman was not going to have a good ending.

The officers processed the scene and searched the surrounding area for clues. Just over an hour later, entry was gained to the boot area, which was finally opened to reveal Maria Korp's body, fully clothed and lying in a foetal position.

'Her skin was so very pale, and she was decaying; her body was breaking down,' Fraser said. 'It was quite shocking and very unpleasant.'

Between the smell and her appearance, the officers knew that Maria Korp was dead. Detective Fraser, nonetheless, checked the victim's vitals and was shocked when her diaphragm moved.

Maria Korp was taking shallow breaths of fresh air for the first time in four and a half days. She was dehydrated, unconscious and barely alive; but she was alive.

'At that point our priorities changed,' Fraser said. 'I yelled to the others that she was still alive and everyone sprang into action. We really were all so shocked because, just by the look of her, we had been certain she was deceased.

'We called the ambos immediately, but because we didn't know what had happened to her, we didn't move her. I did not, for instance, even notice the ligature marks on her neck,' Fraser said. 'I was more concerned for her life and trying to preserve it, at that point, than trying to figure out the cause of what we had thought was a death.

'So I just held Maria's hand and kept talking her. I was virtually in the boot with her. Then I stayed with her in the back of the ambulance, and through the hospital emergency department, just in case she said something.'

Senior Detective Fraser says looking back it was obvious that she wouldn't speak. 'But it would've been a tragedy if she had said something, and we weren't there to note it.'

From that unbelievable moment a truly bizarre murder plot began to come undone. And, even though the police already had their suspicions, what began to unravel was a tale of love and lust; trust and betrayal; manipulation and acquiescence; internet dating, swingers parties and alleged blackmail; psychics and religious shrines; murder and suicide; a bedside vigil and a euthanasia controversy. Most of all it is a story of lies – so many lies.

And most of those lies were told by Maria Korp's husband Joe.

This, however, is not a story about Joe Korp – except for the part he played in destroying the lives of two women; except for the things he put in motion that had such an awful outcome for the children and other family members of these two women; except for the affect it had on his own family.

Nor is this the story of the 'alpha male' that Joe Korp was

incorrectly labelled as by the some in the media. A bloke can only be an 'alpha male' in the company of other men. In the company of women, this man – a strong-willed, egocentric, controlling, charismatic man, with a huge sexual appetite – was simply a manipulator, a bully, a con man.

But again, this is not a story about Joe Korp the bully, the manipulator, the sexual predator.

It is the story of how a manipulative, randy liar ruined the lives of two women and their children. How he convinced one woman to kill another to prove her love for him.

It's the story of how, in the summer of 2005, Tania Herman took the life of Maria Korp.

Tania Herman was 38 years old when she went to jail for the attempted murder of Maria Korp. Before she strangled the wife of her lover Joe Korp, she had never so much as been introduced to the woman. She'd seen her across a crowded school ground at the school that both their children attended – but that was it. All that she knew about Maria Korp she'd been told by Joe Korp. And she should have known – long before it was too late – that her man was a liar.

Eight weeks before Maria Korp had been strangled and thrown into the boot of her own car, she made an appointment with a psychologist. She had a few problems at home and desperately needed help, needed advice; perhaps was even looking for a way out.

In December 2004 Ann Sebire, a registered trauma psychologist with a degree in Criminal Justice, was working as a counsellor for Occupational Services Australia. The OSA Group, with a head office in the Melbourne CBD, has many regional offices. The Group provides counselling services to organisations that are contracted to them.

The Victoria Police is one such organisation; Pacific Brands, and its subsidiaries, another. Under these contracts all staff –

management, members, employees – have access to four free counselling sessions a year. The sessions can be used for any reason, either work related or personal.

On 22 December 2004, an employee of Kayser Lingerie, one of the Pacific Brands companies (located at Coolaroo, north of Melbourne) rang the OSA Group. Head office scheduled a counselling session for her, with Ann Sebire, at the Group's occasionally used Airport West office on 30 December.

As it turned out, the whole building was closed between Christmas and New Year and Ms Sebire could not gain access to the office. With no space to meet in, she set about cancelling her day's appointments, all except the first one with her new client – Maria Korp.

She spotted a woman, with a young boy in tow, in front of the building and approached her. It *was* her 10am client, so she told her she'd have to reschedule.

Maria Korp was agitated and told Sebire that that she needed to see someone straightaway. She couldn't wait while another venue was found, however, as she had other things to do.

'She told me that she couldn't wait, that she just needed someone to talk to because her husband had left her for a slut,' Sebire said.

The psychologist asked Maria if she was at risk. 'She said to me, "My husband is a prick and I need to tell someone as soon as possible."'

Maria was eventually satisfied with a confirmed new appointment, at the same office, in the new year. Sebire suggested that she attend that meeting without her son Damian.

Maria Korp kept that appointment at 11am on 10 January 2005, and another on 17 January; she missed one on 25 January, but attended a rescheduled one on 1 February at 5pm. What Ann Sebire learned of Maria Korp – of her life, troubles, fears, needs, hopes, and her state of mind – in those three sessions was ultimately requested for a witness summons in the case against her client's murderer.

In their first meeting, Sebire learned that Maria was Portuguese and had been widowed by her first husband, who was the father of her 26-year-old daughter. She had later married Joe Korp, from whom she'd recently separated, and they had an 11-year-old son.

'Maria told me that Joe was an Australian and treated her poorly and verbally abused her. She said she did everything, that Joe did nothing and that he treated her like shit,' Sebire said.

Maria told her that 'she looked after their son, worked full time and Joe just went off and had these affairs while she was keeping the house going'. Maria said, 'That man's got problems,' and that his behaviour was all over the place.

Maria told the psychologist that Joe never wanted for anything when it came to the house and children or sexually, and that she was a good wife.

Being a good wife was as important to Maria Korp as being a good Catholic. Born Maria Matilde Martins in 1955 on Madeira, an island of vineyards and citrus groves off the coast of Portugal, she was one of 12 children, two of whom died in childhood. The island then had no mod cons: no TV, phones or running water. Maria and her siblings attended school but also worked hard on the family farm. The local economy was based on barter and the Martins' farm grew vegetables and bran and raised a few cattle.

Like Spain and Italy, Catholicism in Portugal, especially in the 1950s, was more than just religion; more than mass on Sundays. It was the state faith, and touched every aspect of life from birth, through school and work, through married life and old age to death. The local priest was part of everyone's family, marriage was forever and divorce was not contemplated. Maria's family, like most of the people of Madeira, were also very superstitious – which came partly from the faith itself and partly from the residue of local folklore. Evil eyes and curses were as common as blessings and the influence of religious relics.

Maria lost her first love, a childhood sweetheart, to war in Angola. She then married Manuel De Gois when she was 19 years old and migrated to Australia shortly after. They settled in then semi-rural Coolaroo, 19 kilometres north of the Melbourne CBD, before moving to nearby Greenvale. Their only child, Laura, was born in 1978, but when she was just nine, Manuel had a heart attack. Maria had lost her second love, and was a widow at the age of 32.

She met Joe Korp in 1990 at the tyre company where they were both working. He was married but that didn't stop their developing relationship. Maria and Joe married in October 1991; after Joe divorced Leonie, his wife of 13 years.

In the beginning the marriage was a mostly happy one, especially with the birth of their son Damian in 1993. Joe and Maria both worked hard, and built their large dream home on two hectares on Mount Ridley Road in Mickleham. It was their million-dollar pride and joy with five bedrooms, two bathrooms, a theatre room, giant spa, the best fittings, and a three-car garage.

When Maria took her family 'home' to Portugal for a visit, her parents and sister Rosa were happy for her because she was happy – Maria had two beautiful children and a handsome husband she clearly adored; but they found Joe controlling and insincere.

Things were great in the Korp household for about five years or so – until Maria's husband got restless.

Joe Korp had always been a womaniser. For a time at the start of his marriage to Maria it looked like he'd settled down and was happy with one woman. And then he discovered the internet, webcams and the exciting world of online dating, flirting and sex – from the comfort of his own study at home. But he soon progressed from online assignations to real-world encounters, and Joe Korp began getting sex whenever he could.

He blamed his wife for his behaviour – for his need to spread himself around; to have sex with many different women, and even the occasional man in a threesome.

Of course it was his wife's fault, because she wouldn't put out often enough in the way he wanted. He told his brother Gust that 'things had dried up at home' so he *had* to look elsewhere.

According to psychologist Ann Sebire, Maria said Joe was

always screwing other women; that he said he needed other women and needed more than what she offered.

'She told me that she did anything he wanted in relation to sex,' Sebire said, 'but when he wanted her to do "other horrible things, sick things, disgusting things" she had refused because she "wasn't like that; she had only ever been with her first husband and with Joe."'

When Sebire asked Maria what kind of things Joe had asked of her, she said he'd wanted her to join a swingers group, and to have sex with another woman so he could film it.

Some women will do almost anything to keep their man. Maria Korp worshipped at two churches and had turned one of the five bedrooms in her home into a personal prayer room. She told Sebire that she prayed often in her personal sanctuary for a 'safe and honest husband'.

Though her faith was strong, Maria had also gone on the hunt for a more esoteric kind of assistance. She had carried the superstitions of her youth into adulthood and halfway across the world. Her daughter Laura said Maria honestly believed in curses and evil spirits and bad luck – which meant she also believed in the hokum that went with banishing these things from her life.

In 2003 Maria, aided for a time by Laura, had handed over a great deal of money to a clairvoyant 'gypsy' in St Albans. For a while Maria was in daily contact with the crucifix-adorned 'Michael' who sold her expensive things, like prayers and candles. She allowed him to wander the rooms of the Mickleham home to wave incense and attract good fortune into her life.

In the end Michael's good fortune amounted to about $150,000 of Maria's money. The robed pretender was of no more help to Maria Korp than her prayers for an honest husband.

Maria told Ann Sebire, many times during their three counselling sessions, that she would do anything that Joe wanted in a sexual sense – but only with him, not with other people.

'She said she looked after herself and tried to keep herself the way Joe liked, which was fit, thin and well dressed; but she couldn't seem to please him. He continually criticised her and at one stage wanted her to have surgery to her breasts and other things.'

When Sebire had asked what she meant by other things, Maria pointed to her groin and said, 'He wants me to tighten it up.'

'Maria told me that Joe continually verbally abused her about being frigid and that he said he only went outside the marriage because she wasn't stimulating him and making him happy.'

Maria said that Joe had always had affairs but she always took him back. And he'd always wanted to come back – until this latest affair with his 'internet lover'. Tania was her name and she even lived near their house. Maria seemed to think that Tania was a prostitute. Joe had certainly told her that Tania could get him any drug he wanted.

Sebire asked Maria if she wanted to stay in her marriage. 'That's when Maria reiterated about her faith and told me she'd been through a hard time and that it was worth working out.'

'She told me she'd already lost one husband and she didn't want her second marriage to end. Maria also said that Joe wanted to stay in the marriage too but he also wanted the other woman; that he wanted it all.'

Sebire asked her client if she could get Joe to come to a counselling session with her, but Maria said her husband 'thought that all counsellors were lesbians and that they wanted to break marriages, not fix them'.

Towards the end of her first session with the psychologist, Maria said she'd wanted to kick Joe out for good but that he had threatened her with 'knowing people'.

In fact, Maria had kicked Joe out of their house a month before, in December, on the advice of a psychic who made a late-night house call in November. The psychic, no doubt picking up on Maria's distress and obvious conviction that her husband was having an affair, 'psychically', said she felt he was unfaithful. She advised Maria to kick him out. She said he was a good actor, and not to believe him. Luckily, also sensing Maria may have been in real danger, the psychic advised her to contact police if she felt threatened and to get a restraining order.

On 19 December Maria had the locks changed and chucked Joe's clothes out by the front gate. He smashed a window and threatened to break into the house – apparently only because he wanted his computer – and then left. Maria secured a restraining order against him the next day, but by the following Thursday he was back home again.

The Korps separated again in January 2005, during which time Joe told people that his wife had given him permission to get Tania Herman out of his system. But when his mistress dropped him off at his parents' place in Craigieburn on 22 January, for his father's birthday, Joe gave all his attention to Maria, showing her care and affection. He even told his 25-year-old son Stephen, one of two kids from his first marriage, that he was planning to return to Maria to make things work.

He went home with Tania that day, when she came to collect him from the party, but by the end of January he was back in the Mickleham house with his wife, stepdaughter and young son.

Although it upset Tania, it shouldn't have surprised her. Joe had been wandering in and out of their relationship, her house, her life since the very beginning. The fact that he constantly lied to his wife so he could be with Tania should have told her something about his attitude towards the truth, but when you're in love you believe you're the only one, the real one, the one who will win out in the end.

When Joe returned to his marital home in January 2005, he told his girlfriend that he had to; that it was easier, because Maria 'had something on him' and she might get vindictive and turn him in to the cops. He refused to elaborate, so Tania could only imagine what kind of hold the wife had over him that would make him choose a sad and complaining 50-year-old woman over her. But like nearly everything else he'd ever told her, this was simply another in the chain of lies that Joe Korp had been spinning his girlfriend ever since they'd first met.

Tania met Joe online in late 2003. They exchanged photos and hit it off, but didn't meet in person until early 2004. Joe Korp said he was a builder, and single, and that his name was Joe Bonte. The first time they got together, on 11 February, was in Echuca where Tania was living at the time. Joe drove the 180 kilometres from Mickleham, they did a bit of sightseeing around the riverside town, then had sex in his car.

Tania Herman was looking for love, for commitment, for stability. What she got was Joe Korp – a twice-married liar and father of three, who worked in a tyre factory.

Tania was 37 and also twice married with two kids, but this was not something she kept from Joe. In 2004 she was separated from her second husband, Paul Herman, whom she'd met and married after returning to her home town of Echuca in 1992.

Born Tania Lee-Ann Deegan in the tiny nearby town of Rochester in 1966, Tania's family moved to Echuca when she was young. She grew up in the Murray River tourist town, in the heart of paddle-steamer territory, with a sister, Fiona, and two brothers, Steve and Peter.

Years later, Fiona Deegan told a women's magazine, 'We weren't "dragged up" as was insinuated in Tania's court case. Our parents were always there and we had a really good, happy country childhood.'

Tania went to Echuca South Primary School and then St Joseph's College where she finished Year 12 in 1984. She was active, athletic and a good swimmer who, as a teenager, competed in state-level competitions. As an adult she trained for triathlons and belonged to the Echuca Moama Triathlon Club. She was also creative and had a reasonably high IQ, but never managed to use it to her advantage.

Tania Deegan got married for the first time in September 1987, to a much older man, but the marriage ended after a few months. She then moved to Melbourne with a university student from Columbia, and although that partnership didn't last long either it did produce a daughter, Karelita, in 1989.

Tania took on menial jobs and did the single mum thing in Melbourne for a couple more years, before giving up on the big city. She headed home to the Murray River town on the border of Victoria and New South Wales.

She took a job in the galley of the paddle-steamer *Emmylou*, where she met and soon married Paul Herman. They moved to Queensland together for about a year, where their daughter Tayelor was born in 1996, but returned to Victoria where work prospects were better. Back in Echuca the Hermans' marriage was soon getting rocky and finally ended in 2002. That same year Tania's 13-year-old daughter, Karelita, opted to move to Melbourne and live with her father.

Although Paul's family and friends never saw any signs of it, Tania maintained that her husband drank too much, neglected their daughter and was often rough with her. She'd also claimed her first husband had been physically abusive, and years later had another tale of abuse. She told Patrick Newton, the forensic psychologist who assessed her before her trial, that she had been raped and sexually abused from the age of eight, for six years. She refused, however, to disclose the abuser's identity.

Tania's family first learned of this childhood abuse during her trial. Her sister later said, 'That was just dreadful for all of us, because it was the first we'd ever heard of it. And of course it cast suspicion on people who were totally blameless.'

In September 2003, Tania advertised for someone to share her house in Echuca. It was her new housemate, 32-year-old Joyce Rice, who showed Tania the world that was connected to her very own computer. Tania was intrigued by the concept of internet dating and asked Joyce to set her up a profile on a Yahoo personals site.

Though her profile generated interest and, according to Joyce, Tania had a real-world thing with at least one guy, Tania's interest soon started to wane. And then *joek_40*, or Joe Bonte, a handsome and single builder from Melbourne, came online.

Tania was impressed with his looks, the photos of his wonderful home, the fact that he was a well-off, hard-working builder, and boss of his own business. In person he was charming and flattering, always well dressed and dripping with the gold jewellery that complemented his Latino demeanour.

Tania tells a few versions of just when it was she found out that the single and available 40-year-old Joe Bonte was really 45-year-old married Joe Korp, who still lived with his wife, and was the father of two adult children and a then 10-year-old boy. At one stage she claimed he'd told her almost straightaway, when it was obvious they could get serious about each other, but in most versions of her story (including the one given at her trial) it was months before Tania Herman had a clue who Joe Bonte really was.

She must have known by 28 October 2004, though, because by then she had sold her house in Echuca and she and Joe signed a lease on a nice little rental in Greenvale. Not only had Joe moved his mistress into a house nine kilometres from his family home, but he got Tania to enrol her daughter Tayelor in the same school as his son Damian.

The Deegan family never liked Joe Korp – even before everyone found out he was married. Tania's father didn't trust him and thought he was a loudmouth who was always big-noting himself. Her sister Fiona said she and her mother had decided there was a 'blackness' in his eyes. Fiona could not work out why her little sister would ever trust Joe Korp after all his lies, and especially after the car accident – an incident that eventually became known as the Barcelona Fib.

But by then it was too late anyway, Tania was well and truly hooked on Joe Korp. And, given his penchant for letting her go and reeling in her back again, 'hooked' was the perfect word.

In his last online profile, posted on Adult Match Maker in 2005, Joe Korp described himself as 41, straight, athletic and Latino. That was his thing – the cool clothes, the bling, the swagger; and of course his innate sex appeal and machismo.

Psychologist Ann Sebire said Joe Korp was always telling his wife how great he was and that he could get anybody he wanted. This was how he operated; by telling women that he could have 'anyone' but he'd chosen 'them'.

Women either fell for it, or found it sleazy. With Maria and Tania the affect was the same: they felt special, they felt loved, they were conned. Especially Tania Herman.

In reality Joe Korp was no more a Latino than he was a faithful husband. His father, August Korp, is from Austria; and his mother, Florence, is a Koori.

Joseph William Korp was born in Lake Boga, a small community in north-west Victoria not far from Swan Hill. The Aussie kid with a huge passion for football grew up with two brothers, Gust and Kevin, and two sisters, Val and Leanne.

In Lake Boga, and later in the same street in Swan Hill where the Korp family moved in the early 1960s, Joe Korp had a playmate, a little girl, who grew up to be his girlfriend and finally his wife.

Joe had joined the army in May 1975, but was clearly not suited to a life of discipline away from his family, his mates and especially his girlfriend Leonie Stewart. He went AWOL from the Puckapunyal base twice in 10 months just to be with Leonie. The second time he was thrown out of the army.

Leonie Stewart was 17 and Joe 18 when they married in February 1977. They moved to the outer-Melbourne suburb of Craigieburn and Joe started worked at the Dunlop tyre factory in Somerton (which later became South Pacific Tyres), about 15 kilometres from home. Their daughter Mia was born in April that year, and son Stephen came along in 1980. Life was pretty good for the Korps until the early nineties.

Joe Korp met Maria De Gois when she was transferred to his department at South Pacific Tyres in Somerton in 1990. They began a relationship and Joe suddenly decided he needed a new life. After one all-nighter with Maria, he went home and told the unsuspecting Leonie that their marriage was over.

By October the next year Joe Korp had divorced his childhood love, and married Maria. Thirteen years after that, he seduced and lured Tania Herman to Melbourne. But even that wasn't enough for him, because most of the time he was 'dating' Tania he was still having sex with other women he met online. He didn't tell Tania about them, but he did talk her into engaging in swingers parties with him. Joe always maintained he wasn't bisexual, but even before he met Tania – and happily joined in every-way foursomes with her and other couples – he'd had regular threesomes with another 'straight' couple.

Basically Joe Korp liked sex; he liked it a lot. He was a voyeur and an exhibitionist with a large porn collection, which included explicit photos of himself and Tania.

Gust Korp, who knew exactly what his brother was like, had never been entirely convinced by Joe's assurances that he was faithful to Maria in the early years. But then came Joe's excuse that because 'things had dried up at home' he was getting it elsewhere. He told Gust about the sites he used on the internet and boasted about how easy it was to hook up with willing people for casual sex.

For reasons known only to himself, Gust decided to keep an eye on Joe's conquests. Gust knew his way around computers, so he added a program to Joe's PC that enabled him to later download and follow everything Joe did online. Gust later gave this information to police, but admitted even he was surprised by the number of women his brother had 'been doing' and the lies he told them about who he was and what he did for a living.

Although she would have followed him anywhere, the clincher for Tania, what really hooked her, was the 'Barcelona Fib' – otherwise known as the time Joe Korp faked his death.

While they were waiting for her house to sell, Joe and Tania continued to meet in Echuca, and to have romantic interludes at hotels or sex in their cars. The sweetener for talking Tania into the move to Melbourne was Joe's insistence that before they could actually get married, he'd have to get his mother's approval. He'd made a few trips 'home to Barcelona' to visit his family – a perfectly logical reason for him not to be able to see her for a week or more at a time – so Tania was pleased that Joe was so positive about their future he was talking about getting family approval.

Early in August 2004, Joe Korp told his girlfriend Tania that his mother had suffered a heart attack and he had to fly home to Spain urgently. On 14 August, Tania received a cryptic message, in one of her online chat rooms, from a man called Michael who used the alias '*knightriderforty*'. The message asked Tania if it was okay for him to give her mobile number to Joe's brother 'Gus', who'd had some unfortunate news about Joe. When Tania typed back, asking what it was about, 'Michael' said only Gus could tell her but it was 'the worst news for everybody'. Tania gave Michael her mobile number and then waited, and waited, for Joe's brother to ring her.

The next day, desperate to find out what had happened, Tania rang her sister Fiona, the Department of Foreign Affairs and even the Australian Embassy in Spain. Finally that afternoon Gust Korp – or someone claiming to be Gust – rang her mobile and told Tania that Joe had been killed in a car accident in Barcelona. He added that their sick mother had also died when she got the news about her son.

Tania was devastated; she had just lost everything that was important to her. Beside herself with grief, she couldn't believe that the future Joe had planned for her and Tayelor was gone.

Strangely, instead of ringing 'Gus' back (unless his number was blocked it would've been on her mobile, from his call to her) she got online to ask the mysterious Michael to pass on a message from her to be read out at the funeral.

The Deegan family gathered for support. They might not have liked Joe at all, but neither did they want to see Tania so heartbroken and lost.

Fiona Deegan said her little sister just imploded. 'He was everything to her, the man who was going to be her saviour.' She said Tania totally collapsed when she thought Joe was dead.

And then someone from the Foreign Affairs Department rang back and told them that there'd been no Australian killed in Spain.

Fiona, and her mother Daphne, knew instinctively there was something very dodgy going on, and couldn't believe that Tania was so gullible. If Joe Korp was dead anywhere, but especially overseas, it would've made the news or at least the death notices in the newspaper.

Tania tried '*knightriderforty*' again. Michael eventually got back to her and explained that the rest of the Korp family wanted to wait until they got back from the funerals before placing any local death notices.

Tania begged Michael to find out where Joe was buried; she was ready to fly to Spain to say goodbye.

A couple of hours later Tania's mobile beeped with a text message that simply said: *Tan online*. Someone was using the SMS code that Joe usually sent to let her know he was online. With a mix of incomprehension, panic and anger Tania logged back into the chat room where Joe's username was active. She wrote that if it really was Joe in the chat room then he'd better ring her.

When her mobile rang almost immediately, Tania was livid. She shouted at Joe, demanding to know what was going on 'over there'. He was supposed to be getting buried with his mother in Barcelona.

Joe told her there'd been a huge misunderstanding; that he'd only been hurt in a car accident. He was bruised and battered, and in a wheelchair until he recovered, but he was fine and it was her love that would make him better.

By the end of that phone call, Tania Herman was so relieved her lover wasn't dead that he could have told her then and there that he was really a bank robber, or a murderer – or married – for all she cared. Joe wasn't dead; that was all that mattered.

It will never be known whether the Barcelona episode was a married bloke's failed attempt to ditch a needy girlfriend, or a controlling man's plan to ensnare his lover for good and for all, because Joe Korp's motives in most things were murky at best.

But, whatever his reasons, Tania was too enamoured of her man to listen to the warnings or her family, or care what the truth might be.

Or as Tania's barrister, Julie Sutherland, said at her trial, 'After she is told that he is alive, she is then hopelessly, irretrievably and tragically within his thrall. There was no turning back.'

One can only imagine how Tania managed to reconcile Joe's Spanish mother – the one who had died of grief in Barcelona after her son's alleged death in a car accident – with Florence, his Indigenous and very much alive mother who lived in Craigieburn.

Perhaps there was another lie, or 10, that smoothed over that fact, because Joe introduced Tania to his parents, August and Florence, a couple of months later, after she had moved to Greenvale; after she learned about Joe's current wife and kids, including the one who went to the same school she'd just booked Tayelor into.

Patrick Newton, the defence counsel's psychologist, called it 'traumatic bonding'.

Sutherland asked Newton if the aggression in both of Tania's marriages, and the alleged sexual abuse she suffered as a child, could have influenced her dependence on Joe Korp.

Newton agreed it was likely. He told the court that 'with such survivors of abuse … there is often a tendency to seek a strong, virile protector with whom they can feel safe. Regrettably the people whom they are attracted to, who manifest that strong virility and independence, tend to manifest it in dysfunctional ways.'

Newton explained this often set up a cycle of vulnerability and powerlessness, which entrenched the dependency and the need for strength in the partner.

Newton said Tania had a 'dependent personality disorder'. Sutherland said this explained her client's blind devotion to her lover.

Joe Korp was therefore perfect for Tania Herman. Or perhaps Tania was perfect for Joe Korp.

Some women will do almost anything to keep their man. And not long after Tania moved to Greenvale, Joe began talking about the need to get rid of Maria. It was, he claimed more than once, the only way they were ever going to be together. Tania's brother Steve Deegan, who lived in Melbourne and worked in an Elizabeth Street motorcycle shop, was present for some of the couple's 'how to kill someone' chats. He joined in the theoretical talk the first time, until his sister said that she and Joe were thinking of killing Maria. Before that statement, they had discussed poison and electrocution, and then Steve suggested that garrotting by piano wire would be very effective. Given the general scarcity of piano wires, they asked what Steve himself would use if he was planning to garrotte someone, and he said 'a belt'. Following a similar exchange on another occasion, Steve tried to convince his sister to ditch Joe Korp because 'no normal person talked like that'.

Interestingly, by most accounts, even Tania's, Joe Korp didn't use words kill or murder; he always said 'eliminate, deal with, get rid of'; as in, they could get rid of his wife by running her over with a car. This is apparently typical of people attempting to stay one step removed from actual responsibility for a crime, especially one like homicide.

By early January 2005, the couple's plans for 'dealing' with Joe's wife were taking shape.

Meanwhile, Maria Korp's life had become strange indeed. She knew about Tania Herman, she threw Joe out, she took him back, he left again, demonstrated a new affection, and talked of reconciliation and making their marriage work.

When she had her second appointment with her psychologist, on 17 January, Maria was a contradictory mix of relaxed, aware that Joe's treatment of her was wrong and disrespectful, but still angry about his behaviour.

Ann Sebire said, in her written statement for the court, that although Maria still couldn't see a way to fix things, she was smiling as she talked of things that had recently happened.

'This seemed a big step forward psychologically to me, compared to her previous vulnerable state.'

Maria told Sebire that Joe had refused to stop seeing other women and refused to leave either Tania or the family home – not for good anyway.

Even though Maria had started to realise that Joe's behaviour was abusive, despite his never having used physical violence, there was still that underlying thought that there must be something wrong with her because she couldn't keep her husband.

'Maria said that she didn't want the shame of not holding onto Joe,' Sebire said. 'Even though she said that Joe would yell and scream at her and tell her how frigid and useless and boring she was.'

Maria said Joe kept asking her to become involved in sex games with Tania, that he refused to give up his other life, and claimed he had an 'addiction' to his new sex life.

One day, Maria said, she came home from work and Joe snapped, went crazy and dragged her to the garage. He held up a hose and had a knife and he said, 'I'm going to kill myself or I'm going to gas myself if you ever ask me to leave again. I'm going to do it in front of our son.'

Sebire told Maria that this was a clear sign of unstable behaviour and that Joe needed help. 'I told Maria that this was extremely serious and that she and her family were now at risk.'

Sebire reminded Maria that she should report behaviour like that to the police, and to ring 000 if he tried anything like that again. 'That's when she told me that Joe had left again and "was with that slut Tania".'

This was, of course, in January, during Joe's month with his mistress; when he told friends and family he had his wife's blessing to get Tania out of his system.

During the next appointment, on 1 February, Maria explained she'd recently admitted to Joe how much she like talking to her counsellor; how she was getting stronger because of her counselling sessions; and how she told Sebire 'everything'.

Then, according to Maria, a strange thing happened. The day after telling her husband that she told her psychologist everything, Joe came back to the family home and promised to be faithful. He again threatened suicide or self-harm if she didn't take him back.

And – although Sebire wasn't sure who her client meant by 'everybody' – Maria also told her that Joe made an announcement to everybody that he wanted to marry Maria again.

But Maria Korp wasn't about to fall for that line. As she told Sebire in that session, Joe still wasn't planning to give Tania up, so Maria was thinking she would leave her husband. She thought she could live without him now, because he'd done nothing to prove he could be faithful to her.

Sebire said her impression, after that third session, was that Maria was definitely going to leave the marriage but she wasn't going to leave the house.

'She had gained some independence and she utilised her supports – her priest, family, work colleagues, friends and myself,' Sebire said. 'She said the more people she told, the more she realised she didn't have to put up with Joe's behaviour.'

Before Maria left that day, around 6pm, she told her psychologist that she'd ring to make her next appointment.

That Tuesday, however, was the last time Ann Sebire saw or spoke to Maria Korp. Her client was reported missing, by her husband, eight days later.

On Monday 21 February, Sebire was informed that the Airport West office of the OSA Group had had been broken into at about 5am that morning. Nothing, apart from her three-drawer filing cabinet, where she kept her client files, had been touched, and it had been ransacked.

The Moonee Ponds police investigated the burglary but no-one was ever caught.

The break-in may or may not have had anything to do with the 'everything' that Maria Korp told her psychologist about her marriage to Joe Korp. But luckily, as Ann Sebire said in her statement for the court, Maria Korp's files were not at the office that weekend; they were with her.

On Tuesday 8 February 2005, at around 2pm, Joe Korp dropped around to his girlfriend's place. After rummaging through her cupboards he laid some things – including a balaclava, a swimming cap, a hoodie and some white gloves – out on her bed.

This was their murder kit, to go with the latest plan Joe had outlined a few days before. He'd pick Tania up really early and drive her back to his place where she would wait in the garage. He would nick off to put in an appearance work, so he had an alibi; then Tania would strangle Maria, he'd return and meet her down the road a bit, and then she'd drive somewhere with her body and dump the car.

According to Tania's statement to police, just over eight days later, Joe told her he had thought it all through and that she wouldn't be caught because she'd be wearing his shoes, and wouldn't leave any DNA because her hair and hands would be covered.

'He was so convincing about how it would be done that I never for one minute thought that we'd be caught,' she said.

At about 5.15 the next morning Joe Korp took the short drive to Tania's house and found his nervous accomplice ready and waiting for him. She was dressed, as he'd told her to, in the tights and hoodie. Over a quick cup of coffee Joe began revving Tania up with reminders of how their lives were about to change.

'You know what I want you to do,' he told her. 'I want her strangled and dead. She is not to come out of the garage alive.'

When Tania got into the car she found a pair of Joe's runners and a some black tracksuit pants. Joe explained the bigger shoes would confuse things at the scene and the pants would lessen the chance of leaving any fibres behind.

Tania again did as she was told, and put the shoes and pants on while Joe drove them back to his house on Mount Ridley Road. Tania then opened the backpack with the other gear in it and pulled out the bathing cap, balaclava and a leather bag strap. She put the cap on but asked Joe what the strap was for. It was about a metre long.

'I want you to strangle the bitch,' he said.

After they pulled into his garage and the automatic door had closed them inside, Joe told Tania to put the balaclava on and wait in the dark.

Joe Korp then left his mistress and went upstairs to have breakfast with his wife. He returned 15 minutes later, hugged and kissed Tania, told her again that this would work, that she'd be okay.

Then he said, 'I love you, you don't know how much I love you. How much do you love me? Are you going to show me today? I don't want her out of this garage unless she's dead. You've got to do this for me.'

Tania Herman retreated into the dark again after Joe left her alone in the garage to go and secure his alibi.

Dressed bizarrely in her lover's tracksuit and too-big shoes, Tania crouched behind the car parked nearest to the houseand waited. Maria's car, she knew, was the Mazda parked in the centre space.

Tania waited for a woman she'd never actually met, but whom she'd come to hate. She waited for a woman she believed was the impediment to her own happy future, because Joe had told her as much. She waited to 'get rid' of a woman who was already thinking of leaving her husband, leaving Joe Korp free and clear to do whatever he wanted with whomever he wanted.

Tania Herman waited to commit murder in the name of love.

Maria Korp took the internal stairs down to the garage at 6.30. Tania waited until Maria had opened the driver's door to her car before throwing herself forward. She already had the strap wound tight around her gloved hands and stretched taut. She reached it around Maria's throat, and yanked her rival backwards into her own body.

Tania was a good 18 centimetres taller and 18 kilograms heavier than Maria, but that did not stop Maria from fighting for her life. She screamed out for her daughter, and she twisted around to face her attacker and managed to drag the balaclava off.

Unmasked, Tania stumbled in Joe's big shoes and they both crashed to the concrete floor. Tania straddled her victim, and pulled tight on the strap until Maria stopped moving.

Then there was blood, and a body, and a 37-year-old woman facing the horrible reality of what she'd just done.

It's a wonder she didn't panic. She said later that she very nearly did – before, during and after.

She'd could've just fled the scene; disappeared. But she'd been driven there by Joe and the Mickleham house, surrounded by paddocks, was at the head of a long driveway, on a long country road a few kilometres from the nearest highway. If she ran, somebody would be sure to see her, place her somewhere near the scene – near the murder scene.

Tania had no choice, really, but to follow the plan; the stupid, stupid plan.

She dragged Maria's body, heaved it into the empty boot of the Mazda. She picked up her useless disguise and the murder weapon and got into the car. She took off Joe's shoes, chucked them into the dark and put her own runners back on. Then she pressed the automatic door opener and drove out of the garage.

Tania headed not for the hills – which probably would've been more sensible – but for the heart of the city of Melbourne. Not surprisingly Joe was not waiting down the road a bit like he said he'd be. Why would he? He had to be at work for his alibi to work.

It didn't occur to Tania Herman, even then, that if you're *planning* to kill someone and report them as missing then, logically, you should also plan how to dispose of the body so it was never found; or at least get rid of your victim in a way that there'd be no rebound. That would be the sensible thing to do, wouldn't it – unless you were stupid; or not the one in control; or so in love with your co-conspirator that you weren't thinking clearly at all.

It didn't occur to Tania Herman that when the words love and conspiracy crop up in the same plan, then that plan is bound to go pear-shaped. Because while you might actually want to believe that murder is the only way forward for you and your beloved, it never is.

None of that occurred to Tania Herman because, right up until it was too late, she believed Joe's assurances that his plan would work.

Until she realised what she'd just done; and that the plan she'd thought was a bit stupid from the get-go had turned into something ludicrous because her lover hadn't thought beyond just 'getting rid' of the other person.

And that was 'the person', not the body.

And there *she* was, alone – with the body.

And it didn't matter how scared she was because now she had to stick to the rest of Joe's plan – such as it was – because it was all there was.

It wasn't long, however, before Tania Herman discovered that she had been well and truly conned; that her co-conspirator, her lover, her man, never really cared if she got caught or not.

Tania parked the car on Dallas Brooks Drive and, still obeying Joe's instructions, emptied the contents of Maria's handbag out onto the seat to remove anything identifying. She took a wallet, a mobile, some notebooks and the keys with her.

After Tania abandoned Maria and the car, she headed across town to where her brother worked in Elizabeth Street. She nearly had a heart attack when Maria's phone rang as she was crossing Princess Bridge, so she chucked it into the Yarra River. When she reached Steve's work, she lied that she'd had a job interview and asked him to drive her home.

Steve Deegan, although worried about what his sister had really been up to, drove her home to Greenvale, where she then collected her daughter and took her to school.

Just after 10am she met Joe in the car park at his work, something she often did at morning or afternoon tea time. Tania later told police that when Joe asked her if she was okay she'd said, 'What do you reckon? Have you ever been made, you know, to go and kill someone or to go and strangle them and take a life?'

To which, she said, Joe responded, 'No, you took the life for me. I didn't have anything to do with this. You did it.'

Alarm bells yet? Just quiet ones, and still way off in the background.

Tania admitted she wasn't altogether sure that Maria was actually dead. Joe again assured her that everything would be okay. He then told her to take the backpack with the stuff in it to Heathcote, where they used to meet for sex, and burn the lot. He also wanted to know exactly where she'd left Maria's Mazda and asked for the keys, saying he didn't have another set.

Tania drove the 100 kilometres to Lake Eppalock, poured petrol on their murder kit and set it on fire, and got home again in time to pick Tayelor up from school. Even on this strange and violent day, Tania Herman still managed to do the mundane ordinary things that had to be done.

At 1am the next morning, Joe turned up at her place complaining that he'd had to clean up blood on the garage floor. He also had more things for her to get rid of: the sneakers of his that she'd worn, because they also had blood on them; the bleach and scrubbing brush he'd used to clean the garage floor; and, oddly, a pair of diamond earrings.

Joe wanted Tania to take this stuff all the way to Heathcote too, but she insisted the park over the road would do just as well. After school later that day, she took her daughter for a walk in the park and while Tayelor was playing, Tania buried Joe's stuff.

Joe Korp reported his wife missing at 7.30pm on Wednesday 9 February, four hours after she failed to pick up their 11-year-old son from school.

Ordinarily a person, a grown-up person, is not considered 'at risk' until they have been missing for at least 24 ours. There are exceptions, of course, like sick or elderly adults.

But Maria Korp was hale and hearty. Yes, her behaviour was unusual, for her – but not for police accustomed to such things. And the husband had admitted they'd been having marital problems and that his wife was depressed.

The officer at Craigieburn did make the usual preliminary calls, however, to Mrs Korp's friends and workplace, to no avail.

Joe had already rung 'everyone he could think of', he told them though it was later discovered that the one number he had not rung that day in search of his wife was the one to Maria's own mobile phone.

Joe Korp probably figured, and he would have been told as much by the police at Craigieburn, that Missing Persons would not officially action the report until at least Thursday evening…which would effectively mean Friday morning.

So Joe waited for word of his wife; and Maria's daughter Laura and son Damian waited for word from their mother.

Long before the standard waiting period was up, however, the situation changed – for Victoria Police anyway. Within 90 minutes of Joe reporting his wife missing, police were already concerned that this was no ordinary missing person case; that Maria Matilde Korp was neither a runaway wife nor a lost mother.

Just before 9pm that very same night, they received a tip, from an unusual source, that something bad had probably happened to Maria, and that Joe Korp himself may be responsible for his wife's disappearance.

Gust Korp had rung the Craigieburn station and told police that his brother had a girlfriend, Tania Herman, and that his niece Laura had told him she thought she'd heard a scream at their house that morning.

The three officers from Craigieburn who called on the Korp residence in semi-rural Mickleham later that night were, therefore, already looking for clues. They were already watching Joe Korp's demeanour, his reactions, his willingness to help. And, because of the information already received, they weren't too surprised when Korp suggested his *ex*-girlfriend, Tania Herman, as they only person *he* could think of who didn't much care for Maria.

From the first shift the very next day then, Victoria Police were already treating Maria Korp's disappearance as suspicious. The Homicide Squad was already on the case, and officers in the Missing Persons Unit were afraid they would not find the missing woman alive.

It was also the next day that Gust Korp made a formal statement to detectives at the Criminal Investigation Unit at the Broadmeadows station about Joe's online 'dating', and gave police the information he'd collected from his brother's personal computer.

As helicopters searched the Mickleham area for Maria's car, Joe Korp had no idea he was already a person of interest. In fact, straight after his first official interview with CIB detectives at Craigieburn police station on the Thursday afternoon regarding Maria's disappearance, he was placed under surveillance. And by the end of that first full day after reporting Maria missing, several other people, including his alleged ex-girlfriend, had already been interviewed.

While the public was unaware of those details, 'the story' was already gaining momentum. The Friday edition of Melbourne's daily *Herald Sun* had run a small story, basically a request for public assistance in locating the missing mother. Even so, Maria would only have been 'missing' – or reported as such – for about 18 hours by the time that edition of the paper was put to bed on the Thursday night.

Despite the clues and information coming thick and fast from a variety of sources, mostly friends and family, the police still had no real idea of what, indeed if anything, had happened to Maria Korp. They were not taking any chances though, and decided it was time to shine a very big light on the case.

At 11am on Friday 10 February, Victoria Police held an official press conference, at which they supplied photos of Maria Korp and details about her missing car: a maroon Mazda 626, Victorian plates, rego NIW 306. It was barely two days after Maria Korp was last known to have been seen, and only 40 hours since Joe Korp had walked into the Craigieburn cop shop.

Encouraged by detectives, Maria's 27-year-old daughter Laura took part in the media interviews. As a suspect, even though he didn't know it yet, Joe was not included in the police appeal. Laura talked of how worried the family was, and asked for anyone who might know anything about the whereabouts of her mother to come forward or ring Crime Stoppers.

On Friday and Saturday, as family, friends and acquaintances volunteered information, the police realised this case was not going to end well, but even they had no idea just how complicated things were about to get.

On the Sunday morning, 13 February, Laura, Damian *and* Joe appeared on a Channel 7 news report, filmed in their lounge room.

Joe Korp denied having anything to do with the disappearance of his wife. 'No way,' he said. 'I love my wife, I love my wife dearly.'

Tania Herman, meanwhile, was going crazy wondering what the hell Joe was up to. He wasn't responding to her text messages and the cops who'd already searched her house and interviewed her at the Broadmeadows cop shop had said that Joe had told them that he 'used to love Tania' but that he loved Maria more. And now, here he was on TV saying the same thing: that he loved his wife – dearly.

At about 1pm that day, the missing Mazda, which had been found that morning near the Shrine, was finally opened and Maria Korp was found in the boot, alive. She was rushed to the Alfred Hospital where she was diagnosed with hypoxic brain injury; her brain had been starved of oxygen. She had a ligature mark around her neck from the attempted strangulation, was dangerously dehydrated, and had pressure sores and ulcers from laying motionless in the stifling conditions of the car boot. Her skin, in the places where proper blood flow was denied, had literally died and turned black. The doctors feared the worst: that, despite the miracle of being found alive, Maria Korp was unlikely to recover.

Tania Herman was interviewed again, at 10pm that night, by Homicide Squad detectives. She continued to deny any involvement in anything that had befallen Maria Korp.

About 24 hours later, on 14 February, Steve Deegan finished giving police his statement, in which he told them about driving his sister home from the city on the morning that Maria Korp went missing, and of the conversations he'd had with Tania and her boyfriend about ways to kill his wife.

In the meantime, the media was having a field day. TV news

reports had implied there was also something suspicious about the recent death, by heart attack, of Tania's second husband Paul Herman. They were also, of course, going to town on the smut that was circling Tania and the Korps.

Even Maria, already and forever known as 'the woman in the boot', was being dragged through the gutter. The deeply religious woman who had refused to take part in any of Joe's sex games had been 'outed' in the press for her listing on a matchmaking site, with her husband, advertising for sex with other couples. No-one who knew Maria believed she'd have agreed to that; which meant Joe had set her up for that humiliation as well.

It was Joe's Korp's public denials of the current status of his relationship with Tania that prompted Steve Deegan to do what he did next. And he did it to try and save his sister from completely ruining her life for that bastard.

On Wednesday 16 February, wired for sound, he visited Tania at home in Greenvale. It didn't take much to get Tania talking about what had happened, because she was already livid about the way Joe had been treating her and was sick with worry about what she'd done and how it was going to impact on her family.

Steve was also worried that she kept bringing up suicide as a way out for her.

'No, because then he gets away with it,' Steve told her. 'If you're going down yourself, then fuckin' take him with you.'

Tania said she'd leave a note about what had really happened, but Steve said a suicide note wouldn't do it. 'You've got to tell someone.'

'What if I go to the detective and change my statement and tell 'em exactly what happened?' Tania asked her brother. 'Then what happens to me? I go to jail straightaway.'

Steve agreed. 'Yeah, they'll probably arrest you. But if you... tell 'em what he did then they can arrest him as well. He screwed you over, Tan. You know we don't take that.'

A bit later Steve advised his sister, 'If I was in your state at the moment, I'd give Tayelor to Mum and Dad, I'd go to

Broadmeadows police station and I'd confess the whole lot. Him, everything, the whole lot and, being blunt… suffer the consequences. If you give yourself up instead of doing yourself in, that's a lot better for you.

'You were suckered into it by this prick. You were so madly in love with this guy, you would've jumped off a cliff for him.'

Tania finally came around to her brother's way of thinking and asked if he would go with her to the police. He was going to head home to his place, then she would drop Tayelor off there with her parents, who were on their way from Echuca, and then she and Steve would go to the police together.

But the police already had the confession and knew of Tania's intention to hand herself in. The entire conversation had been recorded by the wire that Steve Deegan had worn to help the police get enough information to make two arrests that day.

Detectives turned up at Joe Korp's home shortly after 10.30 and arrested him for the attempted murder of his wife.

Tania Herman was also arrested for attempted murder that morning, moments after she arrived at her brother's house and handed her daughter safely into the care of her stunned parents.

Tania's father Bill went with her in the police car and listened in disbelief as his daughter confessed everything to the detectives who took her into custody.

Joe Korp of course denied everything, and continued to profess his innocence until the very end.

A few days after Maria had been found, her daughter Laura was keeping a bedside vigil and noticed that some of her mother's jewellery was missing. Maria was not wearing her wedding band, her crucifix or her earrings.

Among the things that Tania had buried for Joe after the 'attempted murder' was a pair of earrings. She showed police where she'd disposed of them, in the park near her place. This, coupled with the fact that a tartan blanket had allegedly been found with Maria in the boot, which had been empty when Tania heaved the unconscious woman's body into it, suggested that Joe Korp may have visited the car on Dallas Brooks Drive. Sometime after he had reported his wife missing and before he visited Tania after midnight on the Thursday, Joe Korp – the only person with a set of keys that would open the boot – had probably checked on Maria and just left her there to die slowly.

Released on bail on 9 June 2005, Joe Korp did something that only Joe Korp would do. With his mistress Tania Herman already in jail, and about to be convicted for the attempted murder of his second wife Maria, Joe Korp took refuge from the world, and the media in particular, in the home of first wife Leonie. Despite having had little to do with him for 15 years, she took him into her home.

After pleading guilty to the attempted murder of Maria Korp, Tania Herman faced sentencing on Friday 1 July 2005.

Justice Bernard Teague told her, 'As I pass this sentence, Maria Korp is not dead, but she is close to death. She remains in the Alfred Hospital, having been there now for over four months. Despite the best efforts of doctors and nurses, she has remained unconscious. She is unlikely to survive much longer.

'The attempted murder of Maria Korp was a planned callous attack on a devoted mother of two children in her own home. Maria Korp was not known to you personally. Most, if not all, that you knew about her had been told to you by her husband, Joe Korp. In February 2005, you were passionately in love with Joe Korp. You did to Maria Korp what you had agreed with Joe Korp to do. Your attack was intended to result in her death in a way that would not be traced to you or to Joe Korp.'

Justice Teague noted that when she was interviewed by police on 16 February, Tania made significant admissions and later provided a detailed statement.

'The credibility of much of what is set out in the statement has been verified from independent sources. You have undertaken before me to give evidence at any committal or trial of Joe Korp,' he said.

'I have to weigh against the extremely serious nature of your crime, several significant mitigating factors that operate in your favour. You have pleaded guilty at an early stage. You have no prior convictions. There are many indications of your genuine remorse. I assess the prospects of rehabilitation as excellent.'

Justice Teague said the most significant mitigating factor was Tania's cooperation with the authorities. He pointed out that that might mean she would have to spend some time 'in protection' while in prison.

He told Tania, 'Your choice to assist the authorities has several implications. It warrants a very large reduction in the sentence imposed for purely utilitarian reasons dictated by the public interest.'

Justice Teague sentenced Tania Herman to 12 years in prison, with a non-parole period of nine years.

Twenty-five days later, Victorian Public Advocate Julian Gardner, who had been appointed as Maria Korp's guardian in April, made the decision to withdraw the feeding tube that had been keeping her alive.

Maria was in a vegetative state, able to breathe on her own but receiving intravenous fluids and food through a nasogastric or stomach tube. Doctors predicted she would die within two weeks.

Gardner told ABC Radio, 'I found this a very difficult time personally but the one thing that gives me comfort is that we in the Office of the Public Advocate have been able to protect the interests of this person whose disability meant they couldn't protect themselves.

'One doesn't particularly welcome the sort of uninformed negative comments, but it's important that I've sought to be accountable and explain as well as I could to the public the decision that has to be made.'

The public debate that raged around this issue was another thing that served to belittle what was left of the life of Maria Korp. Pro-lifers and euthanasia advocates argued about the future of a mother who didn't have one. They didn't know her, had no stake in her living or dying – except for their own political agendas – and yet they huffed and puffed.

Deeply religious as she was, Maria's opinion on the subject could only have been guessed at, but the bottom line was that she was never going to regain consciousness.

Julian Gardner told ABC television's *The 7.30 Report*, 'Mrs Korp's medical condition has been declining and it has not been possible to stabilise her condition.

'The treating team at the Alfred Hospital has advised me that her condition is now terminal and that the ongoing provision of medical treatment in the current form is not only futile, but unduly burdensome for her.

'Their clinical view is that she should move to palliative care, and that involves ceasing the provision of artificial nutrition and hydration, that is the provision of food and water, via a peg tube that's essentially inserted in her stomach.'

Gardner disputed reports that this would mean that Maria would suffer some sort of agonising death.

'That is totally incorrect,' he said. 'There are people all over Melbourne every day who die naturally and, as they do, their desire for and their intake of food and water naturally ceases. Their body systems shut down and they cease to feel the need for it.

'I've spoken over many months to palliative care specialists and without fail, without exception, they've advised me that the process will be pain free and free of discomfort, and in accordance with the best palliative care.'

Maria Matilde Korp died just before 2am on Friday 5 August 2005.

Joe Korp hanged himself on 12 August 2005. It was the day of his wife's funeral; the day the woman he'd been married to for 14 years, the mother of his son, had been buried.

Eternally self-centred, this man couldn't even allow Maria Korp the peace and dignity of a funeral unsullied by his dramatics. He held his own private service for Maria at their Mickleham home and declared in journal entries his love for Maria and his desire that they would 'find each other again'.

But not too many people believed Joe Korp anymore. He was about to stand trial for her murder, so most people thought he was just a coward who couldn't face justice.

But there was a rumour that his hanging was unintentional; that it was a stunt gone wrong; that someone was supposed to find him in time, and save him. The rumour was that this grief-stricken 'attempt' to join his beloved wife would convince a jury that he loved her and could not possibly have wanted to harm her.

But no-one saved Joe Korp that day. And given the evidence stacked against him, ultimate justice of the 'what goes around, comes around' kind found him instead.

Ten months later, on 30 June 2006, Deputy State Coroner Iain West delivered his findings at the inquest into the separate deaths of Maria and Joe Korp.

Noting that Tania Herman had already pleaded guilty to the attempted murder of Maria Korp and been sentenced to prison, West said, 'As I am satisfied that the version of events outlined by Tania Herman accurately reflects the circumstances leading to the tragic death, I formally find that Tania Lee-Anne Herman and Joseph William Korp caused the death of Maria Matilde Korp.'

Regarding the question of whether Joe Korp meant to die in his shed on 12 August, West said, 'Following his wife's death on August 5, Joseph Korp was expecting to be re-arrested and to be charged with her murder, and on the 6th he used a video camera to record aspects of his life, to assert his innocence and to state his intention to commit suicide using the orange rope.'

West said that the theory that Korp's death was accidental was 'only one of a number of assumptions that could be made.

'Findings of fact cannot be based on speculation and in the absence of cogent evidence to the contrary, I am satisfied that the deceased intended the fatal outcome of his actions. I formally find that on 12 August 2005, Joseph William Korp, with prior indication of intent, took his own life by hanging.'

Legal findings aside, because Joe Korp signalled his intention, because he sent dozens of text messages and called several people on the night, including a couple of journalists, and because he then waited half an hour before climbing the ladder, the rumours persisted that he expected to be stopped in his suicide attempt.

Whatever the truth of that matter, apparently when Tania Herman learned that Joe Korp was dead, she just said, 'Good.'

Tania Herman was released from prison on Valentine's Day 2014 after serving nine years of her sentence.

# BAD TO THE BONE

Is there anything in the known universe that can explain how a woman, a mother, can participate in the rape and callous murder of a 12-year-old child? It is a shallow excuse to point the finger at her male partner and say that she did it for him, for love. This excuse shatters the moment any weight is added to it, or when the evidence is measured against the story she wants the police to believe.

Much of the media, whose entire industry exists ato use words, to investigate, to inform and to reveal, have trotted out stereotypes, assumptions and reactions.

The controversial psychoanalyst Sigmund Freud made his own attempt to explain those women who participate in predatory sexual behaviour: 'that she is a child being beaten by her father, or watching him beat someone else'.

Gertrude Stein's wonderful short piece makes as much sense as Freud: 'my wife is a cow, is a cow, is my wife, is a cow'.

Even Valmae Beck, convicted child killer, had a more articulate explanation for her behaviour: a lazily extended middle finger given to the waiting media as she was led from court, surrounded by police.

Valmae Beck is dead. Jailed in 1988 for the abduction, rape and murder of a 12-year-old Noosa schoolgirl, she died in hospital on 27 May 2008 after serving 21 years in jail.

Valmae was known to have embarked on a much larger crime spree with her former partner, Barrie Watts, and both were suspected of at least one other murder. Despite the hopes of police that the self-confessed newly born Christian would reveal details of those other crimes, and give surviving families some peace of mind, Valmae Beck took any secrets she had to the grave.

Valmae Beck, who had changed her name to Fay Cram, embraced Christianity, and unsuccessfully applied for parole on three occasions, measured 160 centimetres, and was a morbidly obese 150 kilos.

Because she was addicted to chocolate, the police even resorted to taking packets of Tim Tams to interviews with her, in order to try and elicit a confession. At the end of these meetings, the packet would be empty, as would the file of new information detectives had hoped to fill.

On 5 May 2008, Valmae was taken to hospital and underwent minor heart surgery after complaining of shortness of breath. She had twice previously been admitted to hospital for chest pains: in 2005 and again in 2006. This last time she underwent surgery and was placed in an induced coma in order to improve her chances. But Valmae's recovery was complicated by her morbid obesity, sleep apnoea and complications relating to diabetes. She was taken off life support on 26 May 2008 and died less than 24 hours later.

When the news broke that the most hated woman in Queensland was receiving life-saving surgery, people became hostile and upset. Queensland Premier Anna Bligh was forced to publicly defend the decision and attempt to quell community outrage.

'Whether it is Valmae Beck or any other prisoner, when people turn up sick in our hospitals, doctors have a duty to treat them,' Ms Bligh said.

At the same time, Premier Bligh called on the convicted murderer to assist police with information that may help them solve other crimes. 'Frankly, if there is any opportunity at all for Valmae Beck to put other families out of their distress, then I think she has got an obligation to pass that on,' Ms Bligh said.

Beck either didn't hear the request or still didn't give a damn.

There are now unanswered questions about the death of Valmae Beck herself. Taken from jail to hospital for 'minor' heart surgery, Beck was expected to survive, even with the induced coma.

Police obtained permission to conduct a bedside vigil, in the hope that when she woke she would be willing to answer questions to end speculation over the nature and extent of her crimes, but she just never regained consciousness.

Even today – more than two decades after the fact – speculation remains rife about the events that took place during the relatively brief but toxic relationship between Valmae Beck and Barrie John Watts.

Valmae had been married twice and had six children when, at the age of 43, she met the younger Watts. They got married in Perth, Western Australia, and were living there at the time that David and Catherine Birnie were abducting, raping and murdering women in that city.

While the rest of Perth was reeling in horror at the crimes the Birnies had committed, Valmae Beck's new husband Barrie became fascinated. According to police an evil seed was planted in his fertile mind and, inspired by the Birnies' crime spree, Barrie Watts began to fantasise about 'being the first – and last – lover of young virgins'.

Valmae and Barrie moved to Queensland in 1987 and set up home in Lowood, a small country town in the Brisbane Valley. A farming community of less than 3000 people, Lowood is 70 kilometres west of Brisbane and 30 north-west of Ipswich. When the couple moved to Lowood, they had been together less than a year and their relationship was already floundering.

But during that same time, and in a variety places where the couple just happened to have been, there were numerous reports of missing women, attempted abductions, rapes and murder.

By late 1987, Valmae Beck and Barrie Watts had clearly signalled their sick intentions. On 11 November they drove to Ipswich where they found a 24-year-old woman, Cheryl Ann Mortimer, shopping in Target at the local shopping centre. Armed with a knife, Barrie Watts approached her and tried to force her into his car. But Cheryl fought back and at one point during the struggle she grabbed the knife and managed to escape. She reported the assault and attempted abduction to the police.

Fifteen days later, and 190 kilometres further north, a young woman was relaxing at Castaways Beach near Noosa when she encountered someone who would come to haunt her for the rest of her life.

Noosa and the neighbouring areas are the kinds of places people dream of being able to live in. Beautiful beaches, surrounded and protected by lush forests, this is Queensland's Sunshine Coast. Unlike its ugly step-sister, Surfers Paradise, who sold her soul for the almighty dollar, Noosa retains her charm and her character. Part of the reason for this is that the population has been capped, and the local government has resisted most developers' pleas for high-rise buildings. It is one of Australia's most desirable tourist destinations for surfers and backpackers, and an almost unaffordable dream for people to buy into.

In 1987 Elizabeth Young, a 31-year-old bartender, was at Castaways Beach with her friend Bill Wallace, when her flatmate's black labrador began growling at a stranger. Many years later, when Elizabeth finally broke her silence to the *Sunshine Coast Daily* newspaper, she spoke about the terrible day that has inhabited her nightmares for more than 20 years.

The unshaven, dishevelled-looking man who was walking on the beach that day was wearing KingGee shorts and a work shirt, and appeared to be looking for something.

'He looked like a farmer looking for his cows,' Elizabeth recalled. 'There was something very odd about the way he was dressed; and he wasn't looking at the water. I'd never seen anyone like him on the beach before.

'When the dog started going berserk, I said to Bill, "something is not right here."'

When Elizabeth left the surf and approached the man, she realised she'd seen him at the beach the day before as well, dressed almost identically and behaving in the same bizarre manner.

With a slender 55 kilo frame and long blonde hair, Elizabeth was used to male attention; but she said that when she approached Watts, his reaction froze her blood.

'When I waved to him and said g'day, there was no reaction, no expression. He stared at me with this cold expression. It made the hair stand up on my neck. I thought he was looking for a lost wallet, at first. He was just looking towards the dunes, not towards the water, and kept scouring the dunes, back and forth.'

Concerned by Watts' actions, she and her friend checked out a white dust-covered Kingswood station wagon in the car park – the only other car there apart from their own Land Cruiser.

Because the car looked as if it had been travelling on dirt roads and was not from the local area, they wrote down the plate number and returned to the beach.

Just before 3pm, Watts left the beach so Elizabeth and her friend decided to follow his car. They made it to Noosa Junction before they lost him in traffic.

'He went straight down through the shops, towards Pinnaroo Park,' Elizabeth said. 'We didn't think anything more of it, because he hadn't physically threatened me. But Bill said to me, "This is weird, creepy, I don't want you coming on your own".'

Barely half an hour later, on 27 November, Barrie Watts and his wife abducted Sian Kingi.

Few people who came across Valmae Beck in 1987 would have given her so much as a second look, let alone been scared of her. Short and overweight, with fluffy bleached-blonde hair, she looked for all the world like a dumpy, middle-aged housewife; just another face in the crowd.

So there was no reason for a 12-year-old schoolgirl – a beautiful child who lived in the quiet, safe community of Noosa – to feel threatened by her that afternoon; Valmae Beck looked harmless.

Sian Kingi, dressed in her Sunshine Beach school uniform, was riding her bike home from school. She had taken a path in Pinnaroo Park, near the Noosa Junction shopping centre, when a woman stopped her and asked if she had seen her missing dog – a poodle. There was no reason for Sian to feel alarmed; it was a perfectly reasonable request from a woman who looked old enough to be her grandmother.

Sian, distracted in her helpful search for the poodle, probably didn't even realise the lady had guided her away from the path. All the while, Valmae was luring Sian closer to where her husband, Barrie Watts was lurking in the bushes.

Barrie grabbed Sian and the couple then bound and forced the young girl into their car. They drove 12 kilometres to the nearby national park, where Barrie and Valmae raped Sian several times; and then killed her when they were done.

When Sian didn't come home from school that afternoon her mother went looking for her. She found Sian's abandoned bike in Pinaroo Park but there was no sign of her daughter. Desperately worried, she reported Sian missing to the police. A search of the area followed and schoolmates were contacted, but there was no sign of her.

As night turned to day, fears intensified and the whole community became involved in the search for the missing schoolgirl. As days went by with no sign of Sian, fear turned to dread. Police had begun to privately fear the worst.

Six days later, and 12 kilometres away, a fruit picker stumbled across the small, blood-covered and crumpled body of a young blonde girl, dressed in a school uniform and lying in a dry creek bed. It was Sian Kingi.

News of Sian's disappearance and discovery preoccupied the community and the media. Nobody was immune to the horror when they learned of the extent of the injuries the 12 year old had suffered before her death. One police officer talked about how it was the worst case he had ever come across in 32 years in the job.

Queensland Police Superintendent Alan Bourke was then a

Detective Senior Constable at Sunshine CIB. He recalled that when Sian disappeared that Friday afternoon, there was an initial report that the occupants of a white HQ Holden station wagon were acting suspiciously near where Sian Kingi was last seen.

'There was also a half-baked description of a fattish woman seen arguing with a male at Pinnaroo Park,' he said. 'That's all we had – a white HQ station wagon – so it was pretty vague at the time.'

When police broadcast that description, however, Elizabeth Young came forward and told police she'd been sunbathing at Castaways Beach that same day, when a man had come along and exposed himself. She said the man later got into a white HQ wagon and headed towards Noosa. The woman's boyfriend had scribbled down registration numbers of two cars in the nearby car park. That crumpled and scribbled note, now with the only the last two letters 'LE' and the numbers 429 clearly legible, was the vital clue that police needed.

Detective Bourke and his team went painstakingly through national registration records, matching every possible combination, and eventually found a white HQ wagon with the number LLE 429, registered to a Valmae Beck of the Melbourne suburb of Croydon.

Police then found that a Barrie Watts had struck up a rapport with Beck in Western Australia, where both had spent time in jail. Associates described her as 'a plump woman' and revealed the couple had travelled to Ipswich.

Another breakthrough came when police, already investigating the attempted abduction of two nurses outside Ipswich Hospital, were alerted to another abduction.

Ipswich detective Graham Hall saw the general broadcast on the vehicle with the registration LLE 429 and linked it to another attempted daylight grabbing of a woman at a Booval shopping centre. The woman had fought off a man armed with a knife. Witnesses had written down the rego number of the man's car as LLF 429 or LLE 439.

The attacker had been cut with his own knife in the attempt, and the bloodied fingerprint left on the side of the woman's car proved to be a match for those of Barrie Watts; kept on record by the authorities in Western Australia.

Queensland Police began to close in on Barrie and Valmae. They were found two weeks later in New South Wales, holed up in a hotel at The Entrance. They were extradited to Queensland to face charges in relation to the abduction, rape and murder of Sian Kingi.

When confronted with the allegation, Valmae told police she had no idea what had happened to the missing girl. She claimed she had a fight with Barrie that day and that she'd got angry and stormed off. For his part, Barrie claimed to be so drunk he had no recollection of what had happened that day. They were nothing if not accomplished liars.

When Valmae later changed her mind and decided to confess to the crime, her story was far more chilling and revealing than police could have imagined – for Valmae told them more than she probably needed to.

Police had 'naturally' assumed Valmae was merely an accomplice to the more evil Barrie Watts, one of those pathetic women who would do anything to make her man happy – including stepping over the line to help him commit or cover up a murder.

But Valmae told police that Barrie fantasised about having sex with a young virgin, and that this was the reason they had both kidnapped Sian Kingi. Once she began to open up with particulars of the crime, police were also astonished at the detail she recalled.

Almost from the start, Detective Bourke said, Valmae made full admissions about Sian's murder. 'She took us to the scene – she took us to a lake where he had thrown the weapon in … a knife wrapped in a blanket and other items,' he said. 'She was very emotionless. Watts told us nothing, so we got her version, which was obviously self-serving. We were getting a watered-down version of her involvement in it, but enough that she had obviously planned it.

'[She said] they were looking for a girl, a young girl... [and had been] waiting in the park. I'd describe her as a very cold, calculating person – very careful of what she says ... she really knows the law.'

Valmae's account of the sexual assault of Sian Kingi filled 29 pages of transcript. The police felt at the time that she enjoyed retelling the story; that she was 'replaying it for an audience'.

In secretly recorded conversations between Valmae and Barrie, he showed obvious surprise that she had provided so much detail. 'Why didn't you just tell them I raped her?' he asked.

Barrie John Watts also said to his lover: 'You didn't tell them about the others though.'

In what was one of her more insightful recorded comments, Valmae told her man that, while she gave police an accurate account of what he had done to Sian Kingi, 'The only thing I didn't put in that statement was what happened between her and me ... I just couldn't tell them that.'

Barrie Watts and Valmae Beck appeared in court on 15 December 1987, the day before Sian Kingi should have been celebrating her 13th birthday. If any more proof was needed that Valmae Beck was a willing participant in the crimes, it came when she was giving evidence in court.

Again buoyed by her captive listeners, Valmae recounted at length and in detail the sexual assault of the child. It was as though she were reliving the experience and bragging to a new audience. The testimony, pornographic in nature and chilling in its detail, forced everyone in that courtroom to vicariously experience the assault of a young, defenceless child. It was not the behaviour of a remorseful woman who had simply found herself mixed up with the wrong man.

Valmae's insistence on going into such graphic detail left many people feeling uncomfortable, and several people later expressed their outrage at a justice system that 'allowed this young child to be violated all over again'.

One of the most telling comments Valmae Beck made to the

court was one that left everyone speechless. In talking about Sian Kingi, the 44-year-old murderer told the court: 'Sian never cried, never shed a tear, [she was] a brave little girl, she never uttered a peep. She just did everything he told her.'

The couple were tried separately and in 1988 Valmae Beck pleaded guilty. She was sentenced to life imprisonment for murder, 10 years for rape, and a further three years for deprivation of liberty.

Far from being a passive partner to Barrie Watts, Valmae Beck's involvement in the murder was that of an active participant. She was the one who lured Sian Kingi with the ruse of a missing poodle. During the abduction it was she who undressed the child, tied up her ankles and taped her mouth. While Barrie was raping the girl, Valmae rubbed his penis, gave Sian instructions on what to do, and then helped her husband penetrate the girl. When Barrie Watts began strangling Sian Kingi, the couple's blue heeler began to growl. Valmae took the dog to the car and then came back to watch. She then helped dispose of evidence, drove home and washed their clothes that night.

The sentencing judge described Valmae Beck as callous and depraved.

Barrie Watts described her as domineering and pushy.

Little else is known about Valmae Beck. One of the few insights into the woman came after a regular penpal passed Valmae's letters on to the Brisbane newspaper the *Courier Mail*. The newspaper reproduced some of those letters. Written at a time when Valmae was preparing for her third application for parole, it is hard to measure whether her revelations are the truth, or part of a character reference she was writing in her bid for freedom.

In her chatty, rambling handwritten letters sent between December 2003 and April 2004 while she was in prison in Wacol, Valmae complained to her new penfriend that she felt depressed at times; and labelled her jail conditions at the time as 'inhumane'. Complaining that Wacol was not as comfortable as the jail in Townsville where she had been previously held, and to which she has about to return, she said she dreamt of walking in the rain or visiting exotic rainforests. Among the personal insights she offered were:

> I would have loved to have seen the Amazon plus England and especially Scotland, but I am aware that I will never do it in this lifetime.
>
> I like country life better than the cities. I have worked in the country a lot in the past. I worked as a nanny/housekeeper. I have also done bar work.
>
> I am a cook … I had been doing it on a professional level since I was 18 years old (boy, I wish I could go back). I was a self-taught cook but I have completed a pre-apprentice chef course. I did it in Townsville jail along with five other girls. I came top of the class in all areas. I am also a qualified machinist as I love sewing.
>
> I never got to high school. My mother took me out of school when I was 12 and sent me to work in a clothing factory (she did not like me). I have not had a very pleasant childhood, between my mother giving me away all the time to relatives and strangers, plus the abuse I got from all three of my brothers.

Valmae also wrote about completing a Bible study course before starting the six-month Violent Intervention Program, which ran two hours a day, four times a week.

> We can't refuse to do these programs as it gives us bad reports for parole.
>
> It is going to be very emotional and stressful for a lot because it is dealing with and talking about our crimes and how we became involved in it.
>
> Of course there are people who are in denial about what they have done (not me).
>
> I was beaten 13 times by inmates and set up by staff for this to be done to me. The treatment I received was disgusting.

On other aspects of life inside and before prison, she wrote:

> I don't like grog either … I believe there would be less crimes if there was no grog or drugs.
>
> Some days the food is OK but we get slops as well.
>
> My all-time favourite food is Chinese (yum yum). I love lemon chicken or spare ribs in plum sauce and their fried ice-cream.
>
> I did fried ice-cream for the staff and girls in Townsville jail and made a beautiful sauce to go over it.
>
> I like toasted ham, onion and cheese sandwiches or ham, cheese and pineapple.

Valmae had views about how her crime was being kept alive by the media:

> I am just so fed up with it all. I feel so bad for the victim's family having to relive this horror every few months, what with people who get off on this kind of thing.
>
> Why aren't the victims of crime committees stopping this? Where is there [sic] so-called concern for the families? Don't they realise that what happens to me is God's will, not theirs? I can't stop the media but someone out there must be able to. It's about time it was all put to rest. These people must be allowed to grieve and move on.
>
> Of course the pain will always be there but their wounds are being kept open and idiots (the media, magazines etc) kept pouring salt on the wound.
>
> As for Barrie Watts (my ex-husband) he is in the jail at Rockhampton. He has been up there since about 1994. As far as I know he is still in protection.
>
> We were legally married but I divorced him a few years after coming to jail. His right name is John Fulton Beck. Barrie Watts was his adopted name and he was charged under that name because of his prior criminal record.

He did not know about his real name until about a month before we got married, which was the 19-12-86, then on the 15-12-87 we were in jail so you see I was only married to him for a year.

The 64-year-old, who changed her name to Fay Cramb, had to be moved from a high-security prison in Brisbane to Townsville after she was repeatedly targeted by female inmates. In one bashing, two prisoners clubbed the mother of six with a sock loaded with a jam tin. It caused permanent nerve damage to the side of Valmae's head, which left her partially paralysed in the face.

Fellow inmates were divided in their opinion of living with Valmae/Fay. Some became quite good friends with her and called her Nana Fay; others despised her. One prisoner who served time with Valmae recalled her experiences on an internet forum.

Using the moniker 'Chef on the Run', this former inmate wrote:

I was in jail in Townsville with this awful creature – I was in for something so stupid that I ended up with the authorities as mates … the only thing I could do to FAY CRAMB in order to be utterly cruel (SO not me but hate is hate) was to remove her from her exalted position as 'cook'. She had that position for 5 years prior to my arrival – she instantly loathed me because I started (and finished) a complicated degree in Environmental Studies … AND I cooked!!! At first I grew an enormous garden – I ploughed the land with forks – I refused to eat her foul food – and happily ate my beautiful fresh organic vegies. Then, at long last (took 9 months), the other girls in a secret ballot that Fay Cramb could not manipulate with chocolate and tokens (to buy cokes) – that's what she had done to thwart me in past attempts – I was voted in unanimously as cook (I changed that to chef) – well, the food change was radical but the best part is that Fay sat in her cell … crying for a week … there ARE some of us that make the best of our time in jail – I am highly successful … Fay Cramb is not.

PS I totally agree with keeping her alive to question her –

there was definitely more going on at the time than just dead Sian – they were too 'good' at what they did and videotaped. I spoke with one police officer in Cairns who told me (crying) some dreadful stuff they had done … having been in a medically induced coma myself, it is a very scary place as you are hovering between life and death and very strange things happen in one's head … I say, 'bring her out of the coma' … ask lots of questions.

Another former inmate wrote:

> … Fay Cramb … was transferred to Townsville Womens, where I had the pleasure of meeting this thing. Many of us were unhappy with it and fortunately I was shortly moved to the low security part of the prison, and did not have nothing to do with her. Only days before it arrived I was living in the hut (group of 6 cells), which it then moved into. Many people after leaving her section to come to mine, then had the nerve to stick up for her and say that she didn't deserve to be treated the way she was treated. I can not tell you how this argument made me feel inside, it felt as if they didn't care about what happened to that poor child. I want to let you all know though that there will be no chance of that women [sic] being given parole. Whilst in prison I had the chance to speak to a few screws which had been given information about her and that she could try as many times as she wished to get parole, however, her attempts would be effortless.

One of the more well-known people to spend time in prison with Valmae Beck was former One Nation founder and federal politician Pauline Hanson. Jailed in August 2003 after being found guilty of electoral fraud, Ms Hanson was sentenced to three years in prison. Just three months later she walked out, a free woman, after it was found she had been wrongfully imprisoned. In her short time inside, one of the people Hanson met was Valmae Beck, who was in the protective custody wing with her. After being released from prison, Pauline Hanson gave an interview to *Woman's Day* for which she was apparently paid $150,000.

In the article she described meeting 'Fay Cramb' and telling her, 'If anyone ever hurt my daughter I know what I'd do. I said I believe in capital punishment and I would even push the button myself, and Fay understood that.

'But this woman is so sorry for what she did,' Ms Hanson said. 'She told me: "Pauline, I have to live with this for the rest of my life. No one will be able to understand how I feel about the horrific crime I've committed."'

Valmae/Fay described Pauline Hanson, to her penfriend, as 'a very nice lady'. She wrote:

> I am glad I got to meet her. I believe this was in God's plan for her to meet me and see that I am not the way the papers say I am. Only God, myself and my ex-husband know what happened to bring me here. But a lot of people outside these walls and within don't want to know the truth, they just want to judge me.

Over the years Sian Kingi's family has maintained a dignified silence about their daughter's horrific murder. They have met all requests for comments with a polite 'no comment'. However, Barry and Lynda Kingi broke their silence briefly in 2003, through a family friend, after the blaze of publicity surrounding Pauline Hanson's magazine article about 'life inside' and her perceived support of Valmae Beck. A family spokeswoman said Hanson's comments had reopened old wounds:

> Indeed we are dismayed, but I believe many more will be as disgusted as we are that Pauline Hanson has used this terrible tragedy, which my friends will endure forever more, to financially benefit herself.
>
> She [Hanson] has shown a horrendous lack of judgment here which we believe she should review. She is a mother, which in most women would bring the realisation of the horror of Beck's crime and lead her to encourage the law to keep her behind bars for the rest of her life – in other words, suffer the consequences

of her actions. Without Valmae Beck, this crime would never have occurred. She was an integral part of a predatory pair who set out in a clearly premeditated fashion to abduct, rape and murder. They took this innocent child together.

Beck claims to have suffered guilt and pain and feels she has paid sufficiently to society with the years she had spent in jail. We disagree. She is as guilty as Barrie Watts. The only solace my friends have is in knowing that she stays behind bars and reaps the consequences of her actions.

While in Townsville Correctional Centre Valmae Beck struck up an unlikely friendship with serial child rapist Robert Fardon, who had served almost 30 years in jail for serious sex offences against women and children. They first met at a 'butcher's barbecue' in the prison and quickly became friends. According to people who knew them, they shared visits and found God together before becoming penpals. They spent supervised visits together with the prison chaplaincy team and worked in a prison support group, known as QISPA (Queensland Indeterminate Prisoner Support Association), until Beck was moved to Brisbane in August 2002.

'They shared an uncanny bond as outcasts within the prison system,' a prison source said. 'They also corresponded. At one stage a psychologist was enlisted to peruse the content of the letters they were writing to each other, but exactly what they were hatching never fully emerged.'

Prison records show that in 1998 Fardon asked a pastor if he could buy an engagement ring for Valmae Beck through mail order. The same pastor approached by Fardon had also baptised Valmae and other prisoners in a pond at the Townsville Correctional Centre several years before. The sources said jail management objected to the baptisms, saying they were in poor taste, but the department's head office overruled them. Two other pastors – a married couple who visited Valmae – wanted to adopt her.

A month before the murder of Sian Kingi, during the couple's eight-week crime spree in 1987, another local woman went missing.

Helen Mary Feeney was last seen at a caravan park on 29 October 1987 in Brisbane's northern suburbs. The 31-year-old woman was studying to be a teacher at the North Brisbane College of Advanced Education at Carseldine.

Helen's ex-husband John, with whom she maintained regular contact, reported her missing on 28 November 1987 after she failed to show up for an access visit with their six-year-old son.

Police believed that Barrie Watts killed Mrs Feeney when she disturbed him breaking into her car in the grounds of the North Brisbane College of Advanced Education. A small amount of blood was found in Mrs Feeney's white Holden Gemini sedan, but there was not enough for police to retrieve a DNA profile. Detectives have, however, taken a DNA sample from Mrs Feeney's son, Shea, in the event his mother's remains are ever found.

'We want to be able to declare Helen Feeney dead for her family's sake and to bring them some closure,' Detective Senior Constable Farmer said.

Valmae Beck told police that Helen Feeney had indeed been killed by her partner Barrie Watts. Even though Mrs Feeney's body had not been found, Barrie Watts was put on trial for her murder in 1995. Valmae testified that he dumped and burned Mrs Feeney's body at a rubbish tip near Lowood, where the couple rented a house.

The prosecution case suffered from the lack of a body and the fact that Valmae Beck's testimony was not strong. Barrie Watts was acquitted of murder.

Police suspect Mrs Feeney is buried in a shallow grave somewhere between Lowood and Wivenhoe Dam, because Valmae Beck took police to that area in 1993. She showed them a bush grave that Watts had dug for a woman the couple tried to abduct from a shopping centre near Ipswich.

Valmae had also been questioned about the disappearance of 14-year-old Sophie Helen Woodman, who went missing on 21 March 1980 after leaving her Perth home with a girlfriend and travelling to the eastern states.

Valmae Beck and Barrie Watts have also been linked to the

murders of 20-year-old Sharron Phillips, from Brisbane's outer west; 19-year-old Stella Mary Farrugia; and 10-year-old Adelaide girl Louise Bell.

Queensland Police Commissioner Bob Atkinson, who led the Kingi investigation in 1987, said Valmae Beck had taken a lot of secrets to the grave. But he said police would not give up on learning the extent of the crimes perpetrated by Beck and her 'psychotic killer' husband.

'I don't want to sound pessimistic with that but on balance it's probably more unlikely than likely, but we'll always keep trying,' he said. Mr Atkinson said that while police knew of the deaths of Sian and Helen, and the attempted abduction of two nurses and a woman from a shopping centre – all in 1987 – he was positive there were more victims.

'Given the fact that they were so active, so ruthless, so organised, I find it difficult to believe that the only things they did were the ones we know about,' he said.

He said the positive was that Valmae Beck had fulfilled her sentence of 'life in prison' and justice had been served.

# PART 2: VICIOUS TEENS

Perth, Australia, September 1998. An 18-year old girl kills another teenager by stabbing her 47 times.

Papatoetoe, New Zealand, April 2000. Three teenage girls brutally murder a middle-aged man.

Perth, Australia, June 2006. Two 16-year-old girls strangle their 15-year-old friend.

Perth, Australia, December 2006. Two teenagers drug and bash their 16-year-old friend.

While one could be forgiven for wondering if there's something very bad in the water in Western Australia, these four brutal crimes reflect the pointy end of a disturbing trend: violent crime by young women is on the rise – everywhere.

Australian Institute of Criminology statistics indicate that, between 1995 and 2006, the number of assaults committed by women rose by 40 per cent. In Australia during the nearly two decades from 1984, there was a 209 per cent increase in the number of women going to jail. And, where once their crimes were mostly.drug, theft or property-related, these days they're often likely to be murder, sexual assault and armed robbery.

Discussion could last years, and get more than a little heated, on the subject of just who failed to recognise the trend towards increased female violence – before it was too late. Was it a failing of a blinkered feminism that perhaps didn't want to see any bad that came with the increasing 'freedom' of women? Did no-one notice the downside of successive generations of women trying to claim, maintain and assert their changing identities and roles – and still fit in with the way things really are?

Or does that simply make a long-overdue social movement the scapegoat for the way of the modern world; for a society that has always ignored its own failings?

After all, crime committed by both men and women is up everywhere, as is a new cycle of almost universal disillusionment among the young, of both sexes.

But women, especially young women, are always judged more harshly than males their age for any bad behaviour, and are scorned for any risk-taking or assertiveness. Risk-taking is still seen as irresponsible in a girl, but daring in a boy, while girls' assertiveness is invariably read as aggression.

Apart from the unfair perception, psychologists and criminologists acknowledge that a girl's daring and assertiveness is only a problem when her freedom-to-be-anything translates to not giving a damn about the consequences, or if it's accompanied by an undeveloped, or completely absent, moral sense. Drugs, alcohol and peer pressure add to the mix, as does society's apparent acceptance of an increasingly violent culture.

But there is no question that more women, and much younger women, are committing more crimes of violence, and more violent crimes.

And it has to be said that there is something particularly scary about the sheer viciousness of some teenage girls.

# HELL'S ANGELS

Bordered on one side by the vast Indian Ocean and expanding east to a relentless and unforgiving desertscape, Perth is one of the most isolated cities in the world. Our nearest neighbour of similar size and status is a lazy three-day drive to the east; our closest holiday playgrounds lie to the north and across the sea, in exotic Indonesia. Isolation is a badge we wear with some pride; we like to think of Perth as a large country town, where we're friendly to our neighbours and welcoming of strangers.

Culturally we are a mixed bag. Locals, including a very large English population, regard interlopers and foreigners with some amount of suspicion and distaste. But we're getting there, and pride ourselves on embracing 'others', even if we secretly feel a little wary of them. Our lifestyle is laid back, affluent and dictated by the sun and the sea – we love our sunburnt country. We vehemently protect our family values, bank balances and our rights to be a little bit different from the rest of Australia. We rarely feel the pressure to conform – in part because our isolation leaves us feeling disconnected. We're footy mad, we tolerate gay people, and we embrace every freedom offered to us.

Yet our underbelly is dark. Even a cursory flick through the annals of crime in Western Australia would leave the average person wondering what is in our drinking water. A serial killer in the 1960s terrorised our city and took away our innocence. In the 1980s a husband and wife took serial murder to a terrifying level, and in the 1990s another one stalked Perth's streets. Three women lost their lives to a shadow known as the Claremont Serial Killer, yet nobody has been brought to justice.

So, when 2006 dawned, Perth was a different place; we had grown up a little, were less comfortable about our safety and more wary of strangers. Even so, before the year was out, there would be crimes so shocking, so incomprehensible; our world would change.

For 20 years Catherine Birnie was Western Australia's most notorious female criminal. In 1986 she and her de facto partner David had embarked on a killing spree that only lasted four weeks, but which claimed four victims.

For many years Catherine enjoyed the notoriety of being the most famous prisoner at Bandyup. A small woman, now in her 60s, she has a very unassuming air about her. If you had never looked into her eyes you could be forgiven for thinking she was a suburban housewife; yet she took an active role in the kidnapping and violent murder of four young women.

It is on record, part of the trial transcript, that Catherine played second fiddle and was the 'lesser' criminal of the pair. Yet that is far too simple an explanation and one that Catherine herself laughs about. One of the police officers who conducted the investigation at the time said it was Catherine, not David, who made the hair stand up on the back of his neck.

But that was then – last century even – and Catherine now has competition in the ruthless female killer category at Bandyup Women's Prison.

Collie is a mining town, located 160 kilometres south of Perth. Its population is less than 7000 and like in many small communities, the services and entertainment are limited. Younger people tend to drift to larger towns or cities looking for work, or different opportunities. In June 2006, 15-year-old Eliza Davis was a teenage girl with a dream of becoming a psychologist or forensic scientist. Like many girls her age she was experimenting with the life of an almost-but-not-quite-adult, partying with friends, indulging in the occasional drink, fitting in.

She had no way of knowing when she went to a party with two of her 16-year-old friends on Sunday 18 June that she was stepping into a nightmare. At the party they had all danced, smoked cannabis and snorted 'ice', or crystal methamphetamine.

Eliza then stayed the night. There's nothing unusual in that. It often happens after parties, of any kind; people just sleep over. But in Collie that night, while Eliza slept, her two friends – both girls, who shared the same bed – were planning a most sinister morning-after surprise. They had decided to kill her.

When Eliza got up in the morning her friends, ready-dressed in old clothes, calmly strangled her with speaker wire, and then buried her body under the house. Initially they joined in the hunt for their missing friend, but a few days later walked into separate police stations and gave themselves up. Their admission that they had killed their friend sent shockwaves through Collie and all of Western Australia. Their subsequent confessions chilled even hardened police officers to the bone.

Eliza's killers were a psychologically scarred orphan and a drug-addicted goth, who had a morbid obsession with death and had practiced killing on two kittens. The goth had been raised in a Christian home, but had embraced the angst-ridden emo culture and in recent times had become remote to her family.

Idly chatting during the night and early morning after the party, the girls discovered that neither of them would feel bad about killing someone. In fact it was a subject they had covered before, when a boy offended one of them. That boy was lucky; he lived.

But the teenagers planned how to kill Eliza and even reported her missing, before finally turning themselves into police after deciding the grave they'd dug was so shallow that discovery was inevitable.

'We discussed what would happen if we sort of killed Eliza ... We both admitted we wouldn't care,' one of the girls said in her police interview. 'I said do you want to? She said, yeah; and we did it.'

One of the girls strangled Eliza, while her accomplice held the struggling girl down and pressed a chemical-soaked cloth to their victim's mouth. The girl who twisted the wire around Eliza's throat chillingly described to police how she watched her victim's emotions shift from anger, to fear, to the realisation she was going to die.

'She was face up to me as I was doing it,' she said. 'She started to get scared, she started to cry. It was all blood coming out of her mouth.'

The other girl said: 'She started not being able to get her breath, and we just kept going. She was just yelling at us: "What the fuck, what are you doing? Oh you freaks, what's wrong with you psychos?"'

The girls had trouble getting Eliza's body downstairs and had to rest before they dug the 40 centimetre-deep sandy grave.

'Before we started digging the hole, we just sat there for a bit and had a smoke and a drink.'

The girls said they strangled Eliza that morning because one of them had to return to Perth that afternoon and they wanted a quick and 'non-messy' killing.

'As our friend, we did not really want her to suffer,' one said. 'We knew it was wrong but it didn't feel wrong at all; it just felt right. We were willing to take the risk. We said if we did get caught, shit happens, and we will deal with it.'

One of the killers said she regretted the devastating impact on Eliza's family and friends but did not feel sad Eliza was dead.

Neither of the girls can be named as they were juveniles at the time they murdered Eliza Davis. They were both sentenced to 15 years in prison and have been in Rangeview Juvenile Detention Centre since they confessed to the crime. This year they will both turn 18 and will be moved to Bandyup Women's Prison.

It was a crime that shook Western Australia. How could two teenage girls do this? It was impossible to understand, or even to try and make any sense of it. And then, before the year was over, things in our state got even worse.

December in Perth is a busy time. The shops are crowded with people determined to bend groaning credit cards into further submission, roads are thick with bad drivers, and the local newspaper is desperate for something to write. It's off-season in the footy, and even though we love our cricket it isn't quite the same. Nobody really cares though, because people are preoccupied with shopping for gifts, stockpiling food and bracing themselves for the annual family gatherings. Politicians take their holidays, there's nothing to watch on TV, school is breaking up for the annual extended break, and nobody really notices the news about a 16-year-old girl reported missing, especially when this teenager had run away from home a few weeks before.

Stacey Mitchell was a young, happy, confused, vibrant, fun-loving teenage girl. She came to Australia with her family as a 10 year old when they emigrated from England in 2001. They moved to the southern Perth suburb of Atwell, and Stacey soon made friends. It's never easy for migrant children to fit in to their new home, but Stacey was one of those people who managed it. In September 2006 she got a job at Adventure World as a ride operator. Earning her own income gave her a different level of freedom, as well as the opportunity to meet new friends.

In early December Stacey ran away from home, a rebellion against parental rules for a girl who was beginning to feel the taste of adult temptation and freedom. It isn't uncommon. In Australia around 30,000 people go missing every year – that's 82 every single day. Stacey's photograph, which has subsequently been widely circulated, reflects the excitement of youth, the angst felt by every teenage girl in the world, and her personality. It's also strikingly obvious, behind the mask of her makeup and her cheeky smile, that Stacey Mitchell was young; and innocent.

Sometime in the week before she disappeared Stacey connected with two young women, who were in a new lesbian relationship. They lived in Lathlain, a modest suburb close to Perth, in a house they shared with the slightly older David Haynes. It was around Thursday 14 December 2006 that Stacey Mitchell came to stay with them. It was an arrangement that was to last only a few days, and have devastating consequences.

Lathlain is a really well-kept secret. Even many Perth residents couldn't tell you where it is, yet it lies just five minutes from the city, tucked in behind its better-known neighbours Victoria Park and Burswood. The suburb is named after a former Perth mayor, Sir William Lathlain, and is a strange mix of bland post-war homes and more modern high-density housing. Rutland Avenue runs parallel to the railway line, and it was there in a nondescript house, sitting quietly next door to a block of apartments, that Stacey Mitchell stayed with her new friends at the end of 2006.

At the beginning of December there was nothing to draw anyone's attention to that house. The modest but clean white-brick residence, surrounded by parched lawn and with a shed in the backyard, was nothing a passer-by would look twice at.

The owner's son, David Haynes, lived there; he shared the house with Valerie Parashumti and Jessica Stasinowsky, who'd been a couple for only a month. It was the girls who invited Stacey into their home.

Innocuous it may have appeared on the outside, but inside the house the atmosphere was anything but harmless. This fledgling lesbian relationship had brought together two volatile women. Separately, they were dangerous enough; as a team they defined evil.

Individually, Valerie Parashumti and Jessica Stasinowsky are two very different young women. Jessica was raised an only child by her single mother, and would one day describe how she felt extreme loneliness, and was emotionally barren. Then she met 18-year-old Valerie Parashumti and was immediately drawn to her. It wasn't long before they began a relationship.

Jessica's friends, however, were worried. They didn't like Valerie; they found her freaky and weird, and they tried to warn their friend that this relationship was wrong for her.

But 19-year-old Jessica was finally getting all the love and attention she wanted, and Valerie had found someone who loved and worshipped her. The new couple also found they shared a love for something else, something as destructive as themselves: crystal methamphetamine. Ice.

Valerie Parashumti was an angry young thing, and had already been in trouble with the law before she met the woman she described as her 'co-joined'.

Valerie's parents emigrated from Kosovo to Perth in 1973. They built a life there, found work and had four children – the eldest of whom was Valerie. In May 2004 Nick Parashumti and his wife separated, and this, according to him, left Valerie angry, depressed and withdrawn. Two days after her 16th.birthday his daughter was hit by a car, and soon after that she ran away from home. In a sad father's mind this was the watershed in Valerie's downward spiral into a world of drugs, petty crime and 'meeting monsters'. One of those monsters was Jessica Stasinowsky, whom Nick Parashumti described as 'the Devil's child'.

But even before she met Jessica, there were alarming signs that Valerie Parashumti was willing to cross lines without fear of consequences. She allegedly spent a lot of time with young homeless people involved in the drug culture. Valerie apparently saw herself in these displaced people with whom she spun a bizarre social web.

She had also come to the attention of the police in the northern suburb of Joondalup, where she had thrown a brick through a youth support centre. She was found standing outside with a meat cleaver in one hand and a large kitchen knife in the other. Two days later she was charged with obstructing a public officer when she became violent after an officer took one of her friends into custody.

So, was Valerie already keeping bad company? Or was she the bad company other people were keeping?

Months later, after Valerie met Jessica and they both met Stacey – and despite the desperate attempts of a broken father to explain the inexplicable by blaming the older Stasinowsky for the sins of his daughter – it was Valerie who District Court Judge Antoinette Kennedy described as the 'dominant offender'.

A psychologist, who examined her and tested her, found Valerie had very strong sexual sadistic tendencies and was sexually aroused by physical torture and violence. Combined with her severe personality disorder, he said the likelihood of her committing a murder was 'almost inevitable'.

When Stacey Mitchell was reported missing by her worried parents on Sunday 17 December 2006 the police began making inquiries. Sophie and Andy Mitchell had recently returned from a trip back home to England. Stacey, who had run away a few weeks previously, called them and told them she wanted to come home, but when they didn't hear back from her and were unable to contact her they called the police.

It was a week before Christmas when the WA police began making routine inquiries about the whereabouts of the missing teenager. They hoped, and mostly expected, that she would be home in time to celebrate the festive season with her family. After all, it wasn't an unusual story: girl fights with parents, runs away from home, realises the grass isn't really greener, goes home.

But Stacey Mitchell would never go home again.

David Haynes was a man in unbearable conflict. He was 27 years old with a long history of mental illness and depression, and he knew a secret – a terrible, terrible secret.

Three days after Stacey Mitchell's parents reported her missing David cracked, and what he told the police was shattering. Stacey was dead. Upside down. In a bin. In a shed.

The wheelie bin is ubiquitous in the suburban landscape. The large green rubbish bin on wheels holds 240 litres of material and is provided to every Perth home so residents can dispose of domestic rubbish.

At 3.20am on Thursday 21 December 2006, the WA police opened the shed at the back of David Haynes' Rutland Avenue home, and found the household's wheelie bin. The human remains inside it had been there for nearly four days, in the searing summer heat.

It would take several hours, and a comparison with dental records, before police could confirm what they already knew. It was Stacey Mitchell.

Perth's print media has no competition. Six days a week the *West Australian* delivers news to the locals, and the *Sunday Times* is Perth's rest-day fodder. They are not immune to the isolation and parochialism that determines our culture – they sometimes reflect it, and at other times drive it. But both newspapers showed a decided lack of sensitivity and decency when they began their reporting of this horrendous crime. Until they had a better moniker they named Stacey Mitchell 'The Wheelie Bin Girl'.

Readers remonstrated with them; and family and friends, who were beside themselves with grief, were furious at the dehumanising headlines.

Talkback radio lit up with calls from people who were demanding the death penalty for the culprits. Rumours circulated throughout Perth about 'what really happened'.

People in the street were sickened and saddened; friends were in shock; strangers were appalled; and community backlash was instant and strong. And this was months before any of the facts came to light.

David Haynes did the only other decent thing he could do. He led the police to the Leederville house where Jessica Stasinowsky and Valerie Parashumti were hiding. Four days after the murder of Stacey Mitchell they were in custody.

When these details finally emerged, they were so horrific that nobody even knew how to react. Western Australia was stunned.

So, when did these young women decide to kill Stacey? That is still unclear, but soon after she moved into Rutland Avenue the couple began to get annoyed with her. Jessica was jealous of her lover's friendship with Stacey, and claimed that Stacey would often walk around in a bikini and flirt with Valerie.

The lovers had a discussion about it and, after some exchange of ideas, bizarrely decided the solution was that Stacey had to die. David had also told them he was unhappy with the way Stacey had spoken about one of his male friends, but he baulked at a suggestion they could fix it.

David later said that after this conversation he saw Jessica using a mortar and pestle to grind broken glass. Her intention was to mix it in one of Stacey's drinks.

Sunday 17 December was a typically hot summer day in Perth. The mercury rose to 33°C and all the shopping centres were open for the last-minute Christmas rush. It was also the day that Stacey Mitchell phoned her parents and told them she wanted to come home. For some reason, however, she stayed one extra fateful night at the Rutland Avenue house. During the evening she had a couple of drinks with her friends who, obviously unbeknownst to her, had laced one of her whiskeys with the sleeping pill Stilnox.

A little while later the girls asked David Haynes if he would help them corner and trap Stacey.

He said no. They told him to 'just watch then'.

No, he said again, at which point he was threatened with: 'If you try to stop us you will get hurt.' Valerie Parashumti then instructed him to put on music – loud.

JS Bach wrote the *St John Passion* in the early 1700s. One of his greatest pieces, it is inspired by the gospel of John in the New Testament, and tells the story of the last days of Jesus' life: of His betrayal, mocking and crucifixion.

It is most often performed at Easter, all around the world.

Not at Christmas time, in suburban Perth, and never as the soundtrack to the sadistic, senseless murder that was about to happen.

As the opening aria of the *St John Passion* began to swell, David Haynes walked to his bedroom. On the way he saw Valerie Parashumti with a block of concrete in her hand, and he heard Jessica Stasinowsky yell: 'Now, now, now!'

He heard a thump and a lot of movement; and he heard Stacey cry for help; and then he closed his bedroom door.

It is impossible to know the kind of hell that Stacey endured. Repeated blows to the head with the block of concrete, even after it had broken, were inflicted on her. When she tried to escape to her room she was followed and bludgeoned.

More than 30 minutes went by and Stacey was still fighting for her life, at which point, after a short discussion, Jessica retrieved a chain – similar to a dog lead – and began to strangle Stacey.

As the teenage runaway who'd wanted to go home to her family lay dying, her callous killers checked her pulse and kissed each other.

Almost 40 minutes after the attack began, Stacey Mitchell died a terrifying death. Jessica Stasinowsky later lamented to a prison officer that it was a shame she had died so quickly.

Meanwhile, David Haynes was still in his bedroom and on the verge of a panic attack. He told Jessica that he needed to leave, so she gave him a black T-shirt to put over his eyes and directed him to the front door. She also gave him a mobile phone and said she would call when it was all right to come back.

At 1.40am he phoned Jessica and asked if Stacey was dead. 'Yes,' she replied, and asked David to give them two hours to clean up. He wandered around Burswood until 3.20am when he received a call from Jessica. 'It's still a bit messy,' she said, 'but come on in.'

It is impossible to measure the depth of depravity. That such a callous crime had been committed in the first place would leave every decent human being shuddering with contempt. But everything about the behaviour of Jessica Stasinowsky and Valerie Parashumti beggars belief.

As Stacey Mitchell lay dying her killers kissed passionately over her body. It is a matter of public record that they became sexually aroused by what they had just done; wished they had 'taken their passion further'; and had not the slightest remorse for their actions. They used a mobile phone to video her lifeless, beaten body, and, in that recording, can be heard mocking Stacey's English accent while filming the gruesome scene.

They used their own household wheelie bin to dispose of Stacey's body, and simply wheeled it into their shed. Before they ran off, into hiding, Valerie souvenired a piece of her shattered concrete murder weapon. It was her trophy.

They had not intended to leave Stacey in the wheelie bin. In the days between murdering her and being arrested, the killers discussed ways of disposing of her body. With David Haynes in tow, and equipped with a list that included a chainsaw and spades, they even went to a Bunnings hardware store 'in an effort to see what could be done'.

Various newspapers reported that the killers showed video footage of the murder to one of Valerie's homeless friends, 15-year-old boy, who they also made help them clean up the blood.

Sixteen pink balloons were released into a warm Perth afternoon sky on Wednesday 27 December. Stacey Mitchell's family and friends had gathered at the Atwell skate park to celebrate her life. One pink balloon was let go for every year she had lived. Far too few.

Bandyup Women's Prison lies in a semirural area 22 kilometres north-east of Perth. Built in 1970 to accommodate 147 women, it is the only female maximum-security prison in Western Australia. Since the 1980s overcrowding has been a problem and, compared with its male counterpart, Casuarina, it is antiquated. Aboriginal women are disproportionately represented in the prison population, as are women who have experienced some form of sexual or physical abuse. There are fewer than 20 women incarcerated for murder, yet one-third of them have attracted national newspaper headlines for their crimes.

Bandyup was the only place for Valerie Parashumti and Jessica Stasinowsky while they awaited trial for murder.

With very little to go on, the media appeared content to report speculation rather than fact; to publish rumours and describe reactions. It wasn't until David Haynes faced court for his sentencing hearing in August 2007 that the suppression order on the case was lifted and details began to emerge about the murder.

Suddenly the media, until then bereft of anything real or factual to say, were in a frenzy. But still, even with a smorgasbord of information before them, they all chose to run with a headline that was misleading, irrelevant and only partly true: Lesbian Vampire Killers.

It had emerged during the trial that, during the previous few years, Valerie Parashumti had been part of a vampire subculture. She had been cutting herself and sucking the blood from her own wounds since she was 10 years old, but as she grew up she'd progressed to other people's blood.

This made great headlines and painted Valerie and Jessica as 'freaks' – which they were on so many levels, but not for that reason. The media even tried to offer this 'vampirism' as an explanation for the vicious murder. It was completely misleading. Even the prosecutor later explained to the judge that it had absolutely no relevance to Stacey Mitchell's murder.

The Western Australian gay and lesbian media made a deliberate decision to distance itself from the story. One of the editors had been contacted by a friend of Jessica Stasinowsky, who demanded that she be allowed to tell her friend's 'side of the story'. However, the events she related to the editor could not be substantiated, and did not match with events that later came out in court.

Another of Jessica's friends used her own MySpace page to try and convince people that Jessica Stasinowsky was not much more than a poor misguided fool:

HOW CAN THIS FACE ... MY BEST FRIEND ... BE A MURDERER ... IF THERES A GOD OUT THERE PLEASE EXPLAIN ... Yes Jess is wun of my bets mates and yes she did kill that 16yr old girl Stacey Mitchell, im not exactly sure for the reason behind stacey death but jess'z dad has been on the fone to me and as far as we know jess had a fit of rage after being told that she couldnt come to my party and then her and her new girlfriend valerie decided to bash stacey over the head several times with a brick ... there was a struggle in the house and as Jess and Valerie were highly intoxiacated on chrystal meth, they then dragged the body out the back and put in the bin, to continue going on with life ... [Jess] has called me from bandyup prison and needs all the support she can get, shes not stably mental and needs help, and onlt the people who have knownn jess for as long as i have can help her...... you may have dont sumthing stupid jess but youll always be my hairY love spud xxx

As with most murder trials in Australia, there was a lengthy process of delays and adjournments before the case was heard. Eventually, on Friday 23 November 2007, after expert opinions were sought and found, both women pleaded guilty to murder in Perth Magistrates Court.

In March 2008, in the Western Australian Supreme Court, Valerie Parashumti and Jessica Stasinowsky were each sentenced to life in prison, with a minimum term of 24 years.

Justice Peter Blaxell told the convicted women that they must spend the vast portion of their young lives in jail. He also sentenced them to strict security life in prison, backdated to December 2006. They will not be eligible to apply for parole until 2030.

'Your crime is particularly horrifying and a shocking one, not only because of the young ages of the victim and yourselves,' Justice Blaxell said, 'but because of the casual way in which it was committed, and the lack of any substantial motive.

'It is also very troubling that you do not show any remorse or shame for what you did, but instead appear to be amused and jubilant. In my opinion this inappropriate behaviour is not some form of false bravado but is a true reflection of your attitudes towards the offence.'

Unable to differentiate between the sentences for the killers, Justice Blaxwell found that each bore the same culpability and lack of remorse, and that both had bleak prospects for future rehabilitation.

'You have each had more than a year in custody to reflect upon the evilness of your crime, yet you still lack remorse and obviously place no value on the sanctity of human life.'

Justice Blaxell said he was sickened by the fact the two women used a mobile phone to video the murder scene and later showed others the footage in which they gleefully mocked Stacey. He told the court he was horrified that the couple had each gained a perverse sexual pleasure from the murder; that, at the time, they were sexually excited by the violence of the event.

'You also admit to kissing each other as Stacey Mitchell lay dead or dying; and you, Jessica Stasinowsky, have since expressed regret that the sexual passion at the time did not go further. It is dreadful to have to refer to these admissions, but they do reveal the enormity of the evil in what you did.'

The only time Valerie Parashumti and Jessica Stasinowsky showed any reaction during their trial was when, during the sentencing, Justice Blaxell ordered that they spend their prison time separated from one another.

'It is highly desirable that you should not be permitted to associate together within the prison system, and it is my strong recommendation that you be kept separate and apart,' he said. 'Failing this, it is difficult to see how there will be any genuine change in your attitude which might make it safe for you to be released on parole.' The women were visibly unhappy about that.

After spending almost a year in prison together at Bandyup Women's Prison, Valerie Parashumti was transferred to Greenough Regional Prison, 400 kilometres away, in January 2009.

The prevailing question that lingers over all of these horrific murders is this: why?

Are these young female killers evil? Are they monsters? Is it even possible for them to find redemption?

No satisfactory answers have been found, and nothing has come to light to convince anyone that this was an aberration that will never happen again.

It isn't enough to point to terrible childhoods or the evils of drugs. Nor is it very reassuring that all four killers will be eligible to seek freedom when they are in their 30s and 40s, after spending the **most of the** intervening years in prison together.

Sometime between the couple pleading guilty and being sentenced, Jessica's other best friend wrote on her MySpace page about a recent prison visit:

> went and seen jess in Bandyup on thursday and and she doin ok …well as good as u could be. she had been in solitary and got put into main streme on wednesday and the hole prison had lock down coz approx 18 girls started attacking her in the gym, so for now she is back in solitary until after march. she is very remorseful and wasnt aloud to say much as the cameras and guards were sourrounding us…as we were leaving the prison we were speaking to a few of sum of the other inmates family and friends

and they said that jess should be fune if she cops a cuple of beatings and after that she can start to fight back but, and jess has stated that shes willing to do whatever it takes and will even bow down to them if thats what is necessarey, her exact words were... theres no point being tough and no point being weak whatever happens happens, as far as the other inmates relatives were saying, jess will be fine but valerie is going to get slaughtered in there, apparently she has instigated quiete a few things in the jail already...

Jessica Stasinowsky lodged an appeal against the severity of her sentence. Lawyers filed papers arguing for a reduction of her 24-year jail term, on the grounds that the judge failed to take into account her young age, her personal history and early guilty plea. The appeal was denied on 22 January 2009. Justices Christopher Steytler and Carmel McLure said Stasinowsky, who was 19 at the time of the murder, had 'very little prospect of rehabilitation'.

'It seems to us that, in all of the circumstances of this case, it cannot be said that a non-parole period of 24 years is outside the range of an acceptable exercise of discretion,' the judgement said.

'Were it not for the appellant's age, plea of guilty and favourable antecedents, the brutal and callous nature of the murder might have justified a non-parole period much closer to 30 years.'

Justice Geoffrey Miller said the 24-year term was appropriate and reflected the seriousness of the offence. 'I am of the opinion that the crime committed by the appellant was so high in the scale of crimes of wilful murder that, for this reason, it justified a strict security life imprisonment,' Justice Miller said.

What would the lives of Eliza Davis and Stacey Mitchell be like now, had they not met these vicious and remorseless killers posing as friends?

Their grief-stricken families and friends were robbed of two young women who mattered a great deal to them. They had every right to expect Eliza and Stacey to grow into young women who would pursue careers, fall in love, contribute to society, make people laugh and cry, and who would have been part of the future of this country.

Yet they are gone, having never had the opportunity to have children, or vote, or drive, or discover who they were – and who they weren't. That we have lost them is a terrible tragedy, one that diminishes us all.

# FRENZY

In February 2000 a New Zealand teenager began a life sentence for the frenzied killing of a middle-aged man. She was then the youngest female convicted of murder in New Zealand. Her two accomplices were also sentenced to life for their part in the slaying.

On Thursday 1 April 1999, Raymond Mullins, a 59-year-old self-employed engineer, was bashed with a variety of blunt instruments and then stabbed, repeatedly, to death. He was murdered in his own lounge room, in his warehouse residence in the South Auckland suburb of Papatoetoe. His killers then dragged his body downstairs and stuffed him in the boot of his car.

Mullins was found by two teenage girls, who dropped by the warehouse for a visit. The friends were confronted by a terrible scene on the building's mezzanine floor that could only have suggested something very bad had happened to Ray Mullins. There was blood everywhere, paint splashed all over place, and awful, hateful things written on the walls.

Despite this, the girls followed a trail of blood downstairs to the car outside, where they discovered the body of Raymond Mullins wrapped in a sheet with his feet and hands bound.

Mullins had lived above his factory premises in Plunket Avenue, Papatoetoe, for less than a year. The ground floor of his warehouse contained a workshop for the various boats and trailers he was repairing, and a huge variety of tools and equipment. A set of stairs led to the mezzanine floor, where his living quarters was: a kitchen–dining area that led into a lounge and bedroom.

To the first police at the crime scene the mess upstairs, and no doubt the murder, looked like the work of one of the local youth gangs, the Bloods. The initials BFL – Bloods for Life – were scrawled in paint on the walls. The killer, or killers, had also painted messages implying Mullins had a thing for young girls.

Gang culture is rife in many parts of New Zealand. Of varying ethnicity and criminality, some are motorcycle gangs but others are heavily influenced by American street gangs like the Crips and Bloods of LA. Although only a minority of the nation's criminals are gang members, New Zealand has, according to Ross Kemp in his book *Gangs* (based on his UK TV series), more gangs per capita than any other country in the world.

The violence that runs with many of these gangs is a huge problem for New Zealand police. In Auckland alone it's believed there are as many as 2000 young street gang members. The LA-style gang culture of gangsta rap, bling, souped-up cars, crime and violence pervades the streets of Auckland. Gang colours – blue bandanas for the Crips, red for the Bloods – and a fierce fighting loyalty to their chosen gang is often a life and death matter. There is even a career path within the gangs: from wannabes or prospects, to neighbourhood street crews with territorial clout, to criminal youth gangs, and finally to the adult organised crime networks.

The Bloods for Life clue, written in paint and blood on Ray Mullins' wall, didn't tell the police anything. They were not diverted by such an obvious attempt to sidetrack them. It was clear that most of the paint was thrown around to cover up the blood and other evidence, rather than as an act of gang vandalism, either before or after the murder.

Detective Senior Sergeant Dayle Candy, who led the investigation, said Mullins had a large circle of friends and associates who visited his place regularly, and that one of the teenagers who'd found the deceased had previously been living at the warehouse residence. She said the 17-year-old had begun staying there to escape problems at home.

Detective Candy said that Mullins had been 'loosely described' as the girl's guardian, but not in any official way. Police soon discovered there was a high turnover of 'flatmates' at the Papatoetoe warehouse, and that many of the visitors to Mullins' mezzanine apartment were young women. Or, more specifically, teenage girls.

The murder was looking more and more like a rage-fuelled revenge. The girls who'd found the body – the ex-flatmate and her teenage friend – were eliminated as suspects. But it took Auckland police just five days to gather enough evidence to make three arrests for the murder of Raymond Mullins.

The post-mortem found that Raymond Mullins had suffered extensive injuries, with three general injury areas on his head alone. The pathologist stated these were consistent with forceful hammer blows.

In the left frontal area there were a number of lacerations. The six largest of these, caused by individual blows, had jagged edges and had fractured the skull. In the right frontal area there were four lacerations with irregular edges, and there were three lacerations to the back of the head.

There was a stab wound on the left side of the neck that pierced more than half the thickness of the neck and was consistent with a blow struck with a knife. There were 19 individual stab wounds in the stomach.

The pathologist described four light lacerations or abrasions in the deceased's chest area, which formed what could be the letter 'W'. No significance was attached to the letter but the lacerations were consistent with the use of the tip of a knife and did not appear to have been accidental in their arrangement.

Ray Mullins had other injuries that indicated he had tried to defend himself from the onslaught of blows. The stomach wounds, which included one that penetrated his liver, did not contribute to his death.

The pathologist said death was caused by a combination of the neck wound, which caused bleeding into the airways, and brain damage caused by the head injuries, both of which fatally compromised his respiratory function.

Other crime scene evidence suggested Ray Mullins had also been struck with an ashtray, a chair leg and a saucepan.

'I was just hard-out stabbing him. I felt evil. The place went cold like a freezer, and I knew I had killed him.'

These were the words of young Natalie Fenton less than a week after she took Ray Mullins' life. Natalie had turned 15 years old only three weeks before. She told police she was defending herself from a sexual attack, and that her sister Katrina and their friend Daniella had come to her aid. She admitted they had killed Ray Mullins – in self-defence.

While the victim may well have been a pervert and sexual predator, Natalie Roselyn Fenton was no angel.

Born in March 1984 to a Maori mother and a Niuean father, and with six siblings, Natalie was a primary-school dropout, a prostitute and drug user by age 11, and an armed robber at 13. It was no surprise at all to police that she had graduated to murder.

She told her defence psychiatrist that, for a couple of years from the age of five, she had been sexually abused by three of her father's friends. Her father died when she was eight, leaving her mother to cope with raising seven kids on her own. Natalie was of little help in that department, preferring to run wild. She had ties to the Crips gang and became part of the South Auckland sex worker scene, where she hung out with other young prostitutes and transsexuals who sold their bodies to make money for alcohol and drugs.

Natalie often appeared before the youth and family courts. By the time she was 14 she had a raft of convictions for theft, stealing cars and aggravated assault.

Natalie Fenton was actually out on bail for aggravated robbery when she killed Ray Mullins. She had threatened another girl with a knife, in order to steal her leather jacket.

A hard and brutal life for one so young, but Detective Senior Sergeant Candy said it would be wrong to blame her actions entirely on her background.

'I believe Natalie is a career criminal who was climbing the ladder,' she said.

'I think she had a thirst for violence and needed to see how far she could go. I think she was always going to kill someone at some stage. And I believe it was a challenge to her.'

Melbourne psychologist Ann Sebire agrees that someone's past – even in one so young – is only ever part of the story. Like it or not, she says, 'There are intrinsically bad and evil women out there, just as there are bad and evil men.'

Ms Sebire says it's a given that low self-esteem and an absence of love and nurturing in someone's formative years is a large contributor to who they become; and there are many damaged young people, and adults, who find it hard or impossible to reconcile and live with the effects of childhood abuse. 'But if all victims of sexual assault became perpetrators of violent crime, then the statistics for violence would be higher for women, as women make up the majority of victims of abuse. This clearly is not the case.'

She said it was clear that Natalie Fenton and her cohorts 'had no respect for life, no respect for themselves, no fear of the future, and no fear of an afterlife. Therefore the guilt is less, as there's no conscience'.

People are ultimately defined by their actions; by what they do. And in April 1999, Natalie Roselyn Fenton became a murderer because she decided to kill Ray Mullins.

Natalie first met Mullins when he was cruising for young flesh in 1996. The 12-year-old asked him if he could get her some dope. He could and did.

'He was cool,' she told police after her arrest for his murder. 'He supplied me everything I wanted. But I didn't give him anything, you know. I'm not a ho.'

But she *was* a liar. She told Dr Anthony Marks, the consulting psychiatrist engaged by her lawyer, that not only did she have sex with Mullins at least five times for money, but she miscarried his child in 1998.

Natalie told the police that Ray also fancied her sister Katrina – from the moment she'd introduced them. Katrina, four years older than Natalie and with no criminal record, apparently used Mullins to get money, but never slept with him because she thought he was 'dirty old man'.

There were two versions of what went down in the upstairs living quarters of Ray Mullins' warehouse on the night he died. The version given by the Fenton sisters' friend, Daniella Bowman, was the one with which the Crown prosecuted all three girls, and the one on which they were ultimately found guilty.

While Natalie and Katrina told pretty much the same self-defence story, Daniella Bowman described a premeditated and vicious murder. Either way, what the three young women did to Ray Mullins that evening was shocking.

Until the end of March 1999, the worst thing 17-year-old Daniella Bowman, mother of a two year old, had done – or been charged with – was shoplifting. On the afternoon of Thursday 1 April she went with her friends, Natalie and Katrina Fenton, to Ray Mullins' factory in Papatoetoe. The girls wanted Ray to give them $500 so they could get to another friend's birthday party.

Ray refused to give them any cash so they left the factory, but returned at about 5pm to ask him again. On that occasion they had Daniella Bowman's young son, Jakeem, with them.

Natalie Fenton later told police that she had been upstairs watching television with Ray Mullins, and her sister was downstairs. She said Ray asked her for sex but when she said no, he grabbed her breasts and started to rub her leg.

Natalie said she hit him with an ashtray and yelled out for her sister, who came into the room with a hammer. Natalie said that

Ray was holding her down, so Katrina hit him with the hammer; then she, Natalie, stabbed him several times with a knife. She said that Daniella had also hit Ray, with a saucepan. Then the three of them carried his dead body downstairs and put it in the boot of a car with the weapons they had used.

Natalie also told police that when they dragged the body downstairs backwards, his head hit every step and his false teeth fell out. She said she had to swear at Daniella's kid, who was watching them, to get him to be quiet.

When the police asked her why the dead man was tied up in the boot, Natalie told them, 'I don't know. I just felt so evil that night, I wanted to dump him somewhere.'

Katrina Fenton told police she'd been downstairs at Ray's place when she heard a violent argument between him and her sister, Natalie. The 19-year-old said it sounded like Ray wanted to have sex with Natalie but she was unwilling. When Katrina ran upstairs she saw that Ray was on top of Natalie and holding her down on the bed.

Katina said she believed Ray was raping, or attempting to rape, her little sister so she hit him several times in the head with a hammer she had picked up. She told police she then realised her sister had a knife and had stabbed Ray Mullins several times. Katrina told police she had not intended to kill Ray, just protect her sister.

When Daniella Bowman was interviewed by police she admitted that the three of them had, in fact, planned to kill Ray Mullins while he was watching television.

She said that both Natalie and Katrina Fenton hit Ray with a hammer, and she bashed him with a saucepan. Daniella said she had then got two knives, which she handed to Natalie, who used them to stab Ray.

During the trial in February 2000, Crown prosecutor Aaron Perkins maintained that Raymond Mullins had been taken by surprise and deliberately murdered by the three teenagers.

Natalie Fenton's lawyer, Peter Kaye, said his client was acting in self-defence during the 'frenzied eruption of violence and aggression that took place'. He said that even though it 'might stick in the gullet of some jurors', the defence was seeking an acquittal for the younger Fenton sister.

He said Natalie Fenton was suffering from post-traumatic stress disorder (PTSD) as a result of being sexually abused as a child.

'She was under threat of immediate sexual attack by Mr Mullins. She was alone in that room with him.' Mr Kaye said Natalie was 'entitled to protect herself – and then later on when Katrina came upstairs and got involved and Natalie dashed out and got the other knives, she was acting to defend Katrina'.

Dr Anthony Marks, the defence counsel's consulting psychiatrist, said it was 'thoroughly possible' that Natalie Fenton suffered from PTSD.

'Compared to ordinary people,' he said, 'when victims again face such abuse, they often react in an unpredictable, aggressive and excessive way.'

He said Natalie had told him that she had been involved in prostitution from the age of 11, and had been living on the streets and using drugs and alcohol.

Dr Marks said Natalie had also told him that sometimes a 'dark spirit' came over her and told her what to do. On the night of the killing, she'd said, it was like a blanket over her, and that night she'd also seen the faces of the men who had abused her as a child.

When cross-examined by prosecutor Aaron Perkins, Dr Marks agreed that any diagnosis of post-traumatic stress disorder relied on Natalie Fenton's truthfulness about the abuse she'd suffered as a child, and the sex attack she said Mr Mullins initiated.

One of the dead man's friends told the court that 59-year-old Ray Mullins believed that having lots of young girls around kept him fit and healthy. He said he took that to mean that Mullins was having sexual relations with them.

A statement by a 14-year-old girl, who had been staying with Ray Mullins, was read to the court. The teenager said she'd had sex with him three or four times and, although he hadn't paid her for sex, he did give her money. She said she and another girl once had a threesome with Ray; and that lots of people visited him looking for money for sex. Four glue-sniffers had once offered to have sex with Ray. One of them, her statement said, was a drag queen, and another had a baby by Ray.

None of the accused testified for themselves during their joint trial, but their police statements were admitted as evidence. As were things they told or boasted about to friends and other family members after the crime.

An accused's conversation with someone not involved in the crime can be used as evidence in court, but only for or against that person. So, what Natalie told someone else when her accomplices were not present could only be used for or against her. But if Natalie talked up her crime with an uninvolved friend, in the presence of Daniella, then the evidence of that 'third person' could be used against Natalie and Daniella, but not Katrina.

A variety of witnesses, therefore, told the court the different accounts they'd heard – from the perpetrators themselves – of how, and why, Ray Mullins had been killed. Most versions revealed a case of deliberate murder.

One witness testified that Natalie and Daniella admitted bashing and stabbing a man, and that Natalie had said the man had tried to rape her.

A cousin testified about conversations he'd had with all three girls, with Katrina alone, and with Katrina and her mother. He told the court that Natalie, in the company of the others, had told him that they killed Mullins because of his sexual involvement with children.

He said another time Katrina told him that she, Daniella and Ray had been watching TV when Natalie came up behind Ray with a hammer, and went to hit him with it but missed.

The cousin also told the court that, in his presence, Katrina had told her mother how they had killed Ray Mullins. Katrina had said that, while they were watching TV, Natalie had come up from behind with a hammer. When the first blow had missed Mullins, Katrina said that Natalie panicked so she had helped her out.

An older Fenton sister gave evidence that Natalie, in the presence of Daniella, told her that the three of them had killed Mullins with a hammer and knives, while he was watching television, 'because he deserved it'.

Natalie Fenton, Katrina Fenton and Daniella Bowman were all found guilty of the murder of Raymond Mullins. On 17 February 2000, Justice Chambers sentenced all three to life imprisonment, but with different minimums to serve before being eligible for parole.

Later that year the Fenton sisters appealed against their convictions on the grounds that they should have been tried separately from Daniella Bowman. Their lawyers argued that there had been a miscarriage of justice because their application for their trial to be severed from Bowman's had been refused.

The appeals were dismissed on 14 September 2000.

Melbourne psychologist Ann Sebire noted that, even for a premeditated murder, none of the girls hinted they'd had second thoughts before going through with their crime. They showed no feelings of remorse afterwards and, in fact, seem to have no 'moral' gauge at all.

'They lashed out, they left nothing to chance, and they did the job thoroughly. Once the act was commenced, it was completed with hatred and macabre violence,' Ms Sebire said.

'Why did they do it? Perhaps just because they could; and because they were encouraged and supported by each other. Killing in packs suggests that their behaviour is validated by others; by the company they keep.'

Natalie Fenton came up for parole for the first time in May 2009 – at the age of 25.

The Parole Board said that Fenton's prison history had been 'somewhat rocky' but the Board was 'very pleased with the progress she has made against the background of a childhood marked by extreme abuse and neglect'.

Natalie had been transferred to a new prison at the start of 2009, to start a program in its dependency treatment unit, and was engaging extremely well with the program. The Board said she still had 'real issues dealing with her anger' and would also benefit from an anger management program.

Her parole was denied.

In 2016 the Parole Board became satisfied that Natalie Fenton had learned her lesson, and her progress towards rehabilitation was enough that she no longer posed a danger to the public. She was released from prison in April 2016, now 32 years old, after serving 17 years of her sentence.

A few months later Natalie was back in custody for violating her parole.

# Oh, You Mean This Knife?

Perth woman Karen Lang had been married for 22 years when she embarked on the trip of a lifetime, a two-month bus tour of Europe. It was September 1998. Initially she had planned to travel with her husband, but he couldn't afford to take that much time off work so she set off alone, making new friends and enjoying the experience of a lifetime.

On Thursday 24 September the tour bus rolled into Paris, one of the loveliest, most seductive cities in the world. As Karen's tour bus pulled up outside their hotel the tour guide handed her a note. It requested that she call her brother Michael in Perth.

Fearing that something had happened to their father, Karen phoned home. Her other brother Paul answered the phone and handed her over to Michael. The news he gave her was devastating and left Karen screaming and in need of sedation: her 15-year-old daughter Jessica had been killed in Perth.

Until she spoke with her husband John several hours later, Karen assumed it must have been a motor vehicle accident. But when he rang her close to midnight Perth time, she was barely able to comprehend what he was trying to tell her. Their beloved daughter had been murdered.

Bicton is one of Perth's most pleasant locations. It is tucked on the south side of the Swan River, close to Fremantle and less than 10 minutes from the beach. Prior to European settlement it was a culturally significant location for Aborigines, being a site where fresh water was readily available, and an important camping and ceremonial ground.

In 1830 it was leased as a vineyard where both red and white wine was produced. Then in 1916 the Fremantle Quarantine Station was housed there – all animals had to pass through there on their way into Australia. Between 1947 and 1969 the Point Walter Migrant Reception Centre played an important role in processing new arrivals. By 1998 Bicton was a quiet, relatively established suburb where people went about their business of going to work, paying their mortgages and sending their children to school. The Lang family lived in Yeovil Street.

Jessica Lang was a smart, fun-loving girl who loved nothing better than to socialise with her friends. She was a typical teenager in so many ways, and she found she was growing bored with school. She was eager to get out there and discover what life had to offer, and to experience something new. She was already working part time at Rolloways, a roller-skating rink in nearby O'Connor, and was due to start work as an apprentice hairdresser at the end of September. Jessica had been involved with a guy called Jimmy for a while, and from letters found under her bed it seemed she had become tired of waiting for him to decide whether he wanted to be with her or not.

She started going out with another young man she met at Rolloways. He was working as the DJ there and they had been seeing each other for about a month. Michael Bloom was known as Myk to everyone who knew him.

Before he started seeing Jessica, Myk had been going out with a local woman but he broke off the relationship because she had become too jealous and possessive. Kelly Fuller was an 18-year-old woman from nearby Winthrop who worked at the Mosman Park Vet Clinic.

Winthrop is a middle-class suburb of Perth, only 10 minutes by car from Bicton. Out of reach of most first-home buyers, but adding status to the successful business owner or professional, it would cost more than $700,000 today to buy a home in this former pine plantation. The Fullers were living here in 1998 and Kelly often drove from Winthrop to Mosman Park, a 13 kilometre trip that took her past Jessica Lang's street in Bicton.

Kelly had reacted badly to the breakup with Myk Bloom. He had been her first lover and she wanted him back. Former colleagues described her behaviour at the time as being 'single white female' – a pop-culture reference to a movie that had highlighted the dangerous and obsessive behaviour of a scorned woman.

Kelly Fuller had destroyed Myk's CD collection at one point, and rather than time healing her wounds, it seemed that it was making them hurt more.

Things came to a head when Kelly found out, through friends, that Myk was going out with someone else – Jessica Lang. Her first reaction to the news was to tell friends, 'I am going to kill her.'

Far from an uncommon threat, it is part of the familiar script of many jilted lovers. For most people, however, they're just empty words; a verbal response to the pain of seeing a former lover begin life with someone else. So friends who heard Kelly Fuller express those sentiments paid no attention. They knew she was hurt, they saw that she was acting a little strange, but even in their wildest imagination they never thought she was serious.

September is the favourite month of the year for most sandgropers. Even though winter is mild, Perth people are notorious for hibernating through the annual cold, rainy, windy season.

Come September the world-famous wildflowers begin to bloom, the days turn balmy, and windows and doors are open to the rite of spring.

Thursday 24 September 1998 was one of those spring days that was warm, overcast and cloudy. Rain threatened, but for most of the day it was humid. Kelly Fuller made a phone call to Jessica

Lang's home, and records show it lasted two seconds. A hang-up call? A way of verifying that the teenager was home? Most likely.

Kelly then drove her Nissan Pulsar from Winthrop to Yeovil Street in Bicton, purportedly to visit a mutual acquaintance who was supposedly with Jessica at the time. Strangely, for someone who was popping in to say hello, Fuller wore white gloves and carried a 20 centimetre fishing knife.

According to Kelly's later testimony, she was provoked into attacking Jessica Lang soon after arriving at her Bicton home. Kelly stated that Jessica began taunting her about Myk, and that she hadn't wanted to talk about it.

But no matter how she tried to justify her actions on that fateful Thursday afternoon, the evidence showed that Jessica Lang was stabbed in three separate rooms of the house, that she sustained 47 separate stab wounds to her neck, and that those stab wounds shredded her jugular vein to ribbons, completely severing it.

Kelly Fuller then left the Bicton house and drove back home. In contrast to the frenzied nature of the attack on Jessica Lang, Kelly's actions over the next few hours showed someone who was calm, clear-headed and as cold as ice.

When she got home Kelly showered, washed the steering wheel and door of her Pulsar, and washed the clothes and shoes she was wearing. She then sat down and watched a video. Later she disposed of the used gloves in a rubbish bin at nearby Bull Creek, and wrapped the fishing knife in a tea towel and threw it down a drain near her home.

Kelly calmly kept a physiotherapy appointment, picked up her younger sister from school and took her to softball training, had dinner with the family and later went to bed. At some point during the afternoon she found time to drive back to Jessica Lang's house and smash the back window with a brick, in an effort to make it look like look like an intruder had broken in.

When John Lang arrived home from work that Thursday he walked into a slaughterhouse. It is impossible to imagine what it must have been like for Jessica's father to walk through the front door, expecting the familiarity of coming home, only to be confronted with something barely comprehensible.

Ironically John was in the middle of reading a Patricia Cornwell crime thriller at the time, and in some part of his mind was aware that he shouldn't 'touch a crime scene'. It's funny how the human mind grasps onto things at times of greatest trauma. John called the police, who came immediately.

In shock, and with his mind in terrible turmoil, John was taken to the Fremantle police station where he was questioned for five hours. While it may have seemed awfully unfair to have been an 'initial suspect', it meant John didn't have to be there while the police processed the crime scene.

John had made the terrible discovery early enough that the nightly television news services led their bulletins with the dreadful story. At the time of going to air, details were sketchy but there was enough information that people began calling police with suspicions. One name that came up several times was that of a young woman who had been very jealous of the Bicton teenager – Kelly Renae Fuller.

The most damning phone call came that night from Kelly's best friend. Remy Bridger told detectives that she had helped Kelly dispose of a fishing knife that afternoon. Remy explained to detectives that even though Kelly actually told her she had killed Jessica Lang, she didn't believe it – until she had seen Jessica's house on the news. According to Remy, her friend was known for embellishing and even fabricating stories about people, and about her own life. Remy had simply not believed her until she saw the news.

It was 2am when detectives, armed with the information supplied to them by Remy Bridger, knocked on Kelly Fuller's door. She was taken to Fremantle police station where she was interviewed. Her mother sat with her and listened, in utter horror, as some sort of confession began to unfold. She told police a version of the truth, that she had been provoked because Jessica Lang kept taunting her about her relationship with Myk. She was emphatic that she hadn't gone there to kill Jessica.

Detectives were struck by the cold demeanour of this young killer. She was calm, detached and emotionless. At one point Kelly's mother broke down, almost hysterical as she heard what her daughter had done. It was Kelly who suspended the interview to comfort her distraught mother. In the early hours of the morning Kelly Fuller was charged with the wilful murder of Jessica Lang and remanded in custody.

Fifteen months later the case of Kelly Renae Fuller came before the Supreme Court of Western Australia. The passage of time gave Kelly plenty of time to think about what was about to unfold. No longer caught up in the passion, the rage of seeing her boyfriend in the arms of another woman, Kelly had ample opportunity to develop her story. By then she was 19 years old and had already spent more than a year behind bars – a prelude to what the next phase of her life would bring.

Kelly Fuller stood before Justice White and pleaded not guilty to wilful murder. This meant the case would be heard before a jury. It also effectively meant that the life of Jessica Lang and her family would be put on trial. And it was.

It is a sad indictment on the Australian justice system that victims of a violent crime have their lives torn apart, often by lawyers representing the criminal. In the case of Jessica Lang, she was portrayed as a rebellious party girl who loved to drink, socialise, flaunt herself and behave in a generally irresponsible manner. She was painted as promiscuous, as if this character assassination of a 15-year-old girl could somehow justify her slaughter. According to the evidence offered by Kelly, she had gone to visit Jessica that day, just wanting to talk. She had no intentions of harming the younger teenager.

When asked why she wore white gloves for the visit, she explained that it was cold. This 'fact' was refuted by the data from the Bureau of Meteorology. Asked to explain why she took a 20 centimetre fishing knife with her, Kelly said it was because her employer, the Mosman Park Vet Clinic, was short of knives so she took one from home to cut up dog meat for the hungry animals. Former workmates scoffed at this, saying they had seen the knife, wrapped in a tea towel, under the seat of Kelly's car.

Kelly claimed in court that Jessica had taunted her about her relationship with Myk Bloom. Jessica had a love bite on her neck, and Kelly claimed that the taunting began as soon as she arrived.

Kelly wanted the court to believe that she just happened to take a knife with her, just happened to be wearing gloves, and only wanted to talk. According to her, it was Jessica who pushed her over the edge, because she wouldn't stop bragging about Myk.

The worst thing about the trial of Kelly Fuller was the fact that there were details of the crime that the jury was not allowed to know.

The jury didn't learn that 15 minutes before committing murder, Kelly had purchased Ratsak with the intent of killing the dog she had given Myk Bloom as a present.

The jury wasn't allowed to hear evidence from Myk Bloom that Kelly was obsessive and jealous.

Nor were they allowed to see the crime-scene photos that depicted the bloody violation of a teenage girl stabbed 47 times after being pursued through three rooms of her own home.

Throughout the trial, Kelly presented as a shy, quiet, immature young woman; always in control of her emotions; always acting as though she wasn't quite sure how any of this had happened. She had written to the judge prior to the trial, saying (in part): 'I am just so sorry to everyone that has been affected by this. I wish I could bring Jessica back so her family need never go through the pain and suffering of losing such a vital part of their lives.'

Not sorry enough to spare the family the pain and suffering of a trial. A trial in which the jury essentially heard that Jessica – a brash young vamp – had stolen the boyfriend of the quiet and reserved Kelly Fuller. A trial in which she claimed she went over there 'to talk' but was provoked by the promiscuous and bragging younger woman, so that before she knew it she had wielded the knife, meant for dog meat, making 47 individual thrusts into the flesh of her competitor.

The jury found Kelly Renae Fuller guilty of murder, but rejected the charge of wilful murder. In February 2000 Kelly was sentenced to life imprisonment with a non-parole period of 11 years.

The reaction of Perth people was swift and damning. Compared with every other woman who is serving time in Bandyup Women's Prison for murder, Kelly Fuller appeared to get off lightly. Was it because she was so young at the time of the murder that the jury felt she should have a second chance? Was it because they believed her version of events and considered it plausible that a suburban 18-year-old would go and visit a love rival and just happen to take a knife and gloves with her? Or is 11 years adequate punishment for stealing the life of a girl who will never become a woman?

In August 2009, Kelly received a visit from Karen Lang. Jessica's mother was motivated by a desire to 'move past' the hatred, anger and resentment she held for the young woman who took her daughter's life.

Karen told Channel Nine at the time: 'I just wanted to sit and face Kelly and say some of the things I needed to say to her … Weirdly enough – I don't know why – I've never hated her, so from that point of view she knows I don't hate her.'

Karen said she needed to let go of the need to seek revenge and the need to see Kelly spend the rest of her life in jail.

'I don't want her to stay in jail for the rest of her life if she is not a danger to the community,' she said.

Is Kelly Fuller a danger to the community?

She was denied parole in 2010 but will one day be free to pursue her dreams: to find work, to seek a fulfilling relationship, to have children, to travel – all the things she took from Jessica Lang. And all because of something that had been taken away from her.

# PART 3: OVERKILL

It is the stuff of horror movies, of kids sitting around a camp fire at night trying to scare each other witless. The story of the really, really bad person who comes along and kills someone…and then chops off their head.

Sadly, among the detritus of the criminal world, the dismemberment of a dead body is a reality for some killers. Sometimes they do it to conceal the identity of a body, sometimes to defile it, and at other times they do it for no reason that a thinking person can decipher.

There's another kind of killer who thinks it takes a lot to kill another person. Not in the moral sense, because they've already made the decision to take the life, but in the physical sense. So they poison and burn, or bash and stab, or poison, bash and suffocate their victim – to make sure they're dead.

While the human body can take an incredible amount of punishment and still fight – even without conscious thought – to stay alive, we can also be felled by a single punch and die when our head hits the ground.

Maybe in these cases of overkill, the moral sense does play a part. Maybe deep down the killers know it's wrong, so once they start, they have to be sure, be definite, be absolutely positive their victim is really, really dead – because there's no coming back from this; it's final.

# DINNER AND A MURDER

It is rare indeed for police at the scene of a suspected arson case to be given the name of a likely murder suspect even before the fire is completely under control and a victim located.

But sometimes luck is on their side and investigators just go with the flow.

In the very early hours of Thursday 9 September 2004, fire crews rushed to a blazing house fire in the Melbourne suburb of Bellfield. The fire, at 140 Liberty Parade, had started around 2am but wasn't noticed by neighbours, who called 000, until 2.30. By the time the engines and firefighters arrived there was little they could do to save the residence.

Victoria Police were on the scene by 3am. Standard operating procedure with fires called in to 000 is to dispatch the fire brigade, then notify the local police station. If the fire is at all suspicious, the police officers call in the Arson Squad; and if there are human casualties, the Homicide Squad is also woken up.

As luck would have it that morning, another person who turned up at the Bellfield house fire had vital information – the next best thing to an eyewitness account – so the uniformed officers at the scene were given the heads-up that perhaps Arson and Homicide detectives should attend.

Just before 3am one of the Liberty Parade neighbours had rung a woman who lived nearby, to let her know about the fire raging through the house that she owned and where her male friend lived. The woman, along with her daughter and a neighbour, rushed over but could do nothing but watch her house go up in flames.

The woman tried to run into the house but was restrained by a police officer, to whom she said, 'George must be in there; his van is here.'

She also told the officer exactly who must have set the house on fire to murder George. The police took the woman's details and told her to go home. She did as she was told.

While tackling the blaze, firefighters did indeed find the remains of a partly-clothed male on the floor of the master bedroom at the rear of the house. He was lying face up and was extremely burnt.

From the outset there was little question that the fire had been deliberately lit. The seven bottles of kerosene used as an accelerant, five of which were just left discarded around the house, were a dead giveaway. The arson investigation discovered that there were several seats of fire, and that large amounts of paper had been spread around the house to help the blaze spread as quickly as possible.

Arson Squad detectives discovered that the initial point of ignition was the room where the body was found, which meant that the other fires had been lit afterwards.

The post-mortem revealed that the victim's trachea and smaller airways contained a small amount of soot but bore none of the indicators that suggested smoke inhalation. This meant that the man, although alive at the time the fire began, had been overwhelmed so quickly by the fire itself that he would barely have had time to breathe.

When someone dies – is murdered – as a result of a fire, the case becomes an Arson Squad murder; if a person is killed and a fire is then lit to cover it up, the case is a Homicide Squad murder.

It was quite clear that the house fire at 140 Liberty Parade,

Bellfield, had been set to kill the man who lay incapacitated inside.

It was, therefore, Detective Senior Constable Matthew Height, then of the Victoria Police Arson and Explosives Squad, who led the investigation into the Bellfield fire and the murder of 58-year-old George Marcetta.

Luckily Detective Height and his crew had a place to begin their murder investigation. The owner of the Liberty Parade house, Ms Vasiliki Efandis, knew just who hated her friend George Marcetta enough to do such a terrible thing. Ms Efandis, known as Vicki, was convinced that the man responsible for the fire was one Ivan Bassett.

George Marcetta and Ivan Bassett had been friends for a long time until their falling out earlier in 2004. Nine days before the fire, a solicitor, under instruction from Mr Marcetta and Ms Efandis, had dispatched a letter of demand to Ivan Bassett claiming a debt that was owed to Marcetta.

This alleged debt was the reason, according to Vicki Efandis, that Ivan Bassett would have wanted to kill her man. In subsequent interviews she continued to alert police to the likely guilt of this Mr Bassett, and tell them of the bad blood that had existed between the two men.

George Marcetta's lady was desperate for police to pay attention and get to the bottom of what had happened to the man she loved.

Born in the Victorian country town of Yallourn North in December 1958, Vasiliki Efandis had grown up in a large happy family, attended high school in nearby Moe, and then gone on to tertiary studies in Morwell. She completed a business studies course in 1979, took a job as a caterer at the Royal Women's Hospital in Melbourne, and also worked part time in a nursing home.

In late 1985, not long after ending a relationship with a man she'd been seeing for some time, Vicki Efandis gave birth to her daughter, Atalanti. In 1986 she began an on–off relationship with another man who ran a taxi business and who took on, for a time, the role of Atalanti's stepfather. When the couple separated for good, after more than 10 years together, Efandis started her own housekeeping business.

In 2002, George Marcetta, a Yugoslavian-born 56-year-old divorced father, became one of Vicki Efandis' clients. Marcetta lived alone in Dandenong at the time, as his ex-wife Ionna had retained the family home in Melbourne's east, and his daughter Athanasia had moved to Greece, where she had married in 2002. Marcetta was a successful self-employed painter, with a profitable contracting business. He had loyal staff and many friends, and was regarded as a lovely and generous man.

George Marcetta and the 44-year-old single mother soon became friends and then began a sexual relationship. Over the course of the romance, Vicki Efandis took a great interest in her new partner's business and encouraged him to buy a home closer to where she lived in Ivanhoe, so they could see each other more often.

In 2003 Marcetta sold his house in Dandenong and purchased the Bellfield home with Vicki Efandis. He contributed $100,000 and she contributed $80,000 and, although she never actually lived with him in the Liberty Parade residence, the title was listed in her name alone because it had enabled her to get the first home buyers grant.

Efandis continued to live in nearby Ivanhoe with her 19-year-old daughter Atalanti, but visited Marcetta regularly, and often stayed the night with him.

Although she'd been at the Liberty Parade house on Wednesday 8 September, that was one of the nights she had not stayed with her lover. Vicki Efandis had cooked Marcetta his favourite meal for dinner, spent the evening with him and, some time around 10.30pm, drove the few minutes home to her place in Oriel Road.

As was their nightly, and morning, custom, Efandis sent Marcetta a goodnight SMS at 11.08. He sent a return message 20 minutes later.

Then, just before 3am, she was woken by George Marcetta's concerned neighbour ringing to tell her the Bellfield house was on fire.

So on the night George Marcetta died in the fire that destroyed his home he was, theoretically, alone. The autopsy confirmed that Marcetta died as a result of the fire, and that he was alive when the blaze started but, mercifully, did not survive for very long.

The pathologist's toxicology report, however, revealed why George Marcetta had been unable to escape the inferno that destroyed his home.

Marcetta's body contained such high quantities of the muscle relaxant and sedative oxazepam that he would not have been able to save himself. While suicide was, of course, a possibility, it was almost immediately discounted.

Vicki Efandis' tip about Marcetta's ex-business associate was, therefore, looking good. Ivan Bassett had previously been investigated for stealing from the same property that was now a charred shell.

Earlier that year, on 18 June, local police had responded to a burglary at the Bellfield house. Efandis told police that she had witnessed Ivan Bassett driving away, in his own car, with a trailer load of tools he'd taken from George Marcetta's shed. She alleged that Bassett bore such animosity to his former friend, that he had not only threatened him physically but had stolen equipment worth $23,000. Police were unable to find any sign of the stolen goods, however, so the case went no further.

Then came the fire that destroyed the Liberty Parade house. And again the attention of Victoria Police was directed towards Mr Bassett.

But despite Vicki Efandis' determination to point the finger at Ivan Bassett, the Arson Squad detectives quickly figured out that the one-time friend of the deceased had nothing at all to do with the fire or suspicious death of George Marcetta. Just as he had, in fact, taken no part in the theft of anything from the Bellfield property.

At that stage, of course, the logical question of course was this: what did Vicky Efandis have against Ivan Bassett?

The curious answer was – nothing. Nothing at all.

As Detective Height and his crew pursued their investigation, it became obvious that Ivan Bassett was nothing more than a scapegoat – and not a very good one. Efandis, who had tried so hard to ensure someone was brought to account for the arson and resulting death of her partner, soon became their prime suspect.

And eventually all her attempts to smear the character and reputation of Ivan Bassett were seen as evidence of just how long Vasiliki Efandis had been planning the murder of George Marcetta.

According to Detective Height, Efandis was a clear suspect in the murder by December 2004, two months after the fire. But as the Arson Squad began digging ever deeper in their investigation of Vicki Efandis' involvement in the life and death of George Marcetta, they soon discovered just how far back her plan went.

'She researched this guy by getting to know his ex-wife,' Detective Height said. 'She found out his financial situation, that he had a good cash business, and then she started cleaning his house for money. She started a sexual relationship with him, and then got him to sell his house.

'Marcetta was well liked; he'd help anyone and give them money – that's why she targeted him.

'It was calculated from the start.'

By the time he burnt to death in his own home – one that she claimed he was just renting from her – she had thoroughly infiltrated and taken over his life and finances. In less than two years – without marrying him or even engaging in a live-in relationship – Vicki Efandis systematically acquired a 50 per cent share of George Marcetta's business; technically owned the residence in which he lived; and had re-registered, in her daughter Atalanti's name, a Jaguar that Marcetta had bought and lovingly restored in 2002.

Then, on the night of Wednesday 8 September 2004, Vicki Efandis cooked her man his favourite meal of pork rolls and noodles, and laced it with a large dose of Serapax, the prescription form of oxazepam.

Once George Marcetta was drugged and helpless in his bedroom at the rear of the house, Efandis heaped paper around his unconscious body, and spread more paper in various rooms throughout the house. She then poured between 20 and 28 litres of Sparko Kerosene about the place.

At about 10.30 she drove the kilometre home, spoke to her daughter Atalanti and behaved as if she was in for the night. Once her daughter had gone to bed, Efandis returned to the Liberty Parade house.

At 11.08 she used her mobile to send her last-ever nightly SMS to her lover, who by then was unconscious on the floor beside the bed they'd so often shared. At 11.29 she used George Marcetta's mobile to send the usual response from him to her phone.

Shortly before 2am on 9 September 2004, Vicki Efandis set fire to the master bedroom where the man she'd pretended to care for lay drugged. She set fires in five other rooms and then left the house and drove the short distance home again.

Of the many things that proved her undoing – apart from her foolish determination to direct blame towards an innocent man – the most incriminating were the drugs she used to knock Marcetta out, the accelerant she used to drive the fire, the way she set the fire, and the SMS messages she exchanged to set her alibi.

George Marcetta had never been prescribed any form of oxazepam, but in the previous year Vicki Efandis had been given two prescriptions for Serapax – which she had kept.

Even though Efandis herself, on the night of the fire, had shouted 'murder, murder' the Arson Squad knew, by the order in which the eight fires in the five rooms were lit, that the fire was arson and not an accident or suicide.

The detectives also discovered that, according to the date stamp on the kerosene bottles, the brand of kerosene used as the accelerant in the house fire must have been purchased a long time before the murder. This meant that whoever purchased the seven or more four-litre bottles of Sparko Kerosene had possibly done so for the purpose for which they were ultimately used: to burn down the house at 140 Liberty Parade.

Efandis was also defeated by her otherwise clever attempt to provide an alibi for herself. She could not have known – given it was barely a three-minute drive between their houses – that the mobile phone service for her home in Ivanhoe was served by a different base tower than the Preston tower that served Marcetta's home in Bellfield, a mere 1.1 kilometres away. This fact indicated that both SMS messages exchanged on the night of the fire were sent from 140 Liberty Parade, Bellfield.

One last damning piece of evidence was that, despite having the ready use of three other vehicles, Efandis hired a late-model Ford Falcon on 6 September, three days before the murder. She told no-one that she'd hired the car and did not park it near her own house. It was, however, spotted near George Marcetta's house in Liberty Parade on the night of his death.

This was a big investigation, and it took nearly a year before an arrest was made. The bulk of the case was worked by Detective Height and his small Arson Squad crew, Sergeant John Gibson and Detective Senior Constable Brendan White, although they often drew on other detectives for assistance.

'By December 2004, we had enough evidence to present our case to the court to get permission for telephone intercepts and listening devices,' Height said. 'We took out countless search warrants on financial institutions trying to track the financial side of it, and the motive – that was a big part of the case.'

Detective Height said Efandis got Marcetta 'to put the Bellfield house solely in her name – so she could get the first home buyers grant, or so she told him. She started doing the books on his business over a period; got herself put on the books as a co-director of the business without any financial input; and opened joint bank accounts, primarily to fund the balance of the mortgage.

'It took a while but she slowly got all his assets in her name.'

The investigation found that Efandis had insured the Liberty Parade house, declaring herself the sole beneficiary; and that Marcetta's business, Universe Painting, was changed to the company name of Universal Hi-Tech Pty Ltd, with Vicki Efandis registered as a director, and her daughter Atalanti as secretary.

To cap it all off, in July 2003 George Marcetta cancelled his will, of which his daughter Athanasia had been the only beneficiary, effectively leaving him intestate at the time of his death.

Intestate but with Vicki Efandis in effective control of all his assets and finances.

The police also discovered that George Marcetta wasn't even Efandis' first financial victim, in fact not even her first George; and that the way she'd gone about things with her previous partners was obviously leading up to bigger pay-offs.

'Strangely, she had three partners all called George. George 1, 2 and 3 were all a fair bit older than her,' Detective Height said. 'And she had ripped every one of them off.

'The first one she basically trapped into believing he was the father of her daughter. He paid maintenance her whole life but had nothing to do with her.

'The second one, a taxi driver, was just taken from day one. They were on again, off again for years. One time when they split up, she took him to court and got half the taxi business as a settlement. That's where part of the money came from that she used as her share to buy the house in Bellfield with George Marcetta.

'Even after doing that, for at least the last several months that Vicki Efandis was on with George Marcetta, she was also back on with this taxi driver George again. Apparently Marcetta had become aware of this.'

Detective Height explained that a major part of the investigation, which took a huge amount of time, was trying to identify the kerosene bottles that were used and left at the crime scene.

'We were able to prove that "Sparko" brand Recochem kerosene bottles were only sold to Bunnings and no other outlet at the time. They had a date stamp in the plastic and we got an expert from Brisbane, who makes the bottles, to prove when those bottles would've been made. Then, after checking with Recochem and Bunnings, we were able to show that their stocks of Sparko Kerosene only last on the shelf for a short time before it's all sold and replaced with new stock.

'The thing that really drew us to the labels, in relation to the dating on the Sparko bottles, was the poison safety warning. The old bottles, which is what these were, had a New Zealand number on them; and the new bottles have an Australian number.'

Because 20 to 28 litres of kerosene had been used, investigators went right through all the transaction records at all Bunnings stores across the state, looking for bulk purchases of Sparko Kerosene. Detective Height said they were never able to prove where and when or by whom those bottles were purchased.

'But this was a circumstantial case,' the detective explained. 'The reason it was such a strong case was because each link in the case didn't rely on the next. They were all individual circumstances that pointed to Vasiliki Efandis being the murderer.'

Height said that Efandis had actually tried to be too smart. The exchange of SMS messages was clever but didn't work because of the mobile phone towers.

'She had sensibly paid cash for the Ford Falcon that she hired from Europcar to get around without being recognised. But, as she had to give her drivers' licence to hire it, we were able to prove that she had hired it, and could check the very limited kilometres on it.'

The investigators also realised that part of the set-up over the months prior to the murder was the false burglary reported by Efandis at the same house. Police at the time spoke to Ivan Bassett, who Efandis had said she saw driving away with stolen tools. They realised it obviously wasn't him so the case went no further. It seemed she was just being vindictive and making a lot of allegations towards him.

'Obviously,' Detective Height said, 'she was just setting him up as the fall guy for the murder. But we had to be careful how we danced around everything, as this man still could have been a suspect.'

When the detectives questioned Bassett, he claimed the car that Efandis had 'seen' him driving on the day of the burglary was a wreck at the time and that he no longer owned it.

Detective Height said he was soon able to verify Bassett's statement. 'I was able to prove the car was completely written off and sitting at a wreckers a couple of days prior to the alleged burglary. The second-hand dealer's books were all legitimate and signed off properly.'

Naturally, in the course of any investigation detectives speak to family members, friends and colleagues. 'And we figured that prior to the murder Efandis was probably, from what we can tell, testing drugs on George Marcetta, putting little bits in his food to see what would happen. Marcetta had mentioned to one of his ex-girlfriends that when Vicki had come over and cooked for him, he'd often feel sort of funny afterwards,' Detective Height said.

'Then when the time was right, she's gone and cooked him pork rolls and noodles and put Serapax in it. You don't need a lot of Serapax to kill someone, let alone knock them out. Then she's poured kerosene all throughout the house.'

Even without the telltale empty kerosene bottles the Arson Squad knew, in the early stages of the crime scene investigation, that the Liberty Parade house fire had been deliberately lit.

'The way the kerosene was poured around was what indicated that it was a murder and not a suicide,' Detective Height said, 'because the room with the heaviest burning was the room where the body was – it had been burning the longest.

'There were a lot of fires set in the rooms clockwise off that room going out the back door, but those fires hadn't taken off by themselves because she'd shut the doors after she'd lit them and there wasn't enough oxygen to keep them going.'

In retrospect, the uniformed officers at the scene recall that Efandis' behaviour had been odd. They say she'd made 'a bit of a half-arsed attempt at concern and tried to run into the crime scene' but was easily stopped by police.

Detective Height said the officers realised it was all just crocodile tears. 'Straightaway she was saying that he'd been murdered – and that was before she'd even been told there was a body in the house – and she was already blaming one of his ex–business associates.

'When the police told her to go home, she just did, and they found that sort of a bit chilling too. Because if it was your boyfriend or someone you knew, you would stay there and want to know if he was all right. But she left before even knowing whether the guy was alive or dead, or even in there.'

Detective Height said that everyone involved in the investigation found their suspect very cold and very calculating. Even the listening devices revealed a woman planning her every move.

'She'd sit there alone and have full-on conversations with herself in preparation, like she was interviewing herself and training herself as to what she was going to say.

'Efandis was a very hard woman – completely ruled by money and greed. She used her daughter, as much as everyone else, to create alibis. She tried to get her daughter to say she was home in bed the whole time the night of the fire. And on that night she got her daughter *and* a neighbour to go to the fire with her. She always made sure there were witnesses around when she needed them.'

The investigation took nearly a year and a great deal of work by many police officers. 'We just kept working on it, we were trying to get the maximum amount of evidence to charge her before we showed our hand,' Detective Height said.

Vasiliki 'Vicki' Efandis was finally arrested for the murder of George Marcetta on 5 August 2005.

On the day of her arrest, when her residence was searched, a large number of the tools and electrical items alleged to have been stolen by Ivan Bassett during the burglary of George Marcetta's place in June 2004 were found in the garage at the Ivanhoe home of Vicki Efandis.

During her remand and bail applications in 2005 and 2006, police and prosecutors naturally opposed her release. One of the reasons for not wanting the accused back out on the streets was that Victoria Police had apparently been looking at Vasiliki Efandis for a few other murders as well.

Victoria Police knew that Efandis had been acting as a carer for elderly people; not officially, but through her housekeeping business. She was 'helping' people; happy to do things for them like their shopping or driving them around. But, allegedly, she was then suggesting they should leave their houses to her when they died.

The investigation into every nook and cranny of Vasiliki Efandis' life had revealed that she was the only person in the room when an elderly, and quite wealthy, man died. There was no post-mortem examination in this case because of his age, so there was no indication as to how or why the 90-year-old man actually died. His wife died shortly after that. Efandis again was present.

Police also believed that in the months leading up to George Marcetta's death, she'd already picked out her next victim: an 82-year-old woman. Apparently the only reason that this mark didn't sign her house over to Efandis was because the woman's daughter realised what was happening and stepped in to stop it.

These investigations, ultimately, did not proceed because of the cost involved in exhuming the bodies in question;, and the likelihood that only limited information could be obtained from the bodies, in relation to toxicology, because they were old.

Vasiliki 'Vicki' Efandis stood trial for the murder of George Marcetta in the Melbourne criminal division of the Supreme Court in 2008. By the time she was found guilty and faced sentencing, on 28 November, she had already served 555 days in jail on remand.

As is customary during a sentencing, Justice Stephen Kaye addressed his sentencing remarks to Vasiliki Efandis herself, noting that her murder of Mr Marcetta occurred in circumstances that could only be described as chilling.

'The evidence was that Mr Marcetta was very fond of you,' Justice Kaye told her. 'I am satisfied that, although you affected to reciprocate his affection, in reality you had no sentimental attachment to him at all. Rather, you insinuated your way into his life, gained his trust, and then abused it in the most appalling way. You resorted to lacing his favourite meal with sleeping tablets, in order to prepare him for death.'

Justice Kaye stated that it was clear that she planned and prepared to commit her crime for some time before the day of the fire. He recounted the evidence given during the trial that she had, after arriving at the scene of the fire at around 3.15am, immediately blamed Ivan Bassett for the fire when she spoke to a policeman.

'There is no evidence whatsoever that Mr Bassett played any part in the fire at all,' the judge told her. He added that Mr Bassett had been a sincere and genuine witness and that the jury accepted his denial that he played any part in the fatal fire.

'During 2004, he and Mr Marcetta had some differences,' Justice Kaye said. 'You sought to exploit those differences by implicating Mr Bassett in the fire, in order to escape any accusation against yourself. Further, in June 2004, you falsely reported to the police that Ivan Bassett had stolen Mr Marcetta's tools on 18 June.'

The judge stated, 'I am satisfied that your false report of the thefts relating to Mr Bassett was, in some way, related to your murder of Mr Marcetta. That you made that report, either to exacerbate the differences between Mr Marcetta and Bassett, or, alternatively, to create evidence, in advance of your crime, that Mr Bassett bore such animosity to Mr Marcetta that he would stoop to stealing Mr Marcetta's tools of trade. Those conclusions reinforce my finding that your murder of Mr Marcetta was the product of planning by you over a significant period of time.

'Based on all the evidence,' Justice Kaye told Efandis, 'I am satisfied beyond reasonable doubt, as I consider was the jury, that you had planned, and prepared, your dreadful crime over a period of some time before you committed it on the early morning of 9 September 2004.

'During that period you had abundant opportunity to consider the enormity of the offence you were about to commit, and for the normal human emotions of compassion and sympathy to displace your murderous intentions,' he continued.

'Instead, throughout that period, you proceeded cold bloodedly to plan and prepare your murder of George Marcetta. Your callous ruthlessness was equally characterised by the cunning, evil and devious way you inveigled Mr Marcetta to eat his final meal, which you laced with oxazepam, and then set about burning down the house, in which he was rendered senseless, while he was still alive.'

Justice Kaye told Efandis that he was satisfied that the motive for her crime was greed; that she murdered Marcetta because she believed she would benefit financially from his death. He said she had already gained substantial control of Mr Marcetta's assets and that the only person who stood in the way of her enjoyment of total ownership and control of those assets was George Marcetta.

'You clearly have not felt or displayed any remorse at all for the death of Mr Marcetta,' the judge told Efandis. 'On the contrary, in recorded conversations which you had with friends in December 2004, you spoke most disparagingly of him. In your interviews with police investigators you told them a number of matters which were particularly derogatory of Mr Marcetta.'

Justice Kaye said those things had reinforced his finding that Vicki Efandis felt no affection for Mr Marcetta, and had callously exploited the man's affection and attraction to her in order to murder him for his worldly assets. He believed her conduct, in seeking to lay the blame on Ivan Bassett for the fire and the death of George Marcetta, was also relevant to her lack of remorse and her high level of moral culpability.

The premeditated murder, he said, 'involved a gross breach of trust, and the betrayal by you of another person's genuine love for you.

'The murder by you of Mr Marcetta was callous, cold-hearted and merciless. You showed no pity to your unwitting victim, and you clearly suffered no pangs of conscience as you set about murdering him,' he said.

'It was only fortuitous that Mr Marcetta did not survive for long in the fire. However, you were not to know that. By drugging him and then setting fires around him, you potentially condemned him to die helplessly in the midst of a horrifying inferno. If the medication you had given him had not been so effective, you could have exposed him to a terrifying death.

'You carried out your crime in a most devious, calculating and treacherous way,' Justice Kaye told Efandis. 'You were motivated purely by greed. Mr Marcetta gave you absolutely no cause to murder him. Indeed, on the contrary, he had been generous and loving towards you.'

He said the crime had taken the life of a man who enjoyed life; who was a decent and productive member of the community; and who had loyal friends and employees, some of whom had given evidence during the trial.

Justice Kaye noted, 'The victim impact statements of his former wife, Ionna Marcetta, and his daughter Athanasia Marcetta, are salutary reminders that while Mr Marcetta was the primary victim of your dreadful crime, there are others who have also suffered considerably as a result of it.

'The grief, pain and sense of loss, felt by those who loved him are the inevitable consequence of your wrongdoing.'

Four years and two months after his death, George Marcetta's daughter Athanasia – who had flown from Greece to Melbourne for the sentencing – stood in the Supreme Court of Victoria and waited to see what would happen to the woman who had taken her father.

For the murder of George Marcetta on 9 September 2004, Justice Kaye sentenced 50-year-old Vasiliki Efandis to 24 years in prison, with a minimum non-parole period of 20 years.

This is longest sentence ever handed down to a female murderer in Victoria.

Outside the court afterwards, Ms Marcetta described her father as a hardworking, much-loved man, whose memory would never be forgotten.

Of Efandis she said, 'She is a cold-blooded killer. I think she deserves everything she got. This is what I wanted.'

Vicki Efandis will be 70 years old before she is even eligible for parole.

Athanasia Marcetta said she took pleasure in knowing that the woman who murdered her father would most likely die in prison.

# THE OTHER SIDE OF HER

It is human nature to form judgements about people based on first impressions. Those judgements come from a lifetime of human encounters and experience, are further shaped by the environments in which people live and work, and even by the stereotypes reinforced by television and movies. Consolidated by a media that is driven by speed rather than circumspection, it is hardly surprising that when someone a little different enters the frame they are judged, convicted and sentenced by the court of public opinion, before they can even speak a word in their own defence.

Tracey Wigginton was an imposing, intimidating woman. Standing six feet tall, she hit the scales at 110 kilograms. To complete the picture that was her in 1989, the 24-year-old wore her dyed-black hair cropped close to her skull, sported tattoos that suggested Satanism, and had a female lover. Tracey didn't look like the archetype of the feminine woman, or even the sporty athletic woman; rather, she loomed larger than life.

To a society fed on a diet of youth and beauty, where girls were expected to adopt properly ascribed gender stereotypes, Tracey Wigginton was an anomaly, the kind of woman you'd probably avoid making eye contact with in a casual encounter.

So it took only three words for her own society to pass judgement on her; to have her tried, found guilty, and locked away – even before a police investigation had begun.

Those words were Lesbian Vampire Killer.

On Saturday 22 October 1989, two Brisbane Grammar School rowers were out early for training. As they rowed the Brisbane River, by the small sailing club at Orleigh Park, they saw a man lying slumped near the club building. They also noticed what seemed to be blood splattered on the roller door behind him. The rowers spotted two women jogging, called out to them and asked them to check on the man. To their horror the joggers found that the man was bloodied, almost naked and very dead. It was just after 6am.

When police arrived at the scene, they knew two things immediately: the deceased was not the victim of an accident; and this case was not going to be a straightforward one. The middle-aged man also had too many stab wounds for his death to have been a mugging gone wrong. Clearly this was something much worse, much more vicious and brutal and probably intentional. When one of the police officers tried to turn the body over, his head wouldn't move. The victim had received such a forceful injury to his neck that he'd almost been decapitated.

Strangely, most of the man's clothing was neatly stacked near his body. His checked shirt was under his left arm and his underpants were under his right foot. Robbery, as a motive, was ruled out quickly when his wallet was found wedged under a gap in the roller door. It still contained his Commonwealth Bank keycard, $35 in cash and enough information to identify the murdered man as Edward Clyde Baldock.

During their search of the body, the police also discovered something strange: a second Commonwealth Bank keycard, pushed up towards the toe of one of the victim's shoes, and bearing the name Tracey Avril Wigginton.

Edward Baldock was a 47-year-old council worker, father of five and grandfather. The previous night he had caught a taxi from his home in West End to the Caledonia Club at Kangaroo Point, where he spent the night drinking with his mates. By all accounts the balding, potbellied Baldock was drunk, to the point of stumbling, when he left the Caledonia Club at around 11pm to head home.

Earlier that night, on the other side of town in Fortitude Valley, a lesbian nightclub was pumping up for a big Friday night. Two young regulars – Kim Jervis and her lover Tracey Waugh – were joined by another lesbian couple, Tracey Wigginton and Lisa Ptaschinski. Although Kim, the extrovert, had a touch of colour in her black and green paisley shirt, Tracey Waugh wore a black dress, stockings and shoes; and their friends wore all black. Nothing unusual there: it was Friday night, it was a club, and big girls always look better in black – it hides a multitude of sins. Tracey Wigginton and her friend Kim Jervis also wore pendants with a ram's head on them.

The friends stayed at the nightclub chatting for a while and then left together at around 11.30pm. The owner of the nightclub noticed their departure because it was unusual; they usually stayed much later.

The women got into Wigginton's green Holden Commodore and, allegedly, went hunting for a victim together. About half an hour later, they came across Edward Baldock staggering along the side of the road at River Terrace, Kangaroo Point. They pulled over and offered Baldock a ride home.

They drove to nearby Orleigh Park, where Tracey Wigginton and her friend Kim Jervis encouraged Baldock out of the car, with promises of sex. Jervis got back in the car with the other two women while Wigginton led Baldock down to the riverside.

Tracey began to seduce Baldock. She helped him to undress and took off her own blouse. It was then that her keycard fell out of her pocket. Promising more to come, Tracey made an excuse to go back to the car for something. While she was gone, Baldock picked up keycard and wedged it in the toe of his shoe.

Tracey had returned to her car to get Kim Jervis's knife, but while she was there she talked Lisa Ptaschinski into going back to the park with her. Kim Jervis and Tracey Waugh remained in the car.

As Tracey and Lisa approached their drunken, unsuspecting

target, he turned to greet them. Tracey lunged at him with the knife and stabbed him with such force that she almost severed his spinal cord.

Tracey Wigginton stabbed Edward Baldock 27 times. Both the front and the back of his neck were cut right across and there were deep wounds in his chest. In one thrust, the knife pierced his left nipple and penetrated deeply enough to scratch the man's heart.

After she had killed him, Tracey returned to the car and invited Kim Jervis to come with her to look at the body. She also grabbed a towel from the boot of the car and washed herself and the knife in the river.

It wasn't until later, after she and Lisa Ptaschinski had returned home, that Tracey Wigginton noticed she'd lost her keycard sometime during the course of the evening. She talked her lover into returning with her to the park to try and find the incriminating plastic, but to no avail.

The police, however, had better luck and came knocking on Tracey Wigginton's door the very next day.

When she was first interviewed by the Queensland police, Wigginton denied any knowledge of the murder of Edward Baldock. After all, they had no proof. The presence of her keycard at the scene meant nothing more than the fact that Baldock was in possession of something Wigginton had lost.

Clearly, the police thought otherwise. Tracey was arrested at the end of that interview and taken to a maximum-security prison.

Throughout the course of the day after the murder, the other three women were obviously suffering. Kim made a number of phone calls to Lisa. Even though she knew that Tracey Wigginton was covering up their involvement in the deed, she wanted it to stay that way. But their consciences – or something – obviously got the better of them, because before the day was over all three had handed themselves in to police.

Because of what happened next, though, it can only be supposed that a certain amount of collusion went into their 'surrender'.

It was the video evidence that Lisa Ptaschinski, Kim Jervis and Tracey Waugh gave to police that not only changed the course of the investigation, but also polarised the Queensland community. The women told stories about satanic worship, vampires, mind control and witches' covens. They claimed Tracey Wigginton was a vampire and that Edward Baldock had been killed in order to feed her 'blood lust'.

So, did they spend the day getting their stories straight before handing themselves in to police? Did they fabricate, embellish and lay blame in order that the scales of justice should fall on Wigginton's head and leave them blameless? It is not possible to know. What is known is that once the statements of those three women became known to the media, the case took a turn away from the objective investigation of a cruel and senseless murder, and descended into fairytales of witches, vampires and a big scary bogeywoman.

Rockhampton is a regional city on the east coast of Queensland. Known as the beef capital of Australia, it lies just north of the Tropic of Capricorn along the banks of the Fitzroy River. Not only does it support a strong farming community, but the average of 300 sunny days per year are a boon for the tourism industry.

George Wigginton was the millionaire-owner of a transport company, and he and his wife Avril were pillars of the Rockhampton community. They were unable to have any children, though, so they adopted three little girls: Rhonda in 1942, Dorrell in 1950, and, later, a part-Indian child called Michelle.

Avril Wigginton, however, was a cruel and domineering woman, with a pathological hatred of men. She was sadistically cruel to the two little girls, and often beat them with electrical cords or with a garden hose with a chain attached to it. She would yell at the children, telling them that men were good for nothing and only wanted women for sex.

When Rhonda turned 21 she got married and soon afterwards gave birth to her daughter Tracey. The marriage failed early, and Rhonda moved back home to her parents' place with young Tracey.

Then, when her daughter was only four years old, Rhonda met another man and ran off to Townsville with him, leaving Tracey in the care of her grandparents.

In stark contrast to the way they had treated their daughters, George and Avril doted on their young granddaughter. They formally adopted her, they spoilt her and they spared no expense for her education and other interests. Tracey wanted for nothing, and was lavished with expensive music, dance and elocution lessons. People who knew her as a child describe her as being a pleasant and generous girl, but with a violent temper.

As a teenager Tracey was a devout churchgoer, but gradually developed an interest in the occult and learnt to read tarot cards. When she was 10 years old, she told someone that her grandfather was sexually abusing her. Tracey's story was treated as being a figment of her childish imagination. Tracey was 14 years old when George Wigginton died in 1979, followed two years later by his wife.

After her arrest for the murder of Edward Baldock, Tracey Wigginton strongly denied the allegation that she was a vampire. She told police she had never claimed to be one. She was required to undergo psychiatric assessments before her case could come before the courts.

Dr Jim Quinn, a forensic psychiatrist, interviewed Tracey over several months. He found her to be friendly and likeable, but noticed that she often became forgetful. Sometimes she could not recall things she'd said to him just moments before, and on other occasions even appeared not to recognise him. When she was shown the videotape of her confession to police, Tracey told Dr Quinn she had no recollection of making it.

Friends told Tracey's defence lawyers that she sometimes introduced herself to people as Bobby; and that in that 'persona' her manner seemed rougher and more aggressive than usual.

Dr Quinn began to suspect that Tracey had a multiple personality disorder, and he engaged the services of a renowned clinical psychologist and hypnotist to help him try and unlock the puzzle.

Through hypnosis they were able to speak to Bobby, who told them that she was 16 years old.

In all, Dr Quinn spoke to at least five different personalities. When he asked Tracey, under hypnosis, about the murder of Edward Baldock, it was Bobby who answered. She claimed she had killed Baldock because she was angry.

When Dr Quinn presented his findings and gave his professional opinion that Tracey Wigginton was suffering from multiple personality disorder it was challenged. MPD does not constitute a mental disease or 'abnormality of mind' under the Queensland Criminal Code.

Tracey Wigginton was ruled fit to stand trial.

The trial began on 21 January 1991 but, in a move that surprised many, Tracey sacked her barrister and entered a guilty plea to the charge of murder. In proceedings that lasted nine minutes, Tracey Wigginton was found guilty of the murder of Edward Baldock and sentenced to life in prison, with a minimum of 13 years. The judge also ordered that no details of her short trial could be released to the public, in order not to prejudice the upcoming trial of the other three women.

For the defence lawyers representing the other three women this was good news. Nothing damaging to their cases had come from the Wigginton trial, and they were in the enviable position of already having a woman in prison for the crime with which their clients were charged. Not only that, but Tracey Wigginton's silence meant their clients had nothing but their own version of events to defend.

Apart from the feeding frenzy of the circling media, the only time the words 'Tracey Wigginton' and 'vampire' were mentioned in the same sentence was by her co-accused, who were all fighting to keep themselves out of prison.

Lisa Ptaschinski told police that her lover, Tracey Wigginton, had killed Edward Baldock to feed her hot blood lust. Lisa said that Tracey was a vampire who hated mirrors and sunlight, and went out mainly at night. She claimed Tracey drank pig's blood, which she obtained from a butcher, and told how on four occasions she had cut her own wrist to let Tracey drink the blood.

Kim Jervis had been close friends with Lisa Ptaschinski for several years, and was in a sexual relationship with co-accused Tracey Waugh at the time of the murder and trial. Kim told police they had all planned to kill a random victim so that Tracey Wigginton could feed.

Kim also claimed that Tracey considered herself a vampire and kept live bats. She 'revealed' she had discussed the devil-worshipping hierarchy with Tracey during the week prior to the murder.

It later emerged that Kim Jervis was the one who had an avid interest in vampire culture; and that it was she who owned a bat-covered waistcoat, who loved watching horror movies, and who apparently belonged to a cult, The Gothics, who performed rituals at Toowong Cemetery.

Other friends believed it was Kim Jervis, not Tracey Wigginton, who fantasised about being a vampire. It was Kim Jervis who also bought one of the knives that was used to murder Edward Baldock; and it was she who happened to have it with her on the night.

Tracey Waugh, the fourth person there on the night Baldock died, took no part in his killing. Apart from trying to convince her lover, Kim Jervis, to stay in the car she had the least involvement of any of the four. When she gave herself up, however, she told police that Tracey Wigginton had exercised mind control over the other women on the night of the killing to convince them to go with her.

Tracey Waugh described Tracey Wigginton as a devil-worshipper who could read minds and who feared crosses. Her lawyer told the court that Waugh had been a reserve victim for Wigginton if Baldock, or someone equally suitable, had not been found.

Tracey Waugh was acquitted of any charges and allowed to leave the court a free woman.

Kim Jervis was found guilty of manslaughter and sentenced to 18 years in prison, later reduced on appeal to 12 years.

Lisa Ptaschinski was diagnosed as having borderline personality disorder. It emerged that she had been hospitalised 80 times in the previous five years for drug overdoses and self-mutilation. Lisa was found guilty of murder and sentenced to life in prison. In 2009 she began a resettlement program – aimed at getting her used to life outside prison once she is released – which entitled her to 12 hours of leave every two months, for six months.

Tracey Wigginton was released from prison in January 2012 after serving almost 21 years – almost double her original sentence. She was 46, frail and walked with the aid of elbow crutches. For many years before her release she had expressed horror and remorse for the murder she had committed.

# TIE HER UP, TIE HIM DOWN

Shirley Withers needed her lover restrained so she could force him to sign a property over to her. She wanted him tied up to humiliate him as payback for sexually demeaning her. At least that's what she told her accomplices, the two new 'friends' she duped into helping her.

Shirley seduced an unwitting young couple with money, gifts, drugs and the pretence of friendship, and won their sympathy and loyalty by convincing them she was the victim of her wealthy lover's control and perversions.

Shirley's man, she told them, had treated her like a nobody; had frozen her accounts; was trying to take away her house; had forced her into bondage sex.

When she finally asked for their assistance in finding 'someone' to help her deal with her de facto husband, they felt obliged to provide that aid themselves. After all, she was only asking for help in tying the manipulative bastard up – so that *he* would know what it was like, and so he would give back what was rightfully hers.

In truth, however, Shirley Withers was a scheming, debt-ridden embezzler. She wanted her de facto dead so she could get her hands on his multimillion-dollar assets. More importantly, she needed him dead before he discovered just exactly how much she'd already stolen from him.

Rightly assuming she'd be unable to restrain the man by herself, as he was much bigger than her, Shirley figured she'd need at least one other person to help subdue him. Her accomplice wouldn't need to know, necessarily, that she intended to kill her lover; just that she wanted to humiliate him.

So, while Shirley put a fair bit of thought into how she would commit her crime none of it was even remotely logical. Sure, she was able to find gullible accomplices; yes, she did manage to kill her de facto; granted, she set about covering her tracks. But every single step that Shirley Withers took in her elaborate scheme to murder Melbourne millionaire Peter Shellard led nowhere but back to her.

The news headlines in the months after the cruel and vindictive murder revealed the unravelling of a plot that was never going to hold together. Initial reports of the merely 'suspicious death' of a maverick millionaire soon gave way to these headlines: *Murder 'accused' forced into bondage sex*, and eventually to something closer to the truth, *Woman guilty of bondage murder*.

Unlike the flash of anger or desperate act of self-defence that often results in murder, Shirley Withers had plenty of time to plan her every move. So what went wrong?

Firstly, even though she was effectively a criminal herself, having already embezzled nearly a million dollars from her lover's company, Shirley Withers was no underworld crook. She was just a boutique owner.

Secondly, although she obviously thought her choice was clever, she ignored all the sensible rules of choosing her partners in crime. With no criminal network of her own, she did the next best thing and recruited a couple of desperate low-lifes who were bound to have connections.

Thirdly, she broke the primo contract killer rule of anonymity, thereby discovering the biggest pitfall of hiring a hitman.

Shirley Withers' unwitting accomplices in the murder of Peter Shellard were junkies, and the hitman she tried to hire to kill them, after the fact, was an undercover cop. The junkies went to jail for manslaughter, and Shirley was found guilty of murder, and of incitement to murder.

Peter Shellard was a millionaire luxury car dealer and former real-estate agent. Twice married and father of three daughters, Shellard was director of several companies, owned nearly a dozen commercial and residential rental properties and, at the time of his death, was worth around $15 million.

Shellard left school after Year 11 but, after studying nights for his real-estate licence, opened his own agency in Brighton's very up-market Bay Street. That first business, Peter Shellard Real Estate, laid the groundwork for his future wealth. Among other businesses, he later took control of a Rolls Royce and Bentley dealership, Kellow-Falkiner Motors.

Over the years, as he made his name and fortune, he was variously described as a maverick businessman, an eccentric millionaire, an argumentative bloke, a bit aggressive, even a bit mad.

Shellard had allegedly tried to break into the Caulfield Town Hall – by climbing in through the roof – and was often removed from the premises while trying to use the council office phones.

'Rosecraddock', the house in which he died in North Caulfield, was his own home but also the source of much aggravation for himself and others. Situated on nearly a hectare of land, and one of the grandest houses in an area of grand houses, Shellard had paid $1.4 million for the fifteen-bedroom mansion in 1984. (It was sold in 2007 for a record $7.8 million.)

His original plan to demolish the house and subdivide the prime real estate on which it stood was thwarted when 'Rosecraddock', built in 1857, was given heritage listing to protect it from any such development.

His neighbours, with whom he did not get on, reckoned that

Peter Shellard had tickets on himself; that he regarded himself as the lord of the manor, the local kingpin, and was something of a law unto himself. He'd even tried to have 'Rosecraddock' classified as a place of religion so he wouldn't have to pay taxes. And although his 'estate' – where he kept dogs, illegal beehives, ponies and lots of cars – was surrounded by high barbed-wire fences, these barriers were apparently not designed to keep Shellard in. The owners of adjoining homes said he treated everyone in the area like peasants or tenants, and wandered onto their properties at will, checking out their tool sheds and even parking his cars in their garages.

Local councillors described a host of strange run-ins with Shellard, including the time he demanded that the bodies of his bees be returned after his hives, prohibited by local by-laws, had been destroyed by council officials.

Shellard had bipolar disorder, he was a hoarder of worthless junk, valuable antiques and classic cars, and a bit of a recluse. And yes, according to friends, he was into a kinkier kind of sex. He had been known to frequent Melbourne's Hellfire Club – an S&M bondage salon where he'd enjoyed lots of leather and whipping.

None of this, however, meant that Peter Shellard deserved what happened to him on the night of 7 May 2005. In fact, the horrific way in which he was killed said a lot more about Shirley Withers than it did about Peter Shellard.

Born in New Delhi in 1966, where she'd lived in 'relatively comfortable circumstances', Shirley Withers migrated from India with her family in 1970. Shirley apparently endured a period of physical abuse as a child, but nonetheless successfully finished school and became a bookkeeper. She married and had two children, in 1996 and 1998, but divorced in 2000. Her sons now live with their father.

In 2001, shortly after meeting and beginning a relationship with Peter Shellard, Shirley opened Suzette Boutique, an exclusive brand-name clothing store in Brighton. She also took over the bookkeeping for Shellard's company accounts and various properties. It wasn't long before she became a signatory on the cheque account for Kellow-Falkiner Motors.

As it turned out Shirley didn't have much of a head for business. When she needed stock for her boutique, she simply ordered it, whether the business could afford it or not. And despite all the money she embezzled from her wealthy lover to cover her spending and staff salaries, at the time of Peter's death she still owed $43,000 on credit cards and had a business debt of nearly $300,000.

In fact Shellard's eldest daughter Jenny, who worked part time for Shirley at the boutique, had seen thousands of dollars' worth of outstanding invoices, and often wondered how the staff were paid each week.

In April 2005 Peter Shellard started to get suspicious about his girlfriend's bookkeeping skills. He was worried that Shirley was using his credit card, and although he had cancelled her authority on his accounts, she continued to cash $50,000 cheques using a 'missing' cheque book. In early May, in order to recoup his mounting losses, Shellard decided to sell the East Bentleigh house in which Shirley was living.

That was it. Shirley Withers suddenly faced the prospect of losing her home and being revealed as a thief. She decided it was time to put into action the plan she'd been working on for months. Part of that preparation had involved making a will that she'd hoped Shellard would sign, making her a significant beneficiary of his estate – should he die.

On 6 May 2006 she contacted her dealer friends and asked them to buy some speed and heroin and to find someone to help her tie her lover up so that, unbeknownst to them, she could make sure that Peter Shellard did die.

Stanley Callinicos and Sophia Stoupas, the two drug addicts who were drawn into Shirley Withers' fictional little world, didn't have a lot going for them at the time. Addicts for nearly half their lives, they both had minor criminal records, although neither had a history of violence.

Estranged from their own families, they were easily impressed by the friendship offered by Shirley Withers, especially as it came laden with gifts, and the money to buy more drugs.

It was Shirley's own substance abuse problem that had led her to Stanley Callinicos in the first place. He was dealing to support his and Sophia's habits. Whether Shirley befriended them on purpose, or if the plot to use them came out of the drug dealing, is not clear. But whichever came first, in the few months before the murder Shirley showered Stanley and Sophia with gifts, and with money for their own drugs and for gambling. She treated them to trips to the Crown Casino and other gambling venues and gave Sophia clothing from her store.

Gradually Shirley also began telling them the lies about Peter Shellard that ultimately secured their assistance and unwittingly landed them in jail for manslaughter.

According to family members and the psychologists who testified on their behalf at their trial in 2006, neither Stanley nor Sophia had violent dispositions. Both were of average intelligence and trusting of anyone who showed them understanding.

At 44 years old, Stanley Callinicos had always been easily influenced by strong women with a knack for distorting his judgement. His 20-year drug addiction to heroin and amphetamines meant he had lived the life of a petty crook and spent time in prison, but not for violent crimes. His offences were all for possessing or trafficking drugs, or for drug-related property offences.

Sophia Stoupas' dependent personality and poor judgement meant she too was easily manipulated. Though she'd faced court five times between 1993 and 2004 – on using, possession, and drug-related property and driving charges – she had never served time. Like Stanley's, 31-year-old Sophia's drug-based life began at a young age. Starting with alcohol and marijuana when she left home at sixteen years old, she'd graduated to speed and heroin by the time she was twenty.

Except for their shared drug-fuelled lifestyle, Sophia and Stanley were not each other's main problem. While the drugs and their individual personalities were always going to get them into trouble, they were not necessarily bad for each other.

They were, however, made to order for Shirley Withers. By paying for the drugs to which they were addicted, by giving them other gifts and indulgences, by treating them as something better than the junkies they were, Shirley Withers made them feel special and, ultimately, useful.

Though they were ashamed and remorseful at the part they played in Peter Shellard's death, their recruitment had been easy.

Or, as Justice Kevin Bell said to Stanley Callinicos at their sentencing: 'You are appalled at your conduct in committing the crime to which you have now pleaded guilty, which resulted from you allowing yourself – when drug addicted – to be influenced and duped by Ms Withers, whose false stories about the deceased you stupidly believed.'

Which, of course, was exactly what Shirley Withers had counted on.

In the months leading up to what Shirley allegedly always intended to be murder, she began spinning lies about her relationship with Peter Shellard. She told Stanley and Sophia that he was not paying his bills, that he'd frozen her accounts to deny her access to her own money, and that he sexually and emotionally humiliated her by forcing her 'to do bondage with him'.

It was no doubt clear to them, when she told them of Shellard's intention to sell her home out from under her, that she'd reached the end of her tether. On the day before the attack that ended in murder, Shirley told her accomplices she simply wanted to force Shellard to sign 'her' house back to her by tying him up and humiliating him – so he'd know what that was like too.

The thing is, as anyone who frequents an establishment like the Hellfire Club would tell you, just because someone has a penchant for restraints and kinky sex, that does not make them deviants or control freaks. One person's weird sex life is, after all, another's missionary position.

According to his friends, Shellard enjoyed the whole dressing up in leather and studs thing; he found it erotic. He'd told them his pain threshold, though low at first, had increased after a few visits to the Hellfire Club. That meant, of course, that unless Peter Shellard enjoyed both the S *and* the M of sadomasochism, then his particular turn-on at Hellfire involved being tied up and whipped.

Shirley's stated desired 'to show him what being tied up was really like' was therefore redundant. But Stanley and Sophia had no way of knowing that the being-bound side of bondage sex was something Shellard already knew plenty about. The man was not going to 'learn' anything from what Shirley had planned for them to do to him.

He *would* be utterly humiliated and terrified and brutalised – but it was never in Shirley's plan for him to survive the night.

On Friday 6 May 2005 Shirley Withers asked her friend Stanley Callinicos to recruit someone to help her tie Shellard up. She also asked him to buy her some speed and heroin – some for her to use on Shellard, but the rest for Stanley and Sophia.

As she expected, her friends volunteered 'their muscle' for the job she wanted done.

The three met at a hotel in Cheltenham where they played the pokies together and Stanley bought some heroin. Later that evening they went to Peter Shellard's home. Shirley let them into 'Rosecraddock' with her own key. Stanley brought ropes along to bind Shellard's feet, and Sophia had a pair of handcuffs.

According to Stanley and Sophia – who, even a month later, still believed they were there merely to supply the drugs and help tie Shellard up – Shirley's plan only went awry because the victim proved harder than expected to subdue.

Peter Shellard, wearing only boxer shorts, was woken by his lover and two strangers attacking him in his own bedroom. Shirley put a pillow over his head while Stanley tied his feet and Sophia tried to cuff his hands.

But Shellard fought hard and naturally tried to protect himself: he bit Sophia's finger. Her instinctive reaction was to reach for the nearest blunt object and hit him on the head with it – twice. Stanley also hit Shellard at least once on the head with his open hand during the struggle to restrain him.

With three against one, and a head wound, Peter Shellard didn't stand a chance. He was finally overpowered, trussed with more ropes, electrical cords and dog leads and left lying on his side on the bedroom floor. His attackers then adjourned to the kitchen.

Shirley soon left her accomplices and returned to the bedroom alone with a drug-filled syringe. She injected Peter Shellard with a probably fatal dose of heroin.

A little later Sophia, with Shirley's help, inserted a Proladone suppository into the already dying Shellard. Proladone, or oxycodone pectinate, is a heavy-duty pain-killer but it reacts badly with opiate narcotics, like heroin, and should not be used by people with intracranial pressure or heart problems.

Shirley, Stanley and Sophia all left 'Rosecraddock' at 2am on Saturday 7 May, but went back again at about 8am. On that occasion Shirley first gave some heroin to her accomplices and then entered the bedroom she'd so often shared with Peter Shellard and injected him again.

Nearly eleven hours later, at 6.50pm on 7 May, an hysterical Shirley Withers rang 000 to report finding her partner dead.

Police who attended the scene found Peter Shellard's bound and naked body, draped with a towel, and covered in blood. His home was a mess but a bloody fingerprint was found on a phone in the hall.

Over the next few days, while presenting herself to Shellard's daughters as a woman deeply affected by the loss of the man she loved, Shirley Withers also attempted to secure a share of her late de facto's money. She tried to persuade some of Peter Shellard's debtors to pay their debts directly to her, rather than to his estate.

Shellard's autopsy revealed that the causes of his death were the effects of heroin injection and head injury in a man with coronary artery atherosclerosis. Pathologist and deputy head of the Victorian Institute of Forensic Medicine, Dr David Ranson, said that while it was possible that only one of those three factors actually caused Shellard's death, all three were present at the time and therefore all had some operative effect.

Although the Proladone suppository could also have had dire consequences, it was believed that Shellard was either dead or so close to it when it was inserted that his low body temperature prevented the oxycodone from being absorbed into the urine or blood.

In the meantime Homicide detectives discovered that the fingerprint at the crime scene belonged to one Sophia Stoupas, who lived with a known drug dealer, Stanley Callinicos. It was no time at all, however, before their connection with the real culprit was found. Shirley Withers had used her own phone to call Stanley Callinicos on many occasions, including late on the Friday and early Saturday morning of 6 and 7 May.

Criminal mastermind she certainly wasn't, but it was the next couple of things that Shirley did that led to her complete undoing. Despite the many incriminating and idiotic things she'd already done, she then put the word out that she knew who killed the man she loved and wanted to do something about it.

Her one last bit of stupidity was to hire a contract killer to deal with her accomplices.

'Victor the hitman' – who approached *her* offering assistance – was of course an undercover police officer. It was Shirley, however, and not 'Victor', who first spoke of killing Stanley and Sophia.

Shirley met with her hitman four times between 24 May and 9 June, and at first merely claimed to know who'd killed her lover. She soon admitted to being present during the assault but shifted any blame from herself by telling Victor that it was Stanley and Sophia who had gone beyond her instructions and killed Peter Shellard – the man she loved.

'Peter was my soul mate,' she told Victor. 'I loved him more than anything in the world, right. He was supposed to sign some papers, right, and just be tied up, nothing else. I didn't want him touched.'

She said she was now afraid that Sophia and Stanley would talk.

Victor asked Shirley how she wanted him to hurt her accomplices; whether she'd like them in hospital or turned into paraplegics.

Shirley Withers said, 'Nah, want 'em dead.'

She agreed to pay Victor $10,000 to make that happen, and made two down payments of $1400 and $1600.

When she showed Victor where Sophia and Stanley lived, he asked, 'What do they do?'

'They're nothing,' Shirley Withers told him. 'They're fucking heroin junkies. They stay at home all day and shoot up.'

On their third meeting, Victor produced photos of Stanley Callinicos and Sophia Stoupas so that Shirley would verify that these were the people she wanted killed.

Finally, during their fourth and last meeting, Shirley told Victor that she'd not only helped restrain her lover on the night he died, but that she'd taken part in the assault.

And then perhaps because she believed Victor to be a 'fellow killer', Shirley decided he probably wouldn't care why she really wanted Stanley and Sophia dead, so she also admitted to him that she had in fact intended to kill her lover.

That same day, 9 June 2005, Stanley Callinicos, Sophia Stoupas and Shirley Withers were arrested for the murder of Peter Shellard.

When questioned by Homicide detectives, the reasons Sophia and Stanley gave for assaulting Shellard were the 'reasons' their friend Shirley had given when asking for their help. Stanley admitted to the part he and his girlfriend had played on the night Shellard died, but said he and Sophia had only gone to 'Rosecraddock' to help their friend because her boyfriend had been treating her badly.

That they'd had to hit him to subdue him obviously weighed on the consciences of Stanley and Sophia because not only had it – in their minds – unintentionally contributed to Shellard's death, but it wasn't what Shirley had asked of them. It was then they discovered that Shirley's ultimate goal had always been murder, and that their actions, or overreactions, had obviously not perturbed *her* at all.

When confronted with the ultimate betrayal, that their 'friend' had hired a hitman to kill them, the unwitting accomplices realised just how much they'd been conned.

Already appalled and remorseful at the part they'd played in the death of Peter Shellard, Stanley and Sophia agreed to give evidence against Shirley Withers.

They also pleaded guilty to manslaughter in the Victorian Magistrates Court on 8 November 2006. When they were sentenced nearly three months later, Shirley Withers had yet to come to trial.

Because of this – for their own protection – some of the judge's comments were at that time restricted from publication.

Supreme Court Justice Kevin Bell told Stanley and Sophia, 'It is a matter of great significance that you have both offered to give evidence against Ms Withers in her trial on the charge of murdering Mr Shellard. Doing so exposes you to considerable physical risks. These risks are not hypothetical. Ms Withers attempted to hire a hitman to kill both of you before she was brought to trial. Her attempts to have you killed were discovered and prevented in a covert police operation. Despite the risk involved to both of you, you gave undertakings before me to give evidence on behalf of the prosecution in Ms Withers' trial…The evidence will be of great importance in Ms Withers' trial and will vitally assist her prosecution.'

Justice Bell said that on the issue of remorse for a crime there were few demonstrations more compelling than entering early pleas of guilty and agreeing to give evidence against a co-accused.

'Giving this assistance, despite the risk, goes further,' he told them.

'It shows you are both prepared to do what you can to demonstrate your great remorse for the terrible things you did to Mr Shellard.'

Justice Bell explained that those mitigating factors had contributed to a sentence that was significantly less than would otherwise have been imposed, given the severity of the offence, but that imprisonment was nonetheless called for.

Referring to the then 44-year-old Stanley Callinicos, the judge said, 'For many years you lived the life of a drug addict and a petty criminal with little respect for the law. You have consistently failed to get the message that your drug addiction and criminal offending was leading to a personal disaster and you now stand accused of the crime of killing another human being ... Nothing in your criminal history to date approaches the severity of this crime.

'The evidence reveals you to be a gentle giant with no violent disposition,' he said. 'You are strongly attached to Ms Stoupas and hope to marry her and have children with her on your release... You seem committed to remaining drug free and assisting Ms Stoupas to do so, but whether you can follow through with this is an unknown variable.'

Of Sophia Stoupas, then 31 years old, Justice Bell said she was currently drug free, except for antidepressants. Furthermore, her relationship with her family had improved since being forced by her situation to admit her drug addiction, and she was benefiting from the courses she'd been doing in prison.

'Like Mr Callinicos, you did not intend to kill Mr Shellard,' the judge said. 'You thought you were going to his house to assist Ms Withers to tie him up, force him to sign documents and show him what being tied up was like. You reacted to him biting your finger by hitting him twice in the head with a heavy object...and your actions substantially caused his death. You had no part in the administration of the heroin to the deceased by Ms Withers, which was also a substantial cause of his death.'

Justice Bell noted that, while Sophia had a criminal record it was nowhere near as long as Stanley's, and that she'd not served any time in prison until being remanded on the charges arising out of Mr Shellard's death. He said her history did not suggest she had a propensity for violence.

To both offenders, Justice Bell said, 'Killing another human being – even unintentionally – is deserving of the strongest condemnation. Both of you, acting in concert with each other and Ms Withers, entered Mr Shellard's house and tied him up, during which he was struck to the head with an object.

'Mr Shellard was completely innocent in relation to these events. The experience of being woken from his sleep and assaulted by three people and treated in this manner would have been unexpected, terrifying and demeaning. Yet he was only subdued because you took advantage of finding him asleep and then it was three against one.'

Justice Bell explained his logic in arriving at the same sentence for both offenders. He had considered dealing more leniently with Stanley because it was Sophia who had struck Shellard; but, on the other hand, more leniently with Sophia because her criminal record was not as extensive as Stanley's.

In the end, for the crime of killing Peter William Shellard on 7 May 2005, both were sentenced six years, with a minimum of three and a half before being eligible for parole.

At the time of sentencing, Stanley had already served 361 days, and Sophia, 592 days.


When Shirley Withers fronted the Supreme Court between 26 April and 5 June 2007 – two years after the death of Peter Shellard – she was on trial for one count of murder and two counts of incitement to murder.

By then she'd returned to her original story – or con. Defence lawyer John Dickinson claimed his client had only planned to tie Shellard up, to show him what it was like and to compel him to sign over what was rightfully hers. It was Callinicos and Stoupas who 'got out of hand' and caused his death.

Dickinson maintained that Shirley Withers was 'greatly attached' to Peter Shellard and that she'd hired the hitman because she was angry with her co-accused.

So she owned up to a version of one crime, the lesser one; but not the other.

In April 2007 a jury found Shirley Withers guilty of the murder of Peter Shellard.

Six months later, at her sentencing, Justice David Harper described the case as a very grave instance of a very serious crime. He said that Shirley Withers had planned her course and had done so with deliberation.

The Crown had established, beyond reasonable doubt, that Shirley Withers either intended to kill Peter Shellard, or intended to inflict really serious injury upon him, or acted with the knowledge that probable death or really serious injury would result from what she intended to do to him.

Justice Harper said this intention may not have been conveyed to her accomplices; and that, if they were to be believed, it had not.

'The result of your actions at "Rosecraddock" on 7 May 2005,' he said, 'was the death, in horrific circumstances, of the man with whom you were then sharing your life.

'The horror he must have experienced is impossible for the rest of us fully to comprehend. This was, moreover, an assault which had been planned for a considerable period. And this is true even if the intention to kill was only formed shortly before the death.'

Justice Harper said the almost indescribable trauma that Mr Shellard must have experienced in those last moments of his life continued to resonate in those who were close to him, particularly his three daughters and his brother.

'You invaded your victim's home,' Justice Harper said. 'You then invaded his person in the most demeaning way by injecting him with heroin. An accomplice committed a similar insult by inserting a suppository.

'He must have been terrified. He struggled hard but to no avail. He died from its effects.'

Justice Harper said that the unchallenged evidence at her trial was that Shirley Withers was present throughout all that was done to Peter Shellard.

'Despite this you continue to protest your innocence. As a result, remorse is not a factor for sentencing purposes.'

While the judge *did* take Shirley's pleas of guilty to the charges of incitement to murder into account, he said this was of limited significance as the prosecution case was overwhelming and she'd made her pleas after the trial had started.

'It is true that the undercover police officer made the initial contact with you, and not you with him. At the same time, it was you and not he who first raised the subject of the prospective killings of Callinicos and Stoupas. Having raised it, you thereafter continued to give him instructions to put your scheme into effect, and made several down payments as an earnest of your intentions.

'Yours was not a casual or diffident approach to the prospective deaths of two people. It was purposeful and continued over an extended period,' he said.

In between being found guilty of murder in mid-2007 and being sentenced for her crimes in October 2007, Shirley Withers was still trying to get her hands on her blood money.

Being incarcerated at the time made her attempt not only difficult but downright arrogant and ridiculous. Tasteless is another word that springs to mind.

'Her' house in East Bentleigh – the one that Peter Shellard had been planning to sell to recoup some of the money she had fleeced from his accounts – had been sold the previous year, sixteen months after his murder.

While the Shellard family waited in the six-month legal limbo between the jury's guilty verdict and the judge's sentencing, another case involving Peter Shellard went through a different court.

John Shellard, as executor of his late brother's estate, found he had to fight Shirley Withers for some of the proceeds from the sale of the house that, in one sense, had been the catalyst for Peter Shellard's murder.

An amount of $87,802.69 from the sale was held in trust and Shirley Withers, as the respondent, was laying claim to it. The Victorian Civil Administrative Tribunal (VCAT) logically agreed, however, that crime really shouldn't pay.

On 24 August 2007, VCAT Senior Member Damian Cremean ruled that the $87,000 plus change belonged to the estate of Peter Shellard.

His reasons: 'Having regard to the evidence I have heard in this matter I am satisfied that Peter William Shellard was murdered on or about 7 May 2005...

'I am quite satisfied that the deceased was murdered by the Respondent in company with others (who, apparently, she may have sought to have killed also). There was talk of him being tied up and bashed...

'In such circumstances I accept the evidence without question, of both the police and Mr John Shellard, that the Respondent was defrauding the deceased man over a period of years of large sums of money well in excess of $1,000,000. This may have commenced as early as 2002 but certainly is known to have occurred between 31 October 2003 and 7 May 2005 (the date of the deceased's death).'

Mr Cremean said he was satisfied that the respondent had no entitlement or right to claim any part of the settlement monies.

'I apply in particular the well-established rule that no person shall profit from their own wrong,' he said. 'Any other finding would be unconscionable and wrong.

'I am satisfied that if the Respondent did contribute monies to the purchase of the house or to its upkeep or to payment for services (such as electricity or gas) that such monies were obtained by her out of her having defrauded the deceased.'

Mr Cremean not only ruled in favour of the executor John Shellard, but ordered Shirley – who, unsurprisingly, was not called to give evidence – to pay the court costs.


On 19 October 2007, Justice David Harper sentenced Shirley Josephine Withers to 20 years' imprisonment for the murder of Peter William Shellard.

He sentenced her to seven years for each count of the incitement to murder Stanley Callinicos and Sophia Stoupas. He stipulated that these sentences be served concurrently, but that six years of the first sentence for incitement must be served cumulatively with the sentence for murder.

He then set a non-parole period of 18 years, declaring that she had already served 862 days of that minimum sentence.

In other words, Shirley Withers was jailed for up to 26 years - for outright murder and the unsucessful hiring of a hitman; or for a vicious murder and rhe sucessful hiring of an undercover cop.

In 2010 Shirley Withers' sentence was slashed when, on appeal, the court determined she was only guilty of manslaughter. She was re-sentenced to serve 13 years with a minimum of nine. This made her eligible to apply for for parole in 2016.

# PREDATOR

One day in January 2005, the lives of two New Zealand women collided in tragedy. One was an 83-year-old great-grandmother; the other a 43-year-old career criminal.

Although this particular burglar habitually targeted homes of the elderly, not caring whether they were home or not, she usually just took off if she was seen or caught in the act. But not this time. This time she didn't flee the scene; she didn't just push her victim aside and make a run for it. This time she beat a defenceless old woman unconscious and stabbed her in the heart with a kitchen knife.

Marton, with a population of 4630, is the principal town in the Rangitikei District of New Zealand. The Rangitikei is 4500 square kilometres of lush and diverse landscape, ranging from sand plains on the southern coast, through lush and rolling rural land, magnificent hill country and wild river valleys.

The largest of many small towns that support the essentially rural community of the lower North Island, Marton has long been a producer of butter, flour and wool.

Lying halfway between the cities of Wanganui (35 kilometres

north-west on the coast) and Palmerston North (40 kilometres south-east), Marton is charming and historic, with many grand old residences. Established in the 1860s, and named after the hometown of Captain James Cook, Marton is also on the main railway line between Auckland and Wellington.

In the first few years of the 21st century Marton, and nearby towns like Bulls and Feilding, became popular tree-change or weekender destinations for people escaping the city life of Wellington and Auckland. The Rangitikei district, and the surrounding Manawatu-Wanganui region, had a vibrant creative and cultural life, with active arts and crafts communities and many museums.

Unfortunately, like pretty much everywhere in the world these days, and no matter how otherwise small and idyllic it is, Marton also had its problems. Assaults and robberies were on the increase there as much as anywhere else.

What's worse was that Marton, like many larger places in New Zealand, was plagued by the crime and violence perpetrated not only by common-or-garden-variety crooks, but also by street gangs of restless and angry youths, and territorial criminal groups. Motorcycle and youth gangs – like Black Power, Highway 61 MC, the Darksiders and the Mongrel Mob – had been causing all manner of trouble throughout the region, either committing crimes or fighting among themselves.

In the couple of years prior to the start of 2005, other petty crimes and housebreakings were also on the increase. In fact the houses of many residents in the area had been broken into more than once.

Mona Morriss of the Cobber Kain pensioner complex in Marton, for instance, had been burgled back in 2003. But even after the scare of having her home broken into, the octogenarian continued to live an independent life in her unit. The Wellington Road complex is named after Edgar 'Cobber' Kain, the Kiwi fighter pilot who was the first RAF Ace in World War II, so perhaps some of his fighting spirit had rubbed off on Mrs Morriss and her fellow residents.

Despite her advancing years and small stature, Mona Morriss was active and feisty, though becoming a little frail. She walked often, to and from the local shops, and was always helping other residents of Cobber Kain. She also had a large, loving and supportive family so it wasn't like she was lonely. Mona Catherine Morriss was a much-loved matriarch, a mother of 10 children, with 28 grandchildren and 19 great-grandkids.

Early on Tuesday 5 January 2005, Bryce Meade, on one of his regular visits to his mother-in-law, arrived to find the curtains drawn and the unit's back door locked. He was immediately worried as 'Mum' was usually up and about by then. Meade later told both police and the court that he knew straightaway that something was wrong; he feared she may have passed away in her sleep. He rang his wife Glenys who told him to use his own key to get inside.

'I saw blankets and pillows on the floor and her feet protruding,' Meade said. 'I thought that perhaps she had fallen and grabbed the blankets to keep warm, but as I went further into the room I saw that they were completely covering her.'

Even though he could tell, when he pulled back the blanket, that his mother-in-law was dead, Meade said he felt her body to make sure.

'I noticed the blood and the marks on her chest and thought, "Oh my God," but I still thought she had fallen.'

The Cobber Kain unit, however, soon became an official crime scene, with Detective Sergeant Tim Smith leading the investigation into the brutal murder of Mona Morriss.

The 83-year-old had been beaten and stabbed, and her unit, including the kitchen drawers, had been rifled. It was soon established that she had died on the evening of Sunday 3 January.

Forensic pathologist Dr George Thomas, of Wellington Hospital, performed the autopsy and reported that Mrs Morriss was more than likely unconscious when she was stabbed. He said she had been beaten about the head, and described a number of blunt-force injuries, including a haemorrhage along the inside of her right eye, a fracture of that eye socket, bruising around her left eyebrow, and a linear fracture of her skull that extended to its base. The injuries, he said, could have been caused by fists, kicks or a blunt object, but that the worst of them were consistent with being punched.

Dr Thomas said Mrs Morriss had then been stabbed six times in such a tight area of her chest that it was almost impossible to ascertain the exact direction of each wound. There were seven perforations of the chest wall, and the weapon, a single-edged blade, had also pierced the heart four times. The pathologist said the victim's blouse had been moved aside to provide the killer with better access to the 10-centimetre by six-centimetre area above her left breast, and that Mrs Morriss had bled to death as a result of the stab wounds. Dr Thomas said that there were no injuries to indicate Mrs Morriss had tried to defend herself.

Because Mrs Morriss' blouse had been unbuttoned before she was stabbed, and because of the placement and nature of the stab wounds, the police originally believed there had been a sexual element to the murder.

With no other forensic evidence to support it, however, that theory was soon discarded, especially when a burglary gone wrong seemed to be a far more likely scenario. A series of mostly unsolved burglaries in the homes of elderly people in Marton and surrounding towns pointed to this.

A local woman also told police that she had noticed the suspicious activity of a group of young males in the park near the flats around the time of the murder. And a pet food factory, just 400 metres up the road from the Cobber Kain units, had been broken into on the night Mona Morriss died.

Police soon collared two associates of the Mongrel Mob for the factory break-in, and later investigated two Mob prospects said to have 'left town' in a hurry around the time of the murder. The gang, and its members and wannabes, were eliminated as suspects in the murder.

Police continued to pursue the botched-burglary theory, however, and the more they dug into the spate of break-ins in the small towns of the Rangitikei, the more one name kept coming up. It was the name of a long-time criminal, a habitual and skilled burglar, who was also a drug user, a problem gambler and a non-custodial mother of five.

In May 2005, nearly five months after the death of Mona Morriss, the police brought 43-year-old Tracy Jean Goodman in for questioning.

Raised on a Rangitikei farm, with five brothers and sisters, Tracy Goodman was just 15 years old when she took off to Auckland with her older brother. She soon got into trouble with the law and was sent to the youth training facility at Arohata Women's Prison near Wellington for a time. Over the next few years she discovered there was one thing she was really good at, and although she racked up a string of charges, Tracy Goodman probably committed many more burglaries than the ones for which she served time.

Over the years Goodman also had five children, became addicted to a variety of prescription medications, and wasted a lot of money at the pokies. According to most of the people who knew Tracy Goodman, the prime motivating forces in her life were crime, sex, gambling and drugs. Two of her children had been adopted out, two were cared for in her *whanau* (a Maori word for extended family) and one was living with a caregiver.

By the time she was 40 years old, Goodman had numerous convictions for burglary, illegally entering properties, and receiving stolen goods. She rarely resorted to violence but did have a 1983 conviction for aggravated robbery, assault with intent to injure in 1987, assault with intent to rob in 1989, and common assault in 2001.

In 2000, when Goodman was paroled to the Shiloh Retreat Renewal Centre, she found two new important things in her life: God, and a willing partner in crime. Shiloh is a drug recovery centre in Feilding (31 kilometres from Marton) and Goodman was paroled there to get help with two of her addictions: to drugs like painkillers, Valium and sleeping pills; and to sex. The latter obviously didn't take too well, as it was at Shiloh that she started a sexual relationship with Les Goodman, although she did marry him in 2002.

The Goodmans lived in Palmerston North, from where they hunted the Rangitikei district for likely victims. With Les as the lookout and getaway driver and the efficient and careful Tracy as the housebreaker, the two committed burglaries in Feilding, Napier, Marton, Bulls and even as far away as Hastings on the east coast of the North Island. The career burglar obviously saw nothing incongruous in becoming a Christian and embarking on a new spree of robbing the elderly.

Les Goodman later testified that he and his wife would often return to places she had previously burgled, especially if she knew that her original entry point hadn't yet been fixed, or no security had been added.

Les Goodman said that one day in 2003, when they were prowling through the town of Marton, his wife had spotted an old woman leaving the Cobber Kain complex. She told him to pull over and wait, and she dashed into the units and came out with some cash.

He told police, during their investigation into the murder of Mona Morriss, that after he'd seen a picture of the victim, he recognised her as the same elderly woman who'd left the flats that day.

Even having a courier job didn't deter Tracy Goodman from her criminal activities. Nor did having a problem with the person caring for her son, which had led to her losing access, encourage her to go straight.

Les Goodman reckoned his wife loved being a crim even more than her other addictions. He said that after a burglary her face would literally light up. 'She used to say the rush was better than sex,' he said.

And obviously more enduring, as the Goodman marriage ended sometime in 2004, after Les apparently got fed up with Tracy's jealousy. Her possessiveness often resulted in violence – hers towards him.

In May 2005, when the police first interviewed Goodman about the spate of burglaries in the Rangitikei, she at first denied any wrongdoing. Then she denied any recent criminal behaviour, saying she'd found God and left all that in her past. She also tried to make out that she'd only taken to burglary about two years before, with her husband.

When the police informed Goodman that, because of her long record and her penchant for targeting elderly and vulnerable victims, she was being considered as a suspect in the burglary and murder at the Cobber Kain units in January, she decided to come clean.

Tracy Goodman suddenly realised that confession was good for the soul – or at least for a lesser prison sentence. She did not, however, confess to the murder of Mona Morriss, and in fact claimed she'd never committed any crimes in Marton.

In a videotaped interview with Sergeant Ricky Lewar, Tracy Goodman instead put her hand up for a host of burglaries in her hometown of Palmerston North, and in Napier and Feilding. She nominated 11 houses and flats she had burgled in those towns and admitted to stealing amounts of up to $900.

While some of these places had been unlocked, Goodman told Sergeant Lewar how she would more usually climb in through a window. Describing them as 'back-to-back' burglaries, Goodman admitted she often returned to places where she'd found money. She said her victims were often in the next room, but on one occasion she'd stolen a handbag from a wardrobe while an old lady lay asleep on the bed in the same room.

Goodman was not sure of the exact dates of any of these crimes, but gave precise details of the addresses, whether anyone had been home at the time, how she'd got in, and what she had stolen.

It's unknown whether Tracy Goodman was simply 'confessing all' or describing a modus operandi that showed that, despite the constant likelihood of being seen or caught, she'd never resorted to violence.

She did tell Sergeant Lewar that because she had a job she didn't even need to steal; that burglary was an ugly part of her that she wanted out of her.

'I shouldn't need to do it, but I just keep doing it,' she admitted. 'I hate me for what I do.'

When Sergeant Lewar told her that, on the day of the murder, she'd been seen attempting to enter a house near where Mona Morriss lived, Goodman denied doing any burglaries in Marton and insisted she had nothing to do with the woman's death.

When police later took their likeliest suspect on a drive around Feilding, Palmerston North *and* Marton, Goodman indicated 20 separate places she had burgled. She ultimately admitted to and was convicted of 85 burglaries – in those three towns and in Bulls, Taihape, Stratford, Lower Hutt and Hastings – between March 2004 and February 2005.

Wanganui Police Detective Nick Brunger analysed Tracy Goodman's burglaries and found that 14 of the 85 were committed in Marton. All of them, and most of the others, were committed against victims over 60 years of age; most did not involve forced entry; and in a good 75 per cent of all the burglaries the victim was at home.

Lead investigator Detective Sergeant Tim Smith later said he'd never come across such a prolific female burglar.

'Her associates used to call her The Cat and she was known as the best of the best,' he said. 'She's got no remorse and is one of the most prolific, predatory criminals this country's probably ever seen.'

Her confession certainly resulted in one of New Zealand Police's largest unsolved crime clean-ups. On 1 September 2005 Tracy Goodman was sentenced to seven years' prison for 85 burglaries.

Meanwhile, with their prime suspect locked up in Arohata Prison, Detective Smith's team continued the investigation into the murder of Mona Morris – for nearly another 12 months. Police were drawn from throughout the North Island to work on the case.

By her own admission Tracy Goodman had a habit of returning to the scene of a previous burglary to rob the same person again. Les Goodman's statement implied it was his ex-wife who had robbed Mrs Morriss' unit back in 2003.

Two witnesses placed Tracy Goodman in Marton on Sunday 3 January. One woman foiled Goodman's attempted burglary of her house, two streets over from the Cobber Kain units, at about 5.20pm; the other saw a car just like Goodman's parked near the Wellington Road complex at 6pm.

While much of the evidence they were gathering was circumstantial, the police did have one strand of dark-brown hair, about 60 centimetres long. It was found on the lounge-room carpet in Mrs Morriss' flat, and DNA tests verified that the hair came from someone in Goodman's maternal family. Until January 2005, and just after the murder, Tracy Goodman had long hair, which her associates said she usually tied back, and under a baseball cap, during a burglary.

The issue of why a usually meticulous and practised burglar, with a cut-and-run MO, would suddenly snap so violently could be explained by an accumulation of circumstances.

Because Mona Morriss was often out walking in the town, there may have been a chance that she'd noticed Tracy Goodman on one of the latter's legitimate visits. Goodman had once lived in Marton and often returned to visit relatives there, so she may have thought, or even known, that Mrs Morriss could have identified 'her burglar'.

Because of the custody dispute she was fighting, Goodman would have known she'd lose access to her son if she was arrested again. So this was one time in her life that Goodman couldn't afford to be recognised, and may explain the action she took on that Sunday evening.

On top of this, Goodman may have been in a higher-than-usual state of agitation or aggression that day, having been unable to get a prescription for Temazepam. Goodman was listed as a potential drug seeker who fronted different clinics as a casual patient. On the morning of the murder, she had been very rude and a bit aggro to the staff of a Palmerston North clinic, after the doctor she'd visited had refused to write her a script.

Police had also secured valuable information from Tracy Goodman's ex-husband and some of her friends. Of course, the big problem with Goodman's 'friends' was that they were themselves all criminals.

Detective Sergeant Tim Smith finally had enough evidence to proceed and Tracy Jean Goodman was arrested in mid-2007 and charged with the murder of Mona Morriss. Her trial in the Wanganui High Court, before Justice Mark Cooper, began on Monday 3 September that year.

In his opening speech, Crown Prosecutor Andrew Cameron said that the death of Mona Morriss had all the hallmarks of a burglary gone wrong; that Tracy Goodman had entered the house as a burglar, and walked out as a murderer.

Cameron said that between 6pm and 7pm on 3 January 2005, Goodman had entered Mrs Morriss' flat. Her intention was to steal cash and any small items she could carry but she had killed Mrs Morriss when the elderly woman surprised her in the act.

The Crown argued that Mrs Morriss had heard a noise in her bedroom and when she went to investigate was punched in the head up to four times and knocked unconscious. Cameron said Goodman then got a knife from the kitchen drawer, lifted Mrs Morriss' blouse and stabbed her six times in the left side of her chest.

Cameron told the court that Tracy Goodman was a compulsive burglar with more than 80 convictions. He said she also had drug and gambling problems but that her real motive was her battle to regain custody of her young son.

'She could not afford to be seen, not afford to be detected committing offences,' Cameron said. 'She was cornered in a confined space, on edge and couldn't be caught. She lost it and killed Mrs Morriss.'

The one-time friends who testified against Tracy Goodman had to tell the court about their roles in various crimes, in order to give the evidence asked by the Crown prosecutor.

Helen Chaffe, who had been dealing prescription drugs to the accused, told the court that she recalled Goodman telling her she was 'scared' that one of her elderly victims, who had woken up during the burglary, had recognised her.

Andrea Stratford told the court, 'None of us witnesses have a reason to lie. We're hanging our own necks out, all of us. Helen [Chaffe] has outed herself as a Valium seller. We've all got stuff to be guilty of, but none of us are guilty of murder.'

Stratford said she and the accused had known each for a few years, after meeting in the Shiloh rehab centre, and that Goodman often turned up with jewellery and other stolen goods for her to sell. She admitted she'd once gone along with Goodman on a burglary and had kept a little old lady busy while her friend slipped into the woman's house and stole $600.

Stratford testified that soon after the New Year in 2005, Tracy Goodman had arrived at her place with a radical new haircut that was very short and dyed. She said Tracy was stressed and had a handbag (containing purses and a small blue sewing tape) that she 'could not be caught with'.

Stratford told the court, 'She said she was friggin' shitting herself because something had gone wrong, but she didn't say what. She asked me if she could swap vehicles with me.'

Although Goodman had asked Stratford to get rid of the bag she'd brought with her that day, Stratford simply left it in her shed. The jury was told that the victim's family had identified one of the purses, a black coin purse, and the tape as belonging to Mona Morriss.

Another witness, whose name was suppressed by the court because she was still serving time, testified that she'd recently been in Arohata Prison with the accused and that Goodman had confessed the killing to her.

Tracy Goodman's lawyer, Mike Antunovic, questioned the

relevance of the only DNA evidence in the case. Because the hair found at the crime scene had no root, it wasn't amenable to standard STR DNA profiling. It was instead sent to a laboratory in the United Kingdom for mitochondrial DNA analysis.

Samantha Underwood, who gave evidence about this analysis, and explained that the DNA in the hair couldn't be narrowed to Tracy Goodman but was inherited from her maternal line alone.

Antunovic argued that this evidence provided 'moderately strong' support for the defence proposition that the hair belonged to another member of the accused's maternal blood line, namely Goodman's niece Tracy Mosen.

As Ms Mosen's partner lived in a flat almost directly opposite Mrs Morriss – and Mosen had been visiting him regularly in the months before Mrs Morriss' death – Antunovic suggested that the single 'incriminating' hair had simply blown into Mona Morriss' flat. Or perhaps it was carried inside by Mona Morriss herself, after contact at the clothesline or some other part of the Cobber Kain complex.

The defence also raised the issue of the criminal activities of gangs in the town, suggesting that perhaps the police simply ignored the possibility that Mrs Morriss' killer was connected to the Mongrel Mob.

When questioning the officer in charge of the Marton police station, Antunovich asked if it was true the Mongrel Mob had been 'hitting hard' in the small community, and had been 'thieving and stealing' in the weeks before Mrs Morriss was killed.

Sergeant Peter Wood agreed that the Mongrel Mob had long had a presence in the area but that any connection to the death of Mrs Morriss had been investigated and ruled out.

The defence also used Tracy Goodman's criminal modus operandi to argue why she would not have killed Mona Morriss. Antunovic and his co-counsel Steve Winter told the court that there was no evidence of their client using violence in any of her many burglaries. Mr Winter said Goodman was a highly skilled burglar whose offences numbered into the hundreds and that she was not deterred by the presence of residents in their homes. He said it was significant that there had not been one instance, in all of that offending, of Tracy Goodman being violent to any of her elderly victims despite being confronted, on occasion, by some of those victims. Mr Winter said that in one case Goodman had been assaulted by one of her elderly victims.

The defence maintained it would have been more consistent with Ms Goodman's approach for her to have talked her way out of the situation. At the very least, she would have simply pushed Mrs Morriss aside. Winter said, 'Violence of any scale, and certainly violence of the scale involved here, was inconsistent with her modus operandi as a burglar.'

Finally, on Friday 28 September, after 110 witnesses and four weeks of evidence, testimony and cross-examination, the jury of four men and eight women took eight hours to return their verdict. The foreman announced that the jury had found Tracy Jean Goodman guilty of burglary, and guilty of the murder of Mona Morriss.

At least 20 members of the victim's extended family had been present in court every day throughout the trial. When the verdicts were delivered, the Morriss family began cheering, hugging and crying with joy and relief.

During the sentencing, on Friday 7 December 2007, Justice Mark Cooper said that burglary had been a way of life for Tracy Goodman. Her entry into Mrs Morriss' home was consistent with her pattern of offending; in particular her choice of the elderly, preferably those living alone, as easily burgled whether they were present or not. He said that if she was noticed on the premises that, as a younger, physically fit person, she could reckon on being able to make her escape.

Addressing Goodman, the judge said, 'Tragically for Mrs Morriss, she encountered you as you were rifling through her belongings in the bedroom. I infer from the facts proven at trial that she must have stood between you and the doorway to the bedroom so as to bar your exit from it.

'For some reason, about which one can really only speculate, you were not content to push her aside, as you could easily have done, and leave. Rather, the course of conduct on which you embarked involved knocking her to the ground and as she lay there, possibly unconscious or semi-conscious, you used a knife so as to inflict five or six stab wounds in the vicinity of the heart.'

Justice Cooper said, 'The injuries that she sustained would, of course, have been sufficient to kill anyone and a frail, elderly lady such as Mrs Morriss was plainly no match for you.'

The judge said it was fair to say that there had been two dominating influences in Goodman's adult life, namely drug addiction and what comes close to being an addiction of a different kind, to the crime of burglary.

He said that in the time leading up to the murder, Goodman had been taking a range of pills including Valium, Rivatril and Temazepam. He also stated that she had 125 previous convictions for burglary, 11 for entering property with intent to commit crimes, 11 for theft, and convictions for receiving and fraud.

Justice Cooper said to Goodman, 'You maintain your innocence of the present crimes. You exhibit some remorse for the burglaries to which you previously pleaded guilt, but there is no remorse that I can take into account in relation to Mrs Morriss' murder.

'As a result of the sentence that I will be imposing on you today, you are going to be in prison for a very long time.'

The judge acknowledged the presence of members of the Morriss family in the court. 'I note that many of them attended every day of the month-long trial. It was plain from the evidence that was given by her relatives at the trial that she was a much-loved mother and grandmother…plainly still enjoying life and her family.'

Justice Cooper said Mr Morriss was 83 years old when she died. 'Her death in these tragic circumstances has been plainly devastating for her family who loved her.

'Those left behind,' he said, 'are devastated by their tragic loss, their grief being made so much worse because of the way in which she died. In their own ways, each and every member of this large grieving family has been left with an emotional scar unlikely ever to heal.'

Justice Cooper said that such brutal crimes committed against defenceless elderly people in their homes could not be tolerated, and was conduct that must be denounced in the strongest terms.

'I have decided,' he said, 'to impose a minimum period of imprisonment of 19 years.

Justice Cooper then pronounced, 'Ms Goodman, for the murder of Mona Catherine Morriss you are now sentenced to life imprisonment.'

Goodman was also sentenced to two years on the burglary charge, to be served concurrently with the life sentence and the remainder of her sentence for the 85 burglaries.

After the sentence the Morriss family, in a written statement, thanked the police, the prosecution, and Mrs Morriss' friends and neighbours in Marton.

'May you sleep better knowing that at least one low-life person has been taken to task for her bad deeds in your community.'

The statement also addressed Tracy Goodman, saying that the verdict and sentence in no way made up for the loss of their mother. 'May God or whoever you believe in, never forgive you.'

Detective Sergeant Tim Smith said, 'This was a brutal and callous murder. Life in prison with a minimum nonparole period of 19 years was extremely pleasing after such a heinous crime. Hundreds of other victims from Goodman's burglaries can also take satisfaction from the sentence.'

He said that so many of the people that Goodman had stolen from had not only lost confidence, and a sense of safety in their own homes, but also felt guilty that they could not give jewellery and family heirlooms to their children.

Glenys Meade expressed a desire to one day confront her mother's killer face to face and make her realise what she had done. 'I want her to actually look at me and see what she's done. She's never once looked at us; she's always averted her eyes.'

Tracy Goodman appealed both her conviction and her sentence. The appeal was heard on 23 September 2008. The sentence stands, and Tracy Jean Goodman – who received the longest prison sentence ever given to a woman in New Zealand – will not be eligible for parole until 2026.

# THAT SHOULD MAKE HIM DIE

*This case had all the hallmarks of fantastic fiction. We even charged five people with murder, without a body.*

Detective Inspector Peter Wheeler, Victoria Police, 2009

Karen Randall had man troubles. An on-again, off-again relationship with one of the local guys was currently off. She and Paul had lived together for a while until he started getting rough with her; well, roughed her up, actually. He'd given her a couple of black eyes and a few other bruises. She'd had him charged with assault back in April. He'd copped to it though, and pleaded guilty in the Moe Magistrates Court. She broke up with him after the assault, and then again a month or so later.

Well, you know, small country town – nearly everybody knows everybody or knows someone who does; and there are not that many guys to go around, so you go with what you know until someone better comes along.

Moe's total population was only around 15,000, which meant fewer than 5000 who were anywhere near her own age; less than half were men and most of them were already taken. Karen and Paul had known each other for about six years but had only been together for a couple. By most accounts Paul was a nice guy, except that some of the drugs he did made him aggro – mostly with Karen.

But again – small town, mutual friends, same parties. You can't keep out of each other's way for long, so you learn to ignore or put up with what you can't change. And this is also bogan territory; in fact outsiders joke that Moe is an acronym for Moccasins on Everyone.

Still and all, Paul was getting more than annoying lately. Before Karen and her young son moved to the even smaller nearby town of Mirboo North, Paul kept turning up at her place in Moe banging on the door and windows, begging her to get back with him.

Stupid dope freak. What did she have to do?

No, seriously. What *do* you do with an ex-boyfriend who won't take the hint and leave you the hell alone?

You could get your sister and girlfriends to provide backup while you embarrass him in public and tell him once and for all to take a hike. You could enlist some guys you know to rough him up a bit to make him back off once and for all. Or you could take the advice of a friend, one you haven't known all that long, and then just go along with her outrageous and despicable scheme.

Simple as that.

One Sunday in 1989 a group of friends got together in Mirboo North to commit murder. Their crime was premeditated, brutal and callous. And much like the murder itself, the motive – such as it was – was an absurd overreaction.

The 134-kilometre Grand Ridge Road, unusually true to its name, traverses the ridge of the beautiful Strzelecki Ranges. It winds its way between the Latrobe Valley and South Gippsland, through beautiful scenery that changes from the rolling pastures of rich farmland to fern forests, towering mountain ash and forestry plantations. It's part two-lane rural highway and part unmade rutted road, travelled mostly by farmers, tourists and a lot of logging trucks.

Mirboo North, the only major town on the route, lies halfway along the Grand Ridge Road. It's around 40 kilometres from Moe, the next biggest town.

The main industries in the region, in fact for much of Gippsland, are farming, mostly dairy, but also cattle, sheep and vegetables; forestry; open-cut brown coal mining; the huge paper mill at Maryvale; and the massive Hazelwood, Yallourn and Loy Yang power stations, which use the local brown coal to provide 90 per cent of the electricity for the state of Victoria.

Mirboo North is a hardworking farming community proud of its history and charm, and totally unprepared to play host to one of the most bizarre murder cases in Victoria.

In late 1989, 26-year-old Karen Randall and her younger sister Donna were both in the midst of moving or settling into new homes. Donna was about to have a housewarming for her new place in Moe; and Karen, and her six-year-old son, had been sharing a farmhouse with a friend Rhona in Mirboo North, while she waited to move into her new housing commission house.

Karen and Rhona Heaney had only known each other since August, when they'd started the same office-skills course at the TAFE college in Traralgon, 50 kilometres away. Both single mothers, they had a few other things in common and quickly became friends, even though Karen dropped out of the course after a month. As this was also during the latest break-up with her boyfriend Paul, Karen was grateful for the opportunity to move in with Rhona and her two kids, and get out of Moe.

Rhona had a sometime live-in boyfriend called Steve and through them Karen met their mutual friends the Maslins, Irene and Jano, who also lived in Mirboo North. The burgeoning friendship between the three women – which by default sometimes included Steve, Jano Maslin and Karen's 22-year-old sister Donna – centred around mutual child-minding, parties, motorbikes, drinking and smoking dope.

The Maslins did a bit of dealing, and apparently had a marijuana crop growing in one of the state forests – out Shady Creek way, north of Moe – and sometimes went to stay in another house they had in Geelong, about three hours away, to score or sell.

By the end of October 1989 Karen was waiting on word of her new commission home, partying with her new friends, and still trying to avoid the ex-boyfriend.

The ex, Paul Snabel, was sharing a house with his mate Paul Friend in Moe. Apart from his obsession with Karen Randall, the 28-year-old also had a fondness for the booze and was a bit of a speed freak. That's speed as in the amphetamine; although he did drive a Holden and ride a Yamaha RZ 250.

According to Paul Snabel's housemate, the Karen–Paul relationship was stormy. He said Karen would tell Paul to piss off, and then she'd want him back again.

As far as the housemate was concerned, Paul should dump Karen because she wasn't worth the effort.

As far as Karen was concerned, Paul was getting really irritating.

As far as Karen's friends were concerned, Paul Snabel was dangerous.

Rhona and Irene had seen at least one of Karen's black eyes, courtesy of Paul after Karen had accused him of cheating on her; and Rhona had witnessed arguments between the ex-couple on her veranda at Mirboo North after Karen had moved in with her. Irene and Rhona were angry about Paul's behaviour towards Karen, and worried that he might really hurt her.

But it was the beginning of his end when, at the start of November, Paul did two things that were beyond the pale for Karen's friends. He allegedly followed Karen's son home from school; and he visited her new house – the one she hadn't moved into yet and which she didn't think he knew the address of – and slipped a postcard under the door. It said: 'You make me see red'.

That was too much for Irene Maslin. She was already convinced Paul was crazy, dangerous and quite likely to kill Karen, and now reckoned he might hurt her son too. Being worried on behalf of a young single mum was understandable given Irene had kids of her own, and it probably made Karen feel supported knowing her new friend was pissed off on her behalf – but this was where the overreaction to the 'Paul situation' began to get out of control.

Apparently, being on Irene Maslin's bad side was a pretty scary prospect. She was a big woman; loud, threatening and aggressive. She was a 'with her or against her' kind of personality.

In fact, more than one Mirboo North resident described her as scary.

'People were frightened of her,' one of the locals said after the fact. 'She could chill you to the bone just by looking at you. Irene Maslin was a real Charles Manson.'

There were other rumours about Irene Maslin: that she 'knew people', you know, who fix things; that she knew hitmen who could deal with **shit** that needed dealing with. They were probably just that – rumours; but she *was* a drug dealer so you don't mess with rumours like that.

Not even if you believe she's your friend.

So Karen, who thought she was at her wits' end, consulted that friend. Sometime around 2 November she got together with her sister Donna, Rhona and Irene. One version of the ever-changing story that came out afterwards also placed Irene's husband Jano at this 'planning meeting'.

Irene took the lead; took control. She said something had to be done about Paul Snabel. They all joked about breaking his legs so he'd get the message. Irene then got more serious and talked about 'disposing of Paul'. She and Rhona came up with the idea of injecting Paul with speed laced with something like battery acid. All they had to do was lure Paul to the isolated farmhouse that Rhona and Karen shared on Nicholls Road.

They decided to put the plan into action the following weekend. Donna's housewarming party in Moe was scheduled for the Saturday night and Paul was expected to attend. It would be Karen's job to ring and invite him out to her place, and Donna would encourage him to go out there later, with her. Rhona would get the syringes, and she and Irene would take care of the lethal shot.

They figured it wouldn't take much to talk Paul Snabel into going anywhere that Karen was. Stupid bastard – he wouldn't have any idea what he was really in for.

No-one, at any time, said, 'Hang on a sec, this is wrong; we can't do this.' They all agreed it was really the only way to deal with the problem. And everyone would have a part to play.

On Saturday 4 November, Donna Randall's party in Moe went off as planned. Karen had decided not to go; or rather the conspirators deemed it sensible, because Paul would be there. It wouldn't do for her to be seen anywhere he was – especially that night.

Donna laid the groundwork early in the evening by suggesting to Paul that he go with her out to Karen's at Mirboo North after her party wound up.

To seal the deal, Karen rang her sister's house during the evening and invited Paul to come along later with Donna. She implied he might have another chance with her.

Meanwhile, out at the Nicholls Road farmhouse in Mirboo North, Rhona, Karen, Irene and Jano – and all their kids – had their own party that night. The adults smoked bongs, and Rhona injected Karen and Irene with speed.

Sometime so late on Saturday night that it was really Sunday morning, Paul and Donna left Moe and headed for Rhona's place in Paul's car. Despite being quite drunk, Paul was at the wheel. When they got to the Nicholls Road residence Rhona, Karen and Irene were sitting around the table having a cuppa. Jano had already left, taking Karen's son and his own kids home to his place.

Paul had been partying hard all night and maybe didn't even realise how mixed the messages were around that table. There he was, invited into Karen's house, although she wasn't exactly coming on to him; but everyone was talking to him and being nice, and he was even playing with Rhona's kids. He got bored after a while though and said he wanted to go get his motorbike.

Paul drove his Holden home to Moe. Rhona went with him, to ensure he came back. They returned about 11am and then some of the group went for a ride to Leongatha – Rhona and Paul on his red Yamaha, and Karen on the back of one of Irene's bikes with her.

After the ride, Karen took herself off to bed, Donna lay down on the couch for a sleep, Paul started drinking whisky, and Irene and Rhona started talking speed.

Irene and Rhona offered Paul a hit. Apparently Paul had only ever drunk or snorted the amphetamine before, but it didn't take much to talk him into injecting it. They went into the bathroom.

Irene had laced the speed in the syringe with battery acid, figuring it would give the guy a heart attack – and the whole thing would look like an accident.

When they emerged from the bathroom Irene whispered to Donna, who was still on the couch, that if she didn't want to see what was going to happen she'd better leave. 'He's going to fall any minute and it won't be nice,' Irene told her.

Rhona let herself into Karen's bedroom, and woke her up to tell her, 'We've just given him a dirty shot but he's still standing.'

Working on the theory that if you've been bitten by a poisonous snake you should remain immobile to slow the rate of poison, Irene and Rhona took Paul for a walk, figuring that the exertion would push the battery acid around his system quicker.

Nothing happened. The acid seemed to have no affect on Paul Snabel whatsoever.

After an hour of wandering, they headed back to the house where Paul grabbed one of the motorbikes and started riding around the paddock. When Irene and Rhona began talking about other ways of dealing with Paul, like using a baseball bat or tying him to a tree, the Randall sisters couldn't take the stress anymore and decided to leave.

Donna and Karen headed for the Maslins' place, where all the kids were, including Rhona's, who'd been dropped off sometime after lunch. Also there were Jano Maslin, Rhona's boyfriend Steve, and another guy.

If there was ever a guy in the wrong place at the wrong time it was that other guy. Ian Gillin wasn't even a local – not born and bred anyway. The 22-year-old had moved to the area from Shepparton for work and had got an apprenticeship at the SEC in Morwell. It was there he'd met Jano Maslin and over the next couple of years he and Jano had become good mates, despite a ten-year age difference.

Young Ian had almost become part of the Maslin family and they all shared a love of motorbikes – Jano and Irene had five of them. Ian was tall and strong and useful. He was often at their house for dinner, or to help Jano with building and renovations. The latest project was a swimming pool.

Ian had also known Steve, who was there that day, for a while; even before Steve had started dating another of the Irene's friends, Rhona Heaney. Through all of them, Ian Gillin had met Karen Randall a few times, enough to know she had a sometime-boyfriend who used beat her up. He'd never met the guy himself though, and in fact until that Sunday in November he'd never even met Karen's sister Donna.

While the three men – Jano, Steve and Ian – continued their digging of the pool foundations, the sisters sat around watching, and the kids were playing.

Then Irene Maslin rang home. She spoke to Karen and then to Jano, whereupon Jano asked Ian if he wanted to take a drive with him. whereon

Where they went and what they did in the next hour or so changed Ian Gillin's life forever.

Ian and Jano called in to a shop in the main street to pick up some smokes and soft drink and then headed to Rhona's place on Nicholls Road. When the guys got there they noticed that Irene was in the shed next to the house, so they wandered in there first.

'She had something in her hand,' Ian Gillin told police much later. 'It looked like a syringe and she was filling it up with some stuff. I asked what the stuff was and she said, "It's battery acid.

There's a guy in there who has to go. If someone doesn't do something about him, he's gonna end up killing Karen."'

When Ian and the Maslins went inside, Paul Snabel was sitting on the couch chatting drunkenly to Rhona. She introduced Ian and Paul, and then the two women retreated to the kitchen to make cuppas for everyone. Ever the helpful young man, Ian left Paul and Jano watching TV and went to see if the women needed any help.

They did, but not the kind Ian Gillin was expecting.

Irene pointed to a baseball bat leaning on the kitchen wall and told him, 'I want you to knock this guy over the head.'

Ian figured Irene, who was a bit drunk, wasn't actually serious; at least he hoped not. He took his cup and left the kitchen. Rhona and Irene followed with the other drinks. A little later, when Ian took his cup back to the kitchen, Irene tagged along.

She said, 'Hurry up and do it cause he just has to go,' and then she left the room.

Poor Ian. He never was the brightest spark, but the truth was that for all the 'being part of the Maslin family', the young man was intimidated by his mate's wife.

In fact, Ian Gillin was **shit**-scared of Irene Maslin. Always had been. The way she talked; the way she treated people; the way she ordered Jano around and how he had to do everything at the house; and **do** everything she said, when she said it. Even though they argued all the time it was Irene who was the boss in that family.

Ian Gillin was so scared he was shaking, although part of his fear was not about what Irene wanted him to do, but what she might do to him if he didn't.

He didn't even know this Paul guy. Sure, he knew *who* he was. He knew that he was Karen's skanky ex-boyfriend; that he'd hurt Karen; that no-one liked him – well Karen didn't, and his friends the Maslins didn't …

Ian picked up the baseball bat with his left hand, and returned to the lounge room. He didn't really think he could do it …

And then he just did it..

Ian Gillin walked up behind Paul Snabel, a virtual stranger sitting in an armchair watching TV, and swung the bat into the left side of his head.

Paul, instantly out cold, slumped sideways and started bleeding onto the carpet.

Jano Maslin and Ian Gillin then just stood there, and watched Rhona Heaney unsuccessfully try to inject the battery acid into Paul's arm. She and Irene then tried to inject his ankle instead, until they realised the needle was buggered.

The women and Jano retreated to the kitchen for a moment but when Paul started groaning Irene yelled out to Ian, 'Just hit him again.'

So he did.

When Ian realised Jano was standing next to him he handed the baseball bat to his mate and went outside because he wanted to throw up. Ian Gillin didn't really like the sight of blood, and Paul Snabel was bleeding all over the floor.

Rhona joined him outside, briefly, to see how he felt; and then after a little while Ian re-entered the house – just in time to see Jano Maslin belt the victim twice more on the same side of the head with the same bat.

A couple of minutes later the women emerged from the kitchen, where they'd obviously been discussing what the hell they had to do to finish this guy off.

Irene Maslin bent over Paul Snabel, put a plastic bag over the unconscious man's head and secured it in place with a rubber band around his neck.

'That should make him die,' Irene said. 'He should suffocate.'

While Rhona Heaney busied herself cleaning up the pool of blood with a towel, the rest of them watched and listened as the plastic bag was sucked in and out with Paul's dying breaths.

Once Irene was satisfied that the problem of Paul Snabel had been solved – that Karen Randall's irritating boyfriend was finally dead – she ordered Jano to fetch a tarpaulin and some rope. Jano spread the green tarp out on the floor, then he and Irene lifted Paul from the chair to the tarp, folded it around the body and tied it up.

Jano and Ian carried the bundle outside and put it into the back of the Maslins' family station wagon, while Rhona scrubbed the carpet with a bucket of water, washed off the murder weapon and put it back among her son's toys.

Then, with Irene at the wheel of the Subaru, the three conspirators and their terrified accomplice took the back streets to the Maslin house. Irene and Rhona dropped the guys off and headed north to dispose of the body.

It may seem like there was a lot of aimless riding and driving around going on that day and night, but country people have to travel for most things; they're accustomed to the distances. For the locals of Mirboo North, for instance, it's a half-hour drive to Moe or Morwell, or 45 minutes to Warragul, to go to the pictures or go bowling or to shop in a big shopping centre. Rhona Heaney's trip to the TAFE college in Traralgon took around 50 minutes; and it took an hour or so for the Maslins to get to the necessarily secluded area of bushland where their marijuana crop was hidden.

So it wasn't a random spot in the middle of nowhere an hour from home that the women chose to dump Paul Snabel's body that evening. Irene Maslin knew exactly where she was going: beyond Shady Creek – 30 minutes north-west of Moe and north-east of Warragul – up a dirt track in the dense bush of the 1400 hectare Sweetwater Creek Nature Conservation Reserve. Irene and Jano had been growing dope there for years and the crops had never been found. There was no better place to dump a body.

In fact Irene was so sure Paul Snabel's body would never be stumbled on that the women didn't even bother burying him. After bumping the Subaru over a few logs, when the track virtually ran out, Irene just stopped the car and she and Rhona dragged the body from the back. They made a half-hearted attempt at covering it with a few logs and branches and then simply drove home.

Meanwhile, Jano and Ian had a nice cup of tea in the Maslin kitchen and then offered to take the Randall sisters home. After a small detour to Karen's new house in Mirboo North to grab some clothes, they drove the sisters, and Karen's son, to Donna's place in Moe.

On the drive home afterwards, Ian Gillin finally said to his mate, 'What have we done?'

Jano Maslin told his mate that they'd all be fine, as long as he didn't talk about it to anyone.

When the men got back to the Maslin house in Mirboo North, Rhona and Irene were already there. There was one loose end that still needed fixing, so Jano and Ian took the Subaru and a trailer and headed over to the house on Nicholls Road to fetch Paul Snabel's red and white Yamaha RZ 250.

They drove it straight into Jano's garage where Irene announced they had to strip the bike and dispose of it. The men again did as they were told and, over the next couple of hours, with Irene and Rhona's help, proceeded to take the thing apart.

Jano filed the engine number off and tied up all the wiring in neat left-handed knots. The wiring and smaller bike parts were put into a bunch of plastic bags that he'd brought home from his work at the State Electricity Commission. When they were done, and the Yamaha couldn't be reduced any further, the plastic bags and the larger parts were loaded into the back of the Subaru.

Irene and Rhona wandered inside while Jano and Ian set off on yet another drive to scatter the bike parts as far and wide as they could. The men drove around in the very early hours of Monday 6 November dropping the larger pieces of the motorcycle – like the engine and the frame – into a couple of dams, and the rest of it at two different local tips. They were done and home again by about 4.30am.

And that was it. No logical reason. No bike. No evidence. No body. No murder.

Seven days later, on Monday 13 November, Paul Friend of Moe reported his housemate missing.

Paul Friend had been away himself for a few days – from Sunday 5 November until the following Tuesday – but then he'd made a few phone calls looking for his mate. Paul Friend didn't really start to worry for another three days though; not until Paul Snabel's mother rang their place looking for her son.

All that the Moe police had to go on, to start with, was what Paul Friend knew: the last time he'd seen his mate was Saturday 4 November. They'd watched *Hey Hey It's Saturday* together, then Paul Snabel had gone out. Friend saw him again a few hours later at the housewarming party of a mutual acquaintance. Since then he hadn't turned up for work; and his friends and family had not heard from him.

By the time Detective Senior Constable Michael Grunwald, of the Morwell Criminal Investigation Branch, picked up the case the following weekend, 28-year-old Paul Snabel had been missing for two weeks.

Detective Grunwald began his investigation knowing that Paul Snabel had been in a rocky relationship with one Karen Randall, and that his last known whereabouts was a party in Moe at the home of Donna Randall, the ex-girlfriend's sister.

Grunwald paid a visit to Karen, made a phone call to Donna, and on Sunday 19 November met with both sisters in Mirboo North, at the Nicholls Road residence of their friend Rhona Heaney.

Donna Randall verified that Paul had been at her housewarming party in Moe, and the sisters added that Paul had also dropped by Rhona's place the next day. Karen had been busy packing, getting ready for the move into her new house, and Rhona and Donna were helping.

The last time either of them had seen Paul, they said, was around 5pm when he'd left the farmhouse on his Yamaha.

With that new and in no way incriminating piece of information Detective Grunwald knew that any search for the missing Paul Snabel should begin in Mirboo North, rather than 40 kilometres away in Moe.

No-one who knew him believed that Paul would leave town – not to mention his job, friends and family – without telling anyone, so the natural assumption was that he'd had an accident.

A ground and police chopper search of the area over the next couple of days found no sign of Paul or his motorbike on or off the roads between Mirboo North and Moe.

Then a stroke of luck not only aroused the investigators' suspicions that the Randall sisters possibly knew more than they were saying, but also suggested that Paul Snabel was more than likely a victim of foul play.

Even before the police launched a local media campaign requesting public assistance, the bush telegraph had been working overtime. News of the missing man had spread through the district and locals were already on the lookout for him and his red motorcycle.

On 22 November, Detective Grunwald ordered a search of the Boolarra tip (about 13 kilometres from Mirboo North) after a local boy informed police he'd made some interesting discoveries while foraging there for useful stuff.

The teenager had found more than a dozen motorcycle parts, from what was probably a red Yamaha 250, including a front headlight and rear indicator lights, a mudguard, a rear wheel and tyre, foot rests and a windshield. The subsequent police search of the tip uncovered plastic SEC bags containing motorbike wiring and cables, wound and secured in distinctive bundles.

Over the next couple of days, other tip foragers came forward with bits and pieces from a red and white Yamaha – including a fuel tank and a seat. And on Saturday 2 December a local man found a motorcycle engine in a dam. The Search and Rescue Unit dragged that dam, and another nearby, and in no time recovered a red motorbike frame and front fork.

After the discovery of the first bits of the dismantled Yamaha in November, the Morwell CIB realised it was time to call in the big guns. Detective Senior Constable Peter Wheeler and two other detectives from the Victorian Homicide Squad arrived in the district on Friday 24 November.

Two decades later, Peter Wheeler, now Detective Superintendent, still marvels at how the physical evidence in this case came together.

'This would've gone down as just another unsolved missing person case, if the bike parts hadn't started turning up,' he said.

'It seems that sometimes, as investigators, we make our own luck. In the end it didn't matter that someone had gone to so much trouble to disassemble that motorcycle and scatter the pieces. Kids just happened to be rummaging around in a couple of local tips, at the right time; their parents happened to notice what their kids had found *and* were paying attention to local gossip and the news, and then put two and two together to arrive at a possibility.

'In the end we were able to almost fully reconstruct the motorcycle.'

While the sheer luck of those discoveries still astounds Wheeler, the gradual unravelling of the conspiracy doesn't – nor did it at the time. Although the number of people involved was highly unusual, it was that very thing that doomed the plan to failure. Once the police had an idea of what might have happened, all they had to do was press on with the investigation and bide their time.

'We were soon able to conclude, with certainty, the circumstances surrounding the death of Paul Snabel,' Detective Wheeler said.

In fact, it was the very care that the conspirators had taken in stripping the bike that proved their undoing. At least one piece of the dismantled Yamaha was found in the Boolarra tip on Monday 6 November, only one day after Paul Snabel disappeared. That gave police a new starting point – or rather a likely end point – on their already short time line.

'It was really quite bizarre,' Wheeler said. 'We were able to identify the people responsible who had a substantial role in the scenario leading to that death, which was very much a planned murder in which people had specific roles to play.

'What's more, we got to a point in our investigation, in January 1990, where we had enough corroborating evidence to make several arrests for the murder of Paul Snabel – even though we did not have a body. We still had no idea where he was.'

Earlier, in November 1989, however, all that the investigating officers had were a few bike parts that *might* belong to the missing man's Yamaha; and a 'trail' that kept returning to the Nicholls Road farmhouse and the three women who'd last seen Paul Snabel on Sunday 5 November.

When Rhona Heaney was first interviewed by Michael Grunwald and his colleague Detective Sergeant Shane Downie, on Thursday 23 November, she gave the same account as the Randall sisters, but added that Paul had been drinking all that Sunday, before riding off on his bike at 5pm. The officers executed a search warrant on Rhona's house that day, but found nothing.

Police are always suspicious when statements from more than one person are too similar. In reality, no matter what the situation, no two people see or remember things the same way, so for three women to be telling the same basic story in the same way could only mean it was just that: a story. And it wasn't long before that story – of the last time they'd each seen Paul Snabel – began to change in other subtle ways.

On 24 November, when detectives Grunwald and Wheeler talked to Karen Randall again, she told them that she'd noticed on that Sunday morning that Paul had obviously taken some speed. She also revealed – probably accidentally – that it was Donna who had brought Paul out to the house at Mirboo North. They'd both arrived in his car, but later in the morning he'd driven back to Moe to switch it for his motorbike.

At that stage, none of the women had even so much as mentioned Irene Maslin's name, let alone placed her at the Nicholls Road house.

But again, that's the problem with a conspiracy: the more people in on it, the more people there are to let something slip. And if the players don't see themselves as equally responsible, or if even one person believes they're going to take the fall, the beans will be eventually be spilled and the truth, or a version of it, will come out.

With each interview Rhona Heaney and the Randall sisters added something to their account. Each time it was something apparently insignificant but telling, like: Paul was in a good mood; Paul had taken some speed at the party the night before; Paul had spent the Sunday afternoon drinking; Paul had left at about 5pm; Paul had left at about 4.15; Paul and Donna got to the Nicholls Road house at 5am; and 6am.

On 25 November, when Detective Grunwald talked to Rhona Heaney again, she mentioned Irene Maslin's name for the first time, but only in passing. Rhona told him she'd gone out after lunch on the Sunday, bought bottle of whisky from the pub, taken all the kids to her friend Irene's house, then gone home again.

When the detectives discovered that Karen and Donna were also acquainted with the Maslins – and that it seemed these mutual friends had a very large garage – they paid a visit, with a search warrant. It was Monday 4 December.

Irene Maslin claimed she'd never heard of Paul Snabel before his disappearance had made the news; and that she'd spent all of that Sunday a month before at home with her husband Jano, two other blokes, her own kids and, from lunchtime until about 7pm, Rhona's kids as well.

Jano Maslin's story matched Irene's perfectly, except he admitted having met the missing Paul Snabel a couple of times over at Rhona's place.

The search warrant enabled investigators to collect several items, which would later prove incriminating: some red paint flecks from the otherwise spotless floor of the garage; a file with red paint flecks; and a Yamaha bike tag. They also noticed, with interest, just how neatly Jano Maslin kept his gear, especially the nicely wound wires and ropes, tied with same kind of left-handed knots as the bike cables found in the SEC bags at the tip.

On 18 December, Irene and Jano Maslin took their kids out of school and left town. It was a day after the cops had paid another call on them to ask Jano to answer further questions about Paul Snabel. After consulting his wife, Jano had refused to go with the detectives without talking to a solicitor. A day or so later, Rhona Heaney told officers that as far as she knew the Maslins had just gone on holidays, but she didn't know where.

Around the same time, a very stressed Karen Randall checked

into a private hospital in Frankston, two hours away, to get treatment for drug and alcohol abuse.

Detective Wheeler said the investigating officers kept returning to Karen, Donna and Rhona because with each new statement the women added something new, or neglected to elaborate on something they should have known – according to one of the others.

'As the pressure from the police intensified, the wheels started to fall off because the women not only knew that we were relentlessly pursuing this; **they also knew** that we weren't fully accepting the versions we were being given. We were constantly seeking clarification.'

The detectives got their first real break in the case when the Randall sisters decided to come clean – again with their own versions of the truth. And these new stories of what happened on 5 November clearly put Rhona and Irene in the frame for having 'done something to Paul Snabel'.

When Detective Downie spoke to Karen in hospital on 21 December, she finally admitted that she felt something may have happened to Paul. She claimed that Irene had told her, on the day after he was now known to have disappeared, that Paul would never bother or hurt her again. Irene also warned Karen that she'd have to watch herself and do whatever they told her to do.

It was in that interview that Karen became the first person to put Irene Maslin at the Nicholls Road house on the day that Paul Snabel was last seen. She added, however, that she had no idea when Irene had arrived at her place.

Karen also changed another part of her earlier account, the bit about watching Paul leave her house on his Yamaha at about 5pm. In her new version, she said that Paul was still at the Nicholls Road house when she and Donna left to go to the Maslins'. She also stated that the only people at her friends' place when they got there were Jano, Steve and all the kids; and that Jano had later driven her, and her son and sister, to Moe.

On the same day of Karen's revised statement, Donna Randall was invited to the Morwell CIB office to talk to Detective Downie again. This time she too placed Irene Maslin at her sister's house on 5 November. Donna told the detective that when she and Paul arrived at the house in Mirboo North early on that Sunday morning, Irene, Karen and Rhona were all awake and in the kitchen.

Donna verified that when she and her sister Karen left Rhona's house, Paul was still there, as were Rhona and Irene. She added that she'd overheard Irene and Rhona talking about doing something to Paul, like breaking his legs, but that he was on a bike in the house paddock when she had left to go to the Maslins' place.

When Downie asked why she had previously lied, Donna said that Irene and Rhona had told her to, and that she was scared of Irene. Donna explained that it was between the first phone call from Detective Grunwald on 19 November and the first face-to-face talk she and Karen had with him later that same day that the original story had been made up.

Irene and Rhona had told the sisters exactly what they should tell police: that they had watched Paul leave Rhona's place on his bike at around five in the afternoon. Irene also made it clear that they were *not* to mention that she had ever been at the house that day.

When asked why she thought this meant that something had happened to Paul Snabel, Donna claimed Irene had also said things like, 'I'm polishing my barrels; if one of us is gunna go down, we're all gunna go. If this gets out of hand the big boys are gunna have to deal with it.'

One other new and vital piece of information that Detective Downie acquired from Donna Randall that day was a name – mentioned for the first time and only in passing. Donna said that she and Karen and her nephew had been driven home to Moe from the Maslin house that evening by Jano – and his friend Ian Gillin.

At this stage during their constantly evolving stories – which denied any real knowledge of whatever it was that might have happened to Paul Snabel – the Randall sisters slowly painted (either deliberately or accidentally) some not very nice pictures of their friends Irene and Rhona.

Detective Wheeler said, 'It soon became obvious that the statements, right from the word go, were concocted and part of the concerted effort on the part of all the females who were giving statements, including Rhona Heaney, to give versions that were false and geared towards minimising their involvement or knowledge as to what had occurred.'

In a series of almost-rolling police interviews with Rhona Heaney and the Randalls over the next couple of weeks the story continued to change and a big, ugly picture began to emerge.

On 24 December Detective Downie spoke to Donna Randall again. She told him that around 3am the previous morning she'd been collected by a friend of Irene's and driven to the Maslin house at Corio, near Geelong. When Rhona arrived there later, she had told her friends that the police seemed to know that Irene had been at her place on that Sunday. Although Irene was suspicious that 'someone had been talking' she was doubtful the police had that particular piece of information.

'They're just guessing,' Irene had said. 'Because if they knew these things we'd all be behind bars.'

Rhona added that she thought Karen was their weak link.

Donna also told Detective Downie about another one-on-one conversation she'd had that day. Rhona had told her, she said, that Paul's body had been left in the bush near a drug crop that they'd been growing for about five years.

Rhona had said, 'He'd be rotten there, rotting away … if the animals and things hadn't dragged him off.'

On December 28, Detective Peter Wheeler interviewed the other sister again. Karen Randall was still in the private hospital in Frankston. This time Karen admitted that she, Rhona, the Maslins and everybody's kids had all been at her place on the night of Donna's housewarming. She said the adults had all smoked dope and the Maslin family had stayed the night.

While Karen still maintained that when she and her sister had left the house Paul was fine, she now admitted that from the very next day she knew that something had happened to him. Karen told the detective that Irene had said Paul wouldn't bother her anymore. She claimed Irene had then threatened her.

'When she said that he would no longer bother me, the way that she said it, with evil eyes and an aggressive look on her face, it really scared me and I could tell that Paul was no longer with us. By that I mean that I believed he was dead.'

Karen claimed Irene's threats included the idea that she, Karen, was an accessory and that if she said anything to the police, her head would be blown off.

Karen said Rhona Heaney had later backed up Irene's threats by implying her death would be made to look like a suicide, and that any attempt to leave a note would endanger the rest of her family.

When Detective Wheeler asked if there was anything more she knew about what had happened to Paul Snabel, Karen said that Irene had said things had gone terribly wrong, that there'd been a baseball bat and a lot of blood involved.

Once the Maslins were well and truly in the investigation mix, the police began hearing other rumours, like Irene was into drugs and Paul Snabel had threatened to dob on her.

Given his predilection for dope and speed, Paul was more likely to have been a disgruntled customer or unreliable with his debts, rather than a snitch. And that possibility, of course, could also have meant there'd been a 'falling out' between dealer and buyer.

Detective Wheeler said, 'Because Irene Maslin never gave us anything – no statement, no information, no admitted association – we could never be entirely sure that Karen Randall's "situation" with her ex-boyfriend was the only reason for Irene to believe Paul Snabel should die.'

An interesting – and ultimately never explained – thing that came out of the follow-up interview with the missing man's housemate Paul Friend on 24 November was the mention of a brief appearance of a gun in their house some months earlier. Paul

Friend told the detective that when he'd asked his mate why the gun was there, Paul Snabel had said there were some guys after him.

And of course, according to the Maslins' closest friends, Irene knew people…

'There were so many parties involved,' Detective Wheeler said. 'It wasn't a matter of Mum shot Dad, and was standing in the kitchen with the smoking gun when the police arrived; or one known offender had stabbed another known offender and the police just had to file the paperwork.

'Part of the process during the Snabel investigation was trying to get an understanding of the relationships, trying to develop some kind of motive in our minds, and then trying to come up with scenarios as to what potentially may have occurred.'

Wheeler said he still doesn't believe that the full nature and degree of all the relationships of all the parties was ever fully established, but no amount of theorising prepared the investigators for what they were about to find out.

For despite what Rhona and Irene thought, Karen Randall was not the weakest link in their very cheap chain.

On 29 December, the detectives went to take a statement from someone whose place in the story so far had barely raised a blip on their investigation radar. From then, and over the following 11 days, however, the bizarre and complicated plot to murder Paul Snabel was revealed by the one person who hadn't been in on the plan from the start.

Ian Gillin was the first to tell the cops everything he knew – including his part in it – and the only one, ultimately, not to minimise his role.

However, even Ian, during his first interview, stuck to the Maslin-Heaney lie. After all, Detective Senior Constable Andrew McLoughlin really only wanted to know what he was doing at the Maslin house on 5 November, and who else he'd seen there on the day.

No-one had placed Ian at the Nicholls Road house and in fact, so far, only Karen had mentioned his name at all. She said he and Jano had driven them home that night.

Ian told McLoughlin about his friendship with Jano and, subsequently, his wife Irene; how he often ate at the Maslin home and helped around the place; and how they were digging a pool that day. Yes, he'd met Karen Randall; no, he'd never met Paul Snabel but knew who he was; and he'd only met Donna Randall that Sunday for the first time.

In this first interview, he said that Irene was home when he arrived there but had later gone somewhere; that he, Jano and Steve worked on the pool all day; and that when he and Steve left the Maslin house around 8pm, the Randalls were still there.

This already conflicted with Donna's story that Jano and Ian had driven her home, and other statements that put Irene at Rhona's house from the Saturday night to the Sunday night.

On 5 January 1990, Donna Randall declared that she wanted to add to her previous statements, and emphasised that she had previously not told the truth because she was scared of Irene Maslin.

Donna told Detective Wheeler how Rhona had gone with Paul to Moe in his car and ridden back with him on the Yamaha; that Irene and Rhona had talked Paul into injecting some speed on that Sunday afternoon; and that afterwards Irene had told her that if she didn't want to see what was about to happen to him she should leave because 'he's going to fall any minute and it won't be nice'. Donna revealed she knew her friends had added battery acid to the speed in that syringe.

She also added that when she and Karen were at the Maslins' place later that afternoon, Irene had rung there and then Jano and Ian had left for an hour or so, after which both men had driven her, her sister and her nephew home to Moe.

Detective Wheeler said, 'It was obvious by then that there had been a hell of a lot going on behind the scenes influencing the versions that were being given to us.

'The suspects, as so many of them were by then, were feeling pressure not only from the police making the inquiries and questioning the information that was being given to them, but also from the knowledge that if they didn't fulfil their role in accordance with the instructions they'd been given by Irene Maslin, then the threats made by her would be carried out.'

In that same statement of Donna Randall's, she also mentioned having helped Rhona Heaney deliver her lounge suite to a friend on 18 November, because she was getting a new one. Apparently she couldn't get some stains out of the one she was giving away.

Detective Wheeler said that as the others started to buckle under the pressure, the ringleader did not.

'Irene Maslin was different – in that she never provided a statement to police at all. She was obviously pulling the strings behind the scenes, in terms of influencing what people were saying to police, and was accompanying that with the threats.'

Two days after Donna's revised statement, her sister offered new information. On 7 January, Karen Randall told Homicide detective John Robertson that immediately after Irene and Rhona had given Paul the speed, Rhona had told her it was a 'dirty shot'.

Karen also admitted that Irene had, days later, told her about the battery acid in the syringe, the baseball bat, and the plastic bag that she had finally used to suffocate Paul. Irene had also said they'd had to kill Paul because 'he knew too much'. Karen claimed she assumed that necessity referred to Irene's drug dealing.

In the meantime, the physical evidence was mounting up. Forensic tests matched the paint on the almost completely reassembled Yamaha 250 to the flakes of paint found on the Maslins' garage floor and captured in the grooves of one of Jano's metal files.

Forensic investigators examined the couch that Rhona Heaney had given away because it was stained, and found that an armchair in her house was tinged with blood. They also removed a section of 'cleaned' carpet that had a large bloodstain on it.

The plastic SEC bags in which the cables from the dismantled Yamaha had been found at the tips provided a circumstantial link to Jano Maslin and Ian Gillin, as they both worked for the electricity commission. More directly incriminating, however, was the way that wiring was coiled and tied in exactly the same kind of left-handed knots that Jano used for his own gear in his garage.

On 7 January Ian Gillin gave a second, videotaped, interview conducted outside the home of Irene and Jano Maslin in Mirboo North.

In his new version of the events on that Sunday two months earlier, he said that Irene was not home that morning; that, according to Jano, she was 'out riding with Paul'; that Jano had left his house that afternoon for a few hours. He first said that he alone had driven the sisters home that evening; then later said Jano was also with them.

He told the detectives Wheeler, Robertson and Downie that when he got back to his mate's place from Moe, Irene and Rhona were there. Shortly after, Jano had driven off in the family's Subaru with a motorbike trailer, and returned with a red Yamaha RZ 250.

Ian said it was after midnight when he helped Jano unload the bike into the shed, 'We were told that we had to strip it down.'

He said it was Irene who gave that instruction; and that it was he, Jano, Irene and Rhona who had taken the bike apart.

Ian denied knowing who owned the bike or why they were dismantling it in the middle of the night, but said dumping the parts in the dams had been his idea. Jano had suggested the tips. Ian then took the detectives on a video tour of the four dump sites.

The next day, Monday 8 January, Ian Gillin was taken to Victoria Police HQ in Melbourne to be formally interviewed by the Homicide Squad about the murder of Paul Snabel.

He told them everything.

While Ian had been unaware of the larger plot to kill Paul, he recounted all that he did know. How he had gone with Jano to the Nicholls Road house on the afternoon of 5 November. How he had seen Irene in the garage loading a syringe with battery acid. How she'd told him there was a guy inside who had to go or he might kill Karen Randall. How Rhona Heaney had introduced him to a drunk Paul Snabel. How Irene had told him to hit Paul with a baseball bat. How scared he felt when he realised she was serious, because he knew that if he didn't do what Irene said, it might happen to him.

Ian Gillin told the detectives, 'I picked up the baseball bat ... I sort of started shaking a bit ... Then I didn't know what to do, so I just walked in and knocked him over the head and he fell.'

Ian described how he, and a shocked-looking Jano, had stood by and watched as the women tried to inject the battery acid into Paul's arm and ankle. He admitted that he'd just obeyed Irene when she told him to hit Paul with the bat again; how he later watched Jano Maslin whack Paul twice on the head. He described the blood on the floor; how Irene Maslin had put a plastic bag over Paul's head and they'd watched and listened as he slowly suffocated; how Rhona cleaned the floor and the baseball bat; how Irene and Jano wrapped the body in a tarp; and how he and Jano carried it out to the car.

Detective McLoughlin asked Ian why he didn't try to take the bag off Paul's head.

Ian said, ''Cause I was that scared, I didn't want to really get involved with it.'

'What did you think was going to happen to Paul with the bag over his head?' McLoughlin asked.

'He was gunna die,' Ian stated. 'I reckon if I stepped in and done something about it ... I might've been the next one.'

In trying to explain why he was so scared of Irene Maslin he recounted an incident from a few months earlier, when Irene had left her house in the company of two big guys, who Jano had said were hitmen.

In this formal interview Ian Gillin also admitted that after he and Jano had taken the Randall sisters home to Moe, he had gone with Jano to collect Paul's Yamaha.

Ian Gillin was charged on 8 January 1990 with causing the death of Paul Snabel.

Detective Wheeler later said, 'Getting an insight into Irene Maslin was difficult right up until the end of the investigation when the

Randall girls and Ian Gillin cracked and were interviewed formally as suspects. That's when they finally came out with the true version of what had occurred, and the roles that each of them had played.

'Rhona Heaney was also difficult to get a handle on,' he said, 'but Irene Maslin never provided a version even when she was formally interviewed.'

The day after Ian Gillin was charged, three of the other conspirators were formally interviewed.

Jano Maslin claimed he had been home all day on Sunday 5 November, digging a pool with Ian and Steve; that Rhona Heaney had popped in during the afternoon to pick up Karen's son, and returned later to watch videos; that he did not see Karen or Donna Randall that day at all.

Jano denied having spent Saturday night and Sunday morning anywhere else; he denied any knowledge of dismantling and disposing of a motorcycle; he denied helping with the removal of a body from Rhona's house on the Sunday. He said he didn't 'know' Paul Snabel but admitted to having met him once at Rhona Heaney's house a couple of months before.

Jano Maslin said he had 'no reason to lie'. Detective Sergeant Shane Downie charged him with the murder of Paul Snabel.

Homicide detective Peter Wheeler interviewed Rhona Heaney. She had been advised by her solicitor to say she had no comments to make. She began by saying she'd got her weekends mixed up and that the visitors she mentioned having dropped by her place on Saturday 4 November had actually called in the previous weekend. She said that only she, Steve, Karen and the kids were home that night. She admitted knowing Paul Snabel; that she had met him a few times through Karen Randall.

Rhona refused to comment on who had been at her place in Nicholls Road on the Sunday; whether she'd gone with Paul to Moe to collect his motorcycle; whether she had later helped dismantle that motorcycle; whether she had played an active role in the murder of Paul Snabel; or whether she had helped to dispose of his body.

Detective Wheeler charged 37-year-old Rhona Heaney with murder.

Irene Maslin's formal interview, the same day, was short and virtually silent. She merely stated her name, said she was 32 years old, gave her occupation as 'homebody, home duties care-giver' and asked for a phone book to find a solicitor.

'Irene Maslin was totally uncooperative from the word go,' Detective Wheeler said. 'By saying so very little – and given what we were learning about her from the other parties involved – she came across as a hard, strong woman. She was quite arrogant in her refusal to give anything away.

'We had learned from other sources too that she was active in the drug trade in the Latrobe Valley and had a reputation that caused people to be fearful of the ramifications of not doing whatever she wanted.'

During her interview with Detective Andrew McLoughlin, on 9 January, Irene Maslin sat in seething, stony silence. She smoked several cigarettes, and even physically turned away from the interviewing officers.

McLoughlin eventually informed the care-giving homebody that she would be charged with the murder of Paul Snabel.

Peter Wheeler said two days later the Homicide detectives collected Rhona Heaney from Remand, where she was in custody; and she directed them to the Shady Creek area 'in a concerted effort to try and locate where the body had been dumped by her and Irene Maslin.

'We didn't find the body that day but Rhona Heaney did elaborate on what had happened at her house on 5 November – although her statement was still geared towards minimising her role in things.'

Basically Rhona overlooked everything that happened before Ian hit Paul with the baseball bat. She acknowledged there had been a plan to do something about the way Paul had been treating Karen, but she maintained that her solution would have been to have Jano or Ian punch him and send him home.

She told the detectives that she'd been in another room when Ian hit Paul, but returned to the lounge room afterwards because it was 'her job' to inject Paul with battery acid. She said she couldn't do it and instead went outside to find Ian, to whom, she claimed, she said, 'This is really fucked, I want to get out of here.'

Omitting all other aspects of how the murder actually transpired, Rhona said that the next thing she knew they were all in the Subaru, and then she and Irene headed to Shady Creek. Rhona said she knew Paul's body was in the back but when they stopped in the dark in the bush all she did was drag some branches over to the car because she felt too sick to help Irene with any other part of the body disposal.

It was a week before the Randall sisters were formally interviewed and charged.

Donna was interviewed first, on 19 January, and finally revealed how the plot to murder Paul Snabel had come about; how, at the gathering a few days before her housewarming party, Irene had said something had to be done about Karen's ex-boyfriend before any harm came to her or her son.

Donna detailed how it was her job to get Paul out to the Nicholls Road place on the Saturday night, where Irene and Rhona would inject him with a shot of speed and battery acid.

Donna told Detective Wheeler how the dirty shot had had no apparent effect on Paul and that when it seemed that Irene was instead planning to bash him, she and Karen left the house.

Donna insisted she did not know what happened to Paul until much later. Irene's threats and other 'overheard' conversations between Irene and Rhona soon made her realise they had in fact probably killed Paul Snabel.

When asked why she didn't tell the police the truth any earlier, Donna told Wheeler that she was scared; that she never come across anything like that before.

'I thought if I'd said something to anyone that they probably would've killed me and if I'd gone to the police they'd probably arrest me,' she said.

Karen Randall was then interviewed by detectives Wheeler and Robertson. She explained how Irene was angry, on her behalf, about her ex-boyfriend's behaviour and had talked about disposing of Paul. Karen said it was Irene's idea to lure Paul out to the house at Mirboo North and inject him with battery acid.

Karen said 'her job' was to ring Paul during her sister's party and entice him out to her place. She admitted that on that Saturday night Rhona had injected both her and Irene with speed.

Most of the rest of her story on this occasion matched her previous statement, except that she now acknowledged that, as far as she knew, Paul's death had come about because of her bad relationship with him.

She said that when Ian and Jano returned to the Maslin residence before taking her and her sister and son home to Moe, Jano had said: 'Well, he's not going to bother you again.'

Donna and Karen Randall were both charged with causing the death of Paul Snabel.


Detective Inspector Peter Wheeler is still not convinced the whole truth ever came out.

'We'll never know, with 100 per cent certainty, the full extent of the relationships of the parties involved; and that includes the deceased. Because not everyone talked to us, we'll never know whether there were any other influencing factors as to why these people embarked on their deadly course of action,' he said.

Detective Wheeler believes it's entirely possible that Irene Maslin had that secret extra ingredient – that the police never uncovered – that caused her to be so intent on getting rid of Paul Snabel.

'It's possible that ingredient was even outside the knowledge of those who were interviewed and actually gave what we, and they, believed to be truth as they knew it.

'The fact the people were given an allocated and dedicated role to play in the overall scheme to lure Paul Snabel out to Rhona Heaney's farmhouse, in order to inject him with a mix of battery acid and amphetamines with the idea that that would kill him, says a great deal about Irene Maslin.

'But then – when things went wrong, when he didn't die from

that – the extraordinary behaviour to ensure that it did happen was clearly indicative of the fact that Irene Maslin was very, very keen to ensure that Paul Snabel died that day,' Wheeler said.

'Despite getting nothing from Irene herself, the fact remains that the investigation got to a point in time that there was substantial evidence there to justify the arrest of all the parties for murder – even though we didn't know the whereabouts of the victim. To be able to arrest people and charge them with murder when you don't have a body is fairly significant.

'And then of course the icing on the cake – from a prosecution point of view – was that we were able to locate Paul Snabel's remains, which then provided a whole range of corroboration in terms of the versions we'd been given about how he'd met his death.'

On the day that the Homicide Squad detectives got Rhona Heaney out of jail so she could show them where she and Irene had dumped Paul's body, they had been unable to locate it. Detective Wheeler said the investigators accepted, however, that Rhona's effort to help them was genuine and that where she took them that day was within a reasonable proximity of where his remains might be.

Two weeks later, on 25 January, Detective Sergeant Shane Downie of the Morwell CIB coordinated a combined Victoria Police and State Emergency Services search of an expansive area of bushland around Shady Creek.

Detective Wheeler said this was another example of how luck can play a big role in any investigation. 'That day an SES worker was walking down a bush track and the wind just happened to blow in the right direction at the right time. This fellow got a whiff of something that was a bit off and just walked off the track a short distance into the bush and located Paul Snabel's remains.

'The wild dogs had been into him and scattered him all around the place. He was skeletal at that stage obviously; but there were also some remnants of his clothing,' Wheeler said.

'Most importantly, we found his skull, with the caved-in left-hand side of his head, which was consistent with the information we'd been provided with regarding the use of the baseball bat.

'So it was just an incredible set of circumstances, where on the particular day that we went back and revisited the scene with all those people searching the bushland area, the wind happened to blow at the right time as a fellow was walking by the right spot.'

Detective Wheeler said it wasn't until Paul's remains were found that he and fellow Homicide detective John Robertson – along with two state pathologists, doctors David Ranson and Alison Cluroe – returned to the region to investigate and recover the remains.

While the forensic search grids of active crime scenes are fastidiously thorough, this location was not only *not* the primary scene, it was also nearly three months old and open to the unforgiving elements of a hot Australian summer. Due to the scavenging of wild animals the dump site was also compromised and uncontained; it had no real borders. The pathologists, for instance, found human bones in eight scattered spots. Two parts of the skull were found in two different areas.

Therefore another discovery, by the crime-scene examiner Tony Kealy, could also be put in the category of 'lucky find'. Sixteen metres from the designated centre point of the crime scene he found a 'slightly damaged' log with paint on it. This was later matched to a small dint and some missing paint on the Maslins' Subaru.

Detective Wheeler still says that even though they had enough evidence to charge all those involved, and that they would've been held responsible for their horrendous activities, there was an incredible sense of relief and high degree of satisfaction in also finding the body.

'We were able to put that part of the case to rest as well, which was especially important for the sake of the family,' he said.

But it was Detective Shane Downie who took on the terrible task that day in 1990 of informing Paul's Snabel's parents that they had more than likely found their son, but would need his dental records to identify him properly.

Despite the evidence, both physical and in the statements of their co-accused, Irene and Jano Maslin were at first not committed to stand trial.

'Ian Gillin was only ever going to go down for manslaughter,' Detective Wheeler said. But even though he offered to plead guilty to that charge – and to testify against the Maslins – he was tried for murder, along with Rhona Heaney and the Randall sisters, in 1991.

Ian Gillin was indeed found guilty of manslaughter and sentenced to six years with a minimum of four.

Rhona Heaney was sentenced to 15 years in jail, with a minimum of 10 years.

Karen and Donna Randall each received 14 years, with a minimum to serve of nine.

All four appealed their sentences but only the Randalls were granted new trials.

Detective Wheeler explained the grounds for the retrial. 'Even though they were part of the plot to kill Paul Snabel the sisters did not take part in the actual murder, and in fact were not present at the time. And because the original plan, of which they *were* a party, did not work and the co-conspirators killed him in a manner unknown to the Randalls, it was ultimately decided they should be not be charged with murder.'

Karen and Donna Randall were found guilty instead of attempted murder and both sentenced to four years, with two-year minimums.

At his later trial Jano Maslin was found not guilty.

In the end – nearly four years after the fact, in June 1993 – Irene Maslin pleaded guilty to the murder of Paul Snabel.

'That decision was a consequence of the combination of the convictions of the other parties and the overwhelming evidence that was going to be relied upon in the prosecution case against her,' Detective Wheeler said.

'There is usually a lesser sentence involved by pleading guilty, and Irene and her legal team would've taken that on board as they weighed pros and cons of contesting the matter or throwing her on the mercy of the court.'

Irene decided not to take her chances with a jury.

She was sentenced to 15 years' jail; and was not eligible for parole until 2003.

All of those convicted for their involvement in the murder of Paul Snabel have served their time.

So how does someone like Irene Maslin coerce a group of people – allegedly her friends – to do such a despicable thing?

Detective Wheeler says there was no question the woman was intimidating and that she did have a bad reputation, but it was more than that.

'She was a manipulator, who relied on the fear factor of her notorious reputation. She relished that power and control,' he said.

'Our impressions of Irene were all as a consequence of the interviews with the others involved in the crime, particularly Ian Gillin and the Randall girls. They gave us our only insight into Irene Maslin and the fact that she was the one who had driven the discussion about how something had to be done to get Paul Snabel out of the picture.

'She was the driving force in all the various scenarios considered and, ultimately, was the one who decided on the means by which his fate would be applied. She then allocated tasks and roles to the other participants to ensure that everything would occur in accordance with the plot. It was also she who called the shots when the original plan went wrong,' Detective Wheeler said.

'There was also the strong demeanour that she displayed in terms of the pressure being applied to the other women; so much so that if they said anything that was not in accordance with her script, and which caused the police to focus their attention on her, she was going to take everyone down with her.

'Even during her formal interview with Andrew McLoughlin, when it was obvious their murder plot had come apart at the seams, Irene Maslin remained stone-faced. There was a complete lack of emotion – except for an underlying anger – and absolutely no expression of regret.

'And that's the way she conducted herself to the end.'

# DONE TO DEATH

The fact that there have already been hundreds of stories written about Katherine Mary Knight is testimony to the public interest in her crime. It reflects the horror felt by ordinary people as they began to realise what she did. More than this though, it shows that journalists, writers, psychologists and criminologists – let alone the average person in the street – have struggled to understand what Katherine Knight did. That stories are still being written about her is evidence that people are still unable to comprehend how someone we live with, work with, share our journey through this life with, is capable of something so unspeakably bad.

No matter how fast you read it, or how abbreviated the story of Katherine Knight's crime, it is the kind of story that ought to belong in the annuls of horror fiction. In short, Knight stabbed her partner, John 'Pricey' Price 37 times. After he died, she skinned him and hung his skin on an architrave over the door in his lounge room.

As if that wasn't revolting enough, Katherine then decapitated Price, put his head in a pot with vegetables and cooked it. Next, as though she were an artist inspired by Dante, she baked part of his buttock flesh and plated it up with potato, zucchini, pumpkin, cabbage, squash and gravy. Two places were set at the table, for Price's children, and an accusatory message that had no basis in truth.

Who was this woman?

It is almost easy to dismiss Katherine Knight as a 'nutter'. As the media became more interested, and details began to emerge of not only the crime but the life of Katherine Knight, the story took on the aura of a late-night B-grade movie. This could not be real: the accused was a mother, a functioning member of society. She must also have had serious mental issues. Either that, or he must have been beating her for years and she finally just snapped.

She must have lost her mind. To imagine anything else would have been incomprehensible.

The truth, however, was much harder to digest. Because the truth was that this red-headed, freckled country woman had a history of violence, of being considered capable of just about anything if she was angry. Red flags appeared throughout her life, and at times she came to the attention of authorities. Yet with no point of reference to guide them, aside from a vague sense that there was something 'not quite right', and no laws strong enough to protect those Knight came in contact with, she was able to slip through the net for many years.

One of the unspoken factors that enabled Katherine to reach maturity as a dangerous, violent woman was that she chose tough, country blokes as her victims; men who would rather endure the pain and the trauma of a violent woman than admit that they were victims of domestic violence. Even though people in her local town knew of her reputation, and had plenty of anecdotal war stories, the few times authorities intervened to stop her behaviour, their interventions were hopelessly inadequate.

Katherine Knight was the youngest of twins born in Tenterfield, New South Wales on 24 October 1955. Her sister Joy was born **30** minutes earlier than her. By the time the twins came along, Katherine's mother Barbara already had four sons: Patrick, Martin, Neville and Barry. Six years later their younger brother Shane was born.

From the time she was a small child, Katherine was exposed to violence. Her alcoholic father Ken used violence and intimidation to get sex from his wife, and Barbara regularly told her daughters the intimate details of her sex life, constantly telling them how much she hated men and sex. Added to this were the claims that, up to the age of **11**, Katherine was sexually abused by some of her brothers.

The backdrop to this dysfunctional family, where inappropriate sex and expressions of violence were too often the norm, was a small country town in New South Wales. Aberdeen is a small town nestled in the Upper Hunter Valley. Boasting a population of almost 1800, it is typical of small country towns. Rumour quickly turns to fact, nobody is a stranger, and a strong sense of community is the heartbeat that keeps it alive. For more than **100** years Aberdeen's main industry, aside from the surrounding farms, was the local abattoir. It was Aberdeen's principal employer.

At the age of **15**, Katherine gave up school and went to work at the abattoir with her father and one of her brothers. No matter how anyone spins it, working in an abattoir is the kind of job that requires a strong stomach and an exceptionally pragmatic view of life. Katherine spent her working life surrounded by dead and dying animals and learning how to bone carcasses. The stench of an abattoir is like little else anyone can experience; blood, manure, decomposing flesh, offal and the aroma of human sweat mingle to create a unique *parfum du mort*.

This was the place, the time, the environment that Katherine Knight described as her dream job. Added to the mix was the machismo culture; emotions were weakness, non-drinkers were pussies, women were cooks and sex objects, mates were mates. Professional development was limited. Some would go on to become supervisors, but for most workers it was a mundane, smelly and repetitive job.

Even before Katherine Knight met John Price in 1993 she had spent years in relationships with different men; relationships that would inevitably become violent. Violence of which she was the perpetrator. Twenty years before meeting Price she was married and had her first child. Her husband, David Kellett, couldn't cope with Katherine's possessiveness and violent moods, so he left her and started seeing another woman. In response, she left their two-month-old baby, Melissa, in the middle of train tracks. Had a man not stumbled across the abandoned infant, she would have been run over by a train. Katherine then found a neighbour's axe and began swinging it around in a threatening manner, ranting that she was going to kill people.

Police intervened and took her to St Elmo's Hospital in Tamworth, New South Wales, where authorities diagnosed Katherine with postnatal depression. Kellett resumed the relationship with her, but in 1984 he came home from work one day and she was gone.

Katherine moved back home with her parents and lived with them on the family farm. She went back to work at the abattoir and remained there until a debilitating back injury forced her out. A working life in an abattoir had inured Katherine to violence, and gave her great knife skills. Handling dead flesh every day in a fetid environment, and handling herself in a culture that was masculine and unforgiving, was a peculiar career choice for a woman who gave every behavioural indication of hating men.

In 1986 Katherine met her next partner, Dave Saunders. He became smitten with her and with her insatiable sexual appetite, but it wasn't long before the fights and violence became part of their relationship. In one of her most cruel and spiteful acts, Katherine slit the throat of his two-month-old puppy, and later that day beat Saunders unconscious with a frying pan.

The following year, the couple had a baby girl and called her Sarah. Katherine's worker's compensation payout came through and she was able to pay off their home – a very modest two-bedroom cottage in Aberdeen. The house was nothing to look at, and had the air of neglect about it, but inside the 'art' was rather unique. Stuffed dead animals, rusted garden tools and a saddle and riding crop decorated the walls of the cottage. Home entertainment included a comprehensive video collection that featured themes of horror and violence.

Dave Saunders walked away from the relationship after

another vicious attack, in which Katherine bashed him in the face with an iron and stabbed his chest with a pair of scissors. The theme was constant – she was always accusing him of seeing other women behind her back. They were groundless accusations, but Katherine's imagination was a consistently dark world.

After Saunders left, Katherine had a brief relationship with 43-year-old John Chillingworth, long enough for them to have a son, Eric, in 1991.

By the time Katherine started her relationship with John Price two years later, the pattern of her life was well and truly set. Screaming arguments were the landscape of her days; physical violence her way of having the last word.

John Price was considered to be a good bloke, one of the boys, who would give anyone the shirt off his back. A local man about town and a bit rough around the edges, 'Pricey' was well liked. When he started going out with Katherine Knight a lot of people were concerned. Her reputation preceded her, and more than one of his mates wondered what on earth Pricey was doing getting tangled up with a woman like that.

John Price had been married and had three children. When that relationship ended his ex-wife took the two year old and left the teenage boy and girl with John. He owned his own home, and Katherine soon moved in. It wasn't long before the drinking and fighting began.

When John wouldn't marry Katherine she took revenge. In 1998, knowing that Pricey had helped himself to items from work that had passed their use-by date and had been taken to the company tip, Katherine videotaped these items and showed them to Pricey's bosses. Because of this, Pricey was sacked from a job he had loved and had been working in for 17 years.

He threw her out of his house and ended the relationship, but a few months later they were back together; only this time Katherine wasn't allowed to live with him.

Pricey's mates were frustrated that he had got back with

Katherine and started to avoid him, at least when 'she' was around. To Pricey's friends there was always a sense of inevitability that something bad would one day happen. Katherine was volatile, with a horribly cruel streak. She would accuse him of seeing other women, of all kinds of imagined wrongs, and would fly into the most irrational rages.

On 27 February 2000, the couple had a nasty altercation, when Pricey attempted to end the relationship and put Katherine out of the house. The police were called in to intervene. Two days later, on 29 February 2000, John Price went to the Scone Magistrates Court and took out an AVO against Katherine Knight.

That night at 11pm Pricey was laying in bed, when he heard a car pull up in the driveway. He knew it was Katherine. She came in, got into bed with him, and the estranged couple had sex.

Nobody knows what unfolded after that, because Katherine Knight's version of events is that she fell asleep after having sex, and remembers nothing else until she woke up the next morning.

But at 6am the next day, a neighbour noted that Pricey's car was still in the driveway, which was strange because John Price usually left for work before 6am. When Pricey didn't arrive at work, and nobody could contact him, his employer sent another worker to Pricey's house. He noticed blood on the front doorknob and immediately called the police, who arrived at John Price's house at around 8am.

The first thing the police officers saw, upon entry, was the skinned hide of a man hanging above the lounge-room door. Then, to their horror, they saw a headless body lying on the floor, and then a man's head in a pot on the stove in the kitchen.

Katherine Knight was snoring loudly in the bedroom. She was woken, dressed and taken to the police station for questioning. Figuring they would come for her, wherever she was, but thinking she could outsmart them, Katherine claimed she remembered nothing – thus sowing the seeds of invented madness.

Detectives, the forensic pathologist and crime scene investigators had to rely on their own powers of observation, their years of experience, and the evidence that was available in order to piece together the events of that night.

They knew that John Price was stabbed **37** times, and that several of those stab wounds were so deep they penetrated organs and major blood vessels. They suspected that the murder weapon was a butcher's knife, which had been found lying in the lounge room. Close by was a knife sharpener, which had been recently used.

The pathologist knew that the 'skinning' of John Price was a highly skilled procedure; and estimated that it would've taken about **40** minutes to complete. It was done so efficiently, and in one piece, that they were later able to 'slip John back into the suit of his skin' before they buried him.

Detectives knew that John Price was decapitated; that his head was placed in a pot and cooked; and that parts of his buttocks were sliced off and roasted with vegetables. Detectives also knew that the table was set for two, with place cards bearing the names of Price's two elder children sitting benignly behind the plates of food.

Forensic experts knew that John Price did not die immediately. From their examination of the blood patterns and drag marks they were able to establish that the first part of the attack had taken place while Price was lying in bed in his bedroom. He got off the bed and moved down the hallway, while being stabbed several times in the back. While in the hallway he tried to switch on a light. Blood on the doorknob told investigators that Price had reached and opened the front door, but drag marks showed he came back inside, fell in the hallway and died there. More drag marks showed that he was moved some time after his death.

Police also knew that Katherine Knight was responsible for the tableau of horrors they witnessed. What they didn't know was whether she was insane at the time. Or whether she was provoked. Or had help. Or was simply a very bad woman.

It was obvious that Katherine was setting herself up for a plea of insanity before the case went to trial. She was examined by three separate psychiatrists who eventually gave evidence in court.

All of them agreed: Katherine Knight was legally sane, was suffering from no significant mental illness, and was legally able to tell right from wrong. At least one psychiatrist diagnosed Katherine with borderline personality disorder, but their professional opinions ruled a line through the generally held view that Katherine was a 'nutter'. It also ruined any chance she had of being found not guilty of murder by virtue of insanity.

The case went to trial, before Justice O'Keefe, on 18 October 2001. Katherine Knight was formally charged with wilful murder and entered a plea of guilty.

In his summary of the trial, and as part of his sentencing remarks, Justice O'Keefe made some very strongly worded observations as he created legal history. Katherine Mary Knight was about to become the first female prisoner in Australia whose papers would be marked 'never to be released'. During his summary Justice O'Keefe included these observations:

> The prisoner has pleaded guilty to a murder which falls into the most serious category of murders. I am satisfied beyond any doubt that such murder was pre-meditated. I am further satisfied in the same way that not only did she plan the murder but she also enjoyed the horrific acts which followed in its wake as part of a ritual of death and defilement. The things which she did after the death of Mr Price indicate cognition, volition, calm and skill.
>
> I am satisfied beyond reasonable doubt that her evil actions were the playing out of her resentments arising out of her rejection by Mr Price, her impending expulsion from Mr Price's home and his refusal to share with her his assets, particularly his home, which he wanted to retain for his children. I have no doubt that her claim to amnesia forms part of her plan to affect madness in order to escape the consequences of her acts and to provide a convenient basis on which to rely to avoid detailed questioning by the police and escape punishment.

As I have said, the prisoner showed no mercy whatsoever to Mr Price. The last minutes of his life must have been a time of abject terror for him, as they were a time of utter enjoyment for her. At no time during the hearing or prior thereto did the prisoner express any regret for what she had done or any remorse for having done it; not even through the surrogacy of counsel. Her attitude in that regard is consistent with her general approach to the many acts of violence which she had engaged in against her various partners, namely 'they deserved it'.

In addition the prisoner's history of violence together with her flawed personality cause me to conclude, along with Dr Milton and the other psychiatrists called in the case, that she is without doubt a very dangerous person and likely, if released into the community, to commit further acts of serious violence, including even murder against those who cross her, particularly males. A crime of the kind committed by the prisoner calls for the maximum penalty the law empowers the court to impose.

An examination of the cases referred to by counsel supports the view that I have formed, namely that the only appropriate penalty for the prisoner is life imprisonment and that parole should never be considered for her. The prisoner should never be released.

In September 2006, Katherine Knight appealed her sentence before the New South Wales Court of Criminal Appeal. Through her lawyer she claimed that the killing of John Price was not in the worst category of murder and did not warrant life in prison. Katherine claimed that her sentence was manifestly excessive.

Justices McClellan, Michael Adams and Megan Latham dismissed Knight's appeal. Justices McClellan and Latham agreed the sentence was appropriate.

'This was a violent and cruel crime during which the deceased must have suffered extreme trauma,' Justice McClellan said. 'The crime was the product of a violent personality intent upon claiming the life of her de facto in a relationship which was plainly failing.'

He said Katherine Knight had expressed no remorse for the killing. 'The psychiatric evidence indicates that her personality is unlikely to change in the future and, if released, she would be likely to inflict serious injury, perhaps death, on others,' Justice McClellan said.

Katherine Mary Knight remains imprisoned at Mulawa Correctional Centre. She works in the prison as a cleaner and, according to prison officers, conducts herself as a model prisoner.

# About the Authors

## Lindy Cameron

An independent publisher and crime writer, Lindy is the author of the Kit O'Malley PI trilogy *Blood Guilt, Bleeding Hearts* and *Thicker Than Water*; the archaeological mystery *Golden Relic*; the action thriller *Redback;* and the sf crime *Feedback.*

Lindy is a two-time Readers' Choice Davitt Award winner: for *Bleeding Hearts* (2002); and for *Thicker than Water* (2004). She is also co-author of the True Crime collections: *Killer in the Family* and *Murder in the Family*, with her sister Fin J Ross.

Lindy is a founding member and National Co-Convenor of Sisters in Crime Australia, and the Publisher of Clan Destine Press.

## Ruth Wykes

Writer and human rights activist, Ruth is co-author, with Kylie Fox, of *Invisible Women: powerful and disturbing stories of murdered sex workers*.

Born and raised in country New South Wales, Ruth moved to Perth where she worked at the Western Australian AIDS Council and ran health and education projects at Bandyup Women's Prison.

She then published a monthly magazine for nine years, before giving it away to become a wage slave in order to work on her first crime novel.

Ruth 's lastest move was to the Mornington Peninsula. When not working or writing she reads, gardens, and tries to live in harmony with her environment.

Her next true crime collaboration, again with Kylie Fox, is *Impact: the ripple effect of murder on society.*